Dividing Divided States

Gregory F. Treverton

PENN

UNIVERSITY OF PENNSYLVANIA PRESS

PHILADELPHIA

Published by
University of Pennsylvania Press
Philadelphia, Pennsylvania 19104-4112
www.upenn.edu/pennpress

Printed in the United States of America
on acid-free paper
10 9 8 7 6 5 4 3 2 1

Library of Congress Cataloging-in-Publication Data
Treverton, Gregory F.
    Diviging divided states / Gregory F. Treverton.
        p. cm.
    Includes bibliographical references and index.
    ISBN 978-0-8122-4599-8 (hardcover : alk. paper)
    1. Partition, Territorial.   2. Dismemberment of
nations.   I. Title.
KZ4028.T74 2014
320.l'2—dc23
                                                      2013038740

CONTENTS

ABBREVIATIONS

CPA   Comprehensive Peace Agreement, Sudan

CSR   Convention Relating to the Status of Refugees

EU   European Union

FSU   former Soviet Union

GoS   government of Sudan (north)

IBRD   International Bank for Reconstruction and Development,
                usually known simply as the World Bank

ICCPR   International Covenant on Civil and Political Rights

ICERD   International Convention on the Elimination of All
                Forms of Racial Discrimination

IDPs   internally displaced persons

IMF   International Monetary Fund

INC   Interim National Constitution, Sudan

IOM   International Organization for Migration

OSCE   Organization for Security and Cooperation in Europe

SPLM, SPLA   Sudan People's Liberation Movement/Army, South Sudan

UNHCR   United Nations High Commissioner for Refugees

Dividing
Divided States

Introduction

In the early 1990s, the weary senior director for Europe on the U.S. National Security Council used to kid his colleagues by saying, "Why don't you get going? I've presided over the creation of lots of new countries in my area over the last few years. What have you been doing in your areas?" The flood of new states set loose by the end of communism and the Soviet empire has slowed to a trickle, but it is a continuing trickle. The vote for independence in southern Sudan in January 2011 is the latest instance of a new state but surely not the last. The appendix presents a list of secessions since 1900.

Framing Secession

Secession is a region formally withdrawing from a state or federation to become a separate state. Some care with terms is in order: Formally, the seceding region is not a state until it is recognized as such by the international community, but since in all cases the seceding region aspired to be a state and was ultimately recognized as such, the book sometimes uses the term "seceding state" for regions withdrawing. The resulting states, both old and new, are regarded as the "successor states." If a region seceded, the original state is referred to as the "continuing state," a status that bears particularly on dividing national resources, like international memberships and assets. If the original state dissolves, there is no continuing state.

This book is intended as a guide to those interested in policy formulation on secession—students and practitioners alike. Secession involves not just the states and regions immediately concerned. Neighboring states may have been affected by spillover conflict and surely will harbor some refugees.

The ripples of those spillovers may reach other states as well. States outside the region, like the United States, may feel their security concerns are invoked, and, in any case, they will be looked to as sources of aid and perhaps honest brokering. International organizations will also be important in those roles, and the international financial institutions are likely to be quite directly involved in negotiations over assets and liabilities.

The book does not reach judgments on whether or when secession is a good idea. Nor does it treat many of the issues in international law surrounding secession, such as recognition of new states, about which there is a vast literature. Rather, the policy premise of the book is that if secession is going to happen, better that it be done well—and that doing it well is likely to be facilitated by an awareness that other secessions have confronted similar issues and an understanding of how they handled them.

Still, secessions arise from a stew of nationalism, ideology, long-simmering conflict, artificial borders, changed geopolitical circumstances, and money. States secede for several reasons, all of which will continue to impel secessions. And plainly, how secessions come about will matter when it comes to making policy decisions. Most of the secession cases we draw on were, like Sudan, the result of long-festering dissatisfaction on the part of groups defined by some combination of ethnicity, nationalism, and religion, groups trapped in states whose borders had been drawn pretty arbitrarily by empires, colonial powers, or federations—ranging from the Austro-Hungarian, Soviet, and Ottoman Empires to the European colonial powers.[1]

In only several of the cases we analyze did the secessionists fight on their way to independence, as was the case in Sudan, though in many violence was touched off by the secession itself—most brutally in Bosnia's ethnic cleansing. In numbers, by far the most secessions in the last quarter century issued from the slow collapse of an artificial multinational empire or federation—the Soviet Union, Yugoslavia, and Czechoslovakia.

Perhaps because so many of the secessions were due to the demise of the Soviet empire, many scholars emphasize money as critical. For one, "few regions have the structural requirements for the development of a secessionist movement," which seems, in Africa, truer of the resulting state than of the secessionist movement.[2] Another scholar argues that "separatism results from varying mixes of sheer economic interest and group apprehension."[3] Supporting this argument, one study found that secession movements within the Soviet Union were most strongly motivated by economic concerns, while another argued that "it is the richest, rather than the poorest, ethnic regions which are the most eager to secede since they have the most to lose should they be exploited by other groups that control the state."[4]

One synthesis analyzes secession movements through a cost-benefit analysis lens that does capture some of the ideological underpinnings of secessionism as a type of "membership benefit." This approach moves beyond the arguments that focus almost exclusively on economics. It provides a way to include material considerations in the analysis but takes into account the passions of ideology and nationalism that arise in secessionist cases.[5]

Some of the seceding states—the Baltics, Croatia, Slovenia—did so on powerful economic grounds. However, others, mostly in Africa but also including Bosnia, impoverished themselves in the name of identity or ideology, though they sometimes *thought* they would be better off after independence. South Sudan's leaders made that argument, however unwisely.

In the end, how well a secession goes also depends on a number of factors beyond the seceding region's control. The amicability of the parting plainly is crucial (though resting too much on the assumption that comity will continue can also be dangerous, as it was for Ethiopia and Eritrea). And it did seem the case for many of the issues we examined that richer (or more powerful) states in any secession were both better able to prepare for separation and more able to set the terms of that separation. Some of these wider issues are picked up in the concluding chapter.

The book's premise is that secessions will continue to occur. A betting person probably would look hardest at Africa, where so many artificial borders remain. Europe is also an interesting case. The European Union in the 2010s is in parlous condition. Yet if it holds together, even as a free trade area and not a currency zone, it could provide economic incentive to secession. Within Europe, Catalonia doesn't need Spain, nor perhaps does Dutch-speaking Flanders need Belgium.

The book's purpose is to learn tentative lessons about how dividing states have handled the particulars in their own divorces, from oil and water to security, citizenship, and assets. That purpose is a humble one. The more we dug into the cases, the clearer it became that no one previous experience could provide an easy template for future secessions. Nor can the lessons be more than suggestive, for the number of cases relevant to any given issue is limited. But even though every circumstance has its own particularities, some understanding of the way previous secessions handled the array of issues that most seceding states are likely to confront can help serve as an antidote to the feeling that the problems are entirely new. If the previous cases do not offer pat prescriptions, they do offer lessons to consider along the way, both suggestive and cautionary.

The cases and issue analyses that compose this book were prepared over three years for Humanity United as part of a kind of Track II—nonofficial— diplomatic effort in the run-up to the vote on secession by South Sudan in January 2011. We found, however, that most of the lessons had relevance far beyond Sudan, and the materials have been "de-Sudanized" to make them useful to other regions contemplating secession. While much of the Sudan-specific material has been omitted, Sudan is a kind of background case throughout. That is especially the case for the chapter on citizenship and the concluding chapter, both of which use the Sudan case to illustrate more general questions, like the sequence and timing in which issues should be handled.

One issue that didn't arise in Sudan and thus is not treated here is borders. The African Union estimates that fewer than a quarter of Africa's borders are delimited and demarcated, so borders are an issue for all African states, not just seceding ones.[6] Whether undefined borders become a crucial issue in secession will turn on whether something of value, like oil or water, lies along an undefined border. That was not the case for Sudan. Rather, for the Sudanese and surely for other secessions, what was an issue was rather defined border regions, like Abyei, that contained people divided in their loyalties.

Note on Method, and Guide to Chapters

The next eight chapters present cases and cross-cutting issue analyses for the core issues that many seceding states are likely to have to address; they arose in Sudan, but some set is likely to arise in any secession. Those issues are grouped loosely in three clusters—people, natural resources, and state or national resources. The first cluster includes citizenship, refugees, and security, and what are called "pastoralists," people who regularly move in pursuit of water and grazing land but who, after secession, may find that their traditional movements now cross newly etched international borders. The second includes oil and infrastructure, and water, while the third comprises assets and liabilities, and currency and financial arrangements.

The people issues begin with citizenship, the subject of Chapter 1, a highly sensitive issue, perhaps the core one over which the parties have argued, even fought. For this issue, it seemed less helpful to have full case studies than to lay out the range of issues involved in citizenship and the variety of arrangements states have conceived to deal with it, along with some case examples.

Division is virtually certain to produce refugees, who are almost always vulnerable and thus dependent on some means of security. Displaced persons sometimes are rendered stateless and are at risk of becoming bargaining chips in a broader conflict between old and new countries—the subjects of Chapter 2.

Chapter 3 turns to the question of pastoralists. This issue was crucial in the case of South Sudan but may not be relevant in regions of the world other than Africa. Yet it will arise in some form in other secessions as well, all the more so as climate change lengthens the migrations of pastoralists.

The natural resource issues begin with oil and accompanying infrastructure. Resources are a curse in secession because they are not distributed evenly across the original and would-be seceding state. Oil and gas are a special problem for two reasons, and Chapter 4 examines both of them. One is that while the resource pools are fixed in space, those pools may straddle the boundaries of new states. Second, oil and gas need to be moved toward market through expensive infrastructure, infrastructure that may pass through what becomes with division another country.

Chapter 5 takes up a rather different oil (and other natural resource issue): how to avoid the "resource curse." At best, resource earnings can distort economic development in the short run; at worst, they can become something to fight over. In the long run, there is concern over equity across generations: how can future generations benefit even after the oil reserves are exhausted? The chapter discusses a variety of funds nations have created, both to smooth out revenue fluctuations when resource prices change and to preserve resource wealth for future generations.

The next chapter discusses the challenges that arise when secession produces new claimant(s) on existing water resources, most often river basins. That requires negotiating shares, along with ways to enforce them and handle disputes.

Chapter 7 turns from natural resources to national ones. Dividing assets and liabilities between an old, diminished state and a new, perhaps jubilant one will surely be an emotional issue. Many fixed assets can fairly be allocated to the (new) state in which they exist, but movable assets will be contested, as will ways to share any existing debt burden, all the more so if a visible fraction of the debt was incurred to finance projects that now seem disproportionately housed in one of the states. Military assets are particularly important, hence contentious.

Currency, the subject of Chapter 8, seems an easier matter: as a symbol of sovereignty, shouldn't a new state have its own? That logic is often unstoppable but can be dangerous, for currency is in fact connected to banking and economic policy. Not surprisingly, secession cases among richer countries produced better outcomes on this score.

The final chapter lays out conclusions. The case study chapters concentrate on the specifics of dealing with the issue in question. Yet looking across the cases and issues also sheds light on the broader, contextual factors that sculpt any secession. The conclusions reflect on those, using the Sudan case as one in point. For instance, sequencing matters—what is important to try to do early and what can be deferred?—and leadership are critical. The leaders of the parties need to have the stature and credibility to do more than issue grand pronouncements; they need to be able to make painful compromises, and make them stick.

Reframing issues can make them more tractable. Yet, the contextual factors that help most—above all trust and amicable relations—are likely to be in the shortest supply. In that sense, the knowledge that other secessions have handled these issues—and the lessons suggested along the way—can help boost trust.

Each issue (except citizenship) is treated in a broadly similar way, and each chapter follows a similar structure. Once we decided which issues were important, we looked for cases in which the issue had been handled, well or badly, ideally in cases that ranged across different regions of the world. We present each case using a similar template—first a brief statement of the issue and the outcome; then a longer discussion of the course of the dispute or discussion; then finally an assessment and discussion of the possible lessons from the case. We have also looked across cases for comparisons and lessons.

As a policy guide, the chapters in this book present the results of the process in a somewhat reverse order. If this were a purely academic book, it would lay out the cases, then present the lessons. Here, though, to make it easy for busy policy-minded readers, we present the lessons that resulted from looking across the cases first, in most cases ending with a table to illustrate those lessons graphically. The cases then follow, and readers who are intrigued or dubious or simply want more can sample the cases as they see fit.

PART I

People

CHAPTER 1

Citizenship

The first people issue is citizenship. It is the essence of state sovereignty, for it identifies "us," and separates "us" from "them." Thus, if ensuring the safety of refugees is usually the most acute challenge of secession, the most enduring one is creating citizenship processes that will be fair and be regarded as such by all the states involved in the secession.

For instance, in Sudan at secession, as many as two million southerners were internally displaced persons (IDPs) living in the North. In addition, there were both southerners and northerners who were not IDPs but lived and worked in the other region—southerners who were members of a military joint integrated unit or civil servants in Khartoum, the capital, and northerners who had settled in the South and been resident there for years, owning businesses and property. Thus, it was necessary not just to safeguard the movements of IDPs and others who became refugees with secession and wanted to return to their chosen homeland but also to establish some process by which those who wanted to stay could become, if not citizens, at least permanent residents with some legal protection.

This chapter proceeds somewhat differently from the others. Rather than laying out specific cases in some detail, it elaborates models, bases, and principles of citizenship, then illustrates them with examples from other nations. Using Sudan as an example, a final section spells out the rights of people who wind up located in the state to which they do *not* feel allegiances in the immediate aftermath of a formal division.

Drawing on the experience of other nations, in principle there are three models of citizenship—single citizenship, dual citizenship, and long-term (or permanent) residence without citizenship. The two other main policy choices are the *basis* for determining citizenship and the *principles* on which the process ought to be based.

Models, Bases, and Principles of Citizenship

There are no universally accepted international norms or standards that compel states' decisions on citizenship when they divide or fracture. Under international law, states have the authority to establish criteria for citizenship.[1] However, as discussed in more detail in the last section of this chapter, international organizations and institutions have adopted nonbinding declarations concerning citizenship when states divide.[2] These declarations generally discourage discrimination in determining citizenship in the context of the breakup of a state and advocate providing people who are affected by that breakup with the option to freely choose their future citizenship.[3] That duty not to discriminate includes actions not only against individuals but also against their *property* based on people's choice of citizenship.[4] The presumption is that anyone holding the nationality of the predecessor state at the time of division has a right to citizenship in at least one of the resulting states, and that anyone with established residence in the region that secedes will acquire the nationality of the new state.[5] In general, state principles for citizenship when states divide should "respect, as far as possible, the will of the person concerned," and provide for a reasonable time in which the choice can be made.[6] They should also discourage linking the citizenship decision to property rights, and prohibit discrimination based on race, ethnicity, religion, language, or political opinion.

Basic Models of Citizenship

Single

This is straightforward. In a secession, it would mean that residents of the seceding state would automatically become citizens of it unless they chose otherwise. Those, say, northern and southern Sudanese living in the "other" state would have the right to choose, under some conditions, of which state to become a citizen. In cases elsewhere in the world, the "condition" is residence, with those seeking citizenship in the "other" required to prove some continuing residency in that other state. All those accepting or choosing citizenship in the seceding state would lose their citizenship in the original state.

Dual

This would be similar to the above except that, perhaps under some conditions, those people living in the "other" state might be permitted to acquire a new citizenship in the new state without losing citizenship in the original state. This choice would entail negotiating arrangements for which laws dual citizens would be subject to, where they would pay taxes, which army they would be subject to being conscripted into, and the like. The presumption would be that most of the arrangements would be based on the primacy of the state in which a person *resided*.

Long-Term (or Permanent) Residence Without Citizenship

At least thirty countries in the world have provisions permitting citizens of other nations to reside in them without citizenship. Indeed, in an increasingly globalized world where people may want or need to reside in another country primarily for economic reasons but have little interest in citizenship, some analysts have begun discussing "sojourner rights." These might permit people to work where they need to but not acquire health care, social security, or other specific benefits of citizenship.[7]

For some, though not all, of the countries that permit permanent residence, that status is a way station to full citizenship. In general, permanent residents have the same rights as citizens except that they usually cannot vote or run for office, hold government jobs, or sometimes own certain kinds of property. Often, but not always, they are restricted from jobs in the national security area. That is not the case in the United States, where permanent residents not only are subject to U.S. taxes, but also were subject to conscription into the U.S. military when the country had a draft. Now, they can serve in the U.S. military; indeed, that service may be a fast track to citizenship.

The risk of permanent residence is that it may become a second-class status. The German case is instructive. Germany—and, on a smaller scale, Belgium and the Netherlands—reached agreements with a number of countries to send *Gastarbeiter* ("guest workers"), low-skill industrial workers, to fill jobs

Table 1.1. Models, Bases and Principles of Citizenship

Model of citizenship		Basis for determining citizenship		Principles for process
MODEL	EXAMPLES	BASIS	EXAMPLES	
Single—must choose one or the other	Czech Republic	Specific residence requirement	Czech Republic, Serbia	Free choice of persons concerned
Dual— permitted to hold several	Slovakia, Serbia			No discrimination against persons or their property
Long-term residence— permitted to live and work but not to vote	United States, Germany	Residence plus other conditions	Croatia Macedonia	Citizen in original state has right to at least one citizenship in successors Reasonable time to make choice

during the boom of the 1960s and 1970s. In Germany, the largest influx was from Turkey. The workers were given the right to live and work for two years, with the expectation that they would return home afterward. Some did, but others stayed and brought their wives. Their children were given the right to live in Germany but not citizenship. They came to form separate communities, sometimes quite large ones scarcely integrated in broader German society and sometimes the target of extremist politicians.[8] Table 1.1 summarizes the models, bases, and principles for citizenship.

Citizenship Examples from Other Countries Dividing

The situation of Czechoslovakia is similar to that of Sudan in that prior to the 1993 dissolution of the country, it had two levels of citizenship, one national (Czechoslovakian) and the other regional (Czech or Slovak). When the country divided, both of the resulting countries granted national citizenship to their former regional citizens. And both allowed citizens who had held regional citizenship in the other region to apply for citizenship in their newly independent states. However, the new Czech Republic also applied a residence requirement to Slovakian nationals desiring Czech citizenship, requiring them to demonstrate uninterrupted residence for two years in the Czech Republic. The two states also differed in that Slovakia allowed for dual citizenship, while the Czech Republic did not.

So, too, Slovenia, Croatia, and Macedonia all took slightly different approaches to citizenship in their respective new states following independence from Yugoslavia. As in the Czechoslovakia case, each new state's laws automatically granted citizenship in the new state to individuals who were previously citizens of their respective former republics. However, for others wishing to apply for citizenship, Croatia also imposed a residency requirement, requiring "habitual residence," in its case defined as five years, in addition to some other conditions. In contrast, Slovenia and Macedonia allowed citizens from all of the former Yugoslav republics to apply for citizenship, although the latter applied a number of conditions, requiring applicants to have fifteen years of residence in the former Yugoslavia, be at least age eighteen, receive personal income, and apply within a year.

Similarly, Serbia and Montenegro made somewhat different choices about citizenship following Montenegro's declaration of independence in 2006. In particular, Serbia allowed Montenegrins who held a registered residency in Serbia prior to the succession to apply for Serbian citizenship, and allowed for dual citizenship. In contrast, in March 2008 after the referendum Montenegro enacted legislation that precluded dual citizenship except through separate agreements with other countries, although it did allow Montenegrins who had gained Serbian citizenship after the 2006 succession to retain these citizenship rights until Serbia and Montenegro concluded a formal agreement. Unfortunately, as of 2011, such an agreement had not been concluded, with Montenegro opposing and Serbia supporting the idea of letting those initially allowed to keep both citizenships to retain them.

Ethiopia and Eritrea opted for a kind of dual citizenship when they divided in 1993, agreeing—but only after the Eritrean referendum—to continue to respect traditional rights of people to reside in another territory.[9] That state of affairs continued for three years, though the two states could not agree on permanent citizenship arrangements for Eritreans living in Ethiopia. The issue remained stalled amid disagreements over borders and trade when civil war erupted between the two countries in 1998. The Ethiopian government revoked the citizenship rights of Ethiopians who had voted in the Eritrean final status referendum, equating voting with a forfeiture of Ethiopian citizenship. Ethiopia forcibly expelled 75,000 Eritreans, a move condemned by the international community. For its part, Eritrea also subsequently expelled Ethiopian citizens from its territory, though the numbers were much smaller. This humanitarian aftermath of the war remains a sharp point of contention between the parties.

Principles and Special Considerations

The models and examples suggest several critical principles in handling citizenship during secession.

Establish the Basic Principle Permitting Choice in Light of Residence

The first presumption is that people should be allowed to choose their citizenship. The second is that, in general, it will be based on residence. In all the cases, the starting point was that those people residing in the territory of the new state would become citizens of that state unless they chose otherwise. The harder issue is dealing with those who regard themselves as "belonging" to the state other than the one in which they reside. For them, special provisions or agreements may be required.

Think Carefully About Dual Citizenship and Permanent Residence

In thinking of special provisions, dual citizenship is tempting. It can be complicated, and it can become a bone of contention, as was the case, tragically, in Ethiopia and Eritrea and, less dramatically, in Serbia and Montenegro. The complications are clear in the Sudan case. On one hand, dual citizenship would be less on the agenda if, for instance, formal independence meant that southerners in the Khartoum civil service or in joint military units returned to the South. So, too, northerners who had long residence and business in the South might have found it best to become citizens of that state. The challenge was the southern IDPs who in principle wanted to return to the South but were prevented by economics from doing so, at least for some time. At a minimum, some agreement on their rights was necessary, perhaps in the form of dual citizenship or permanent residence for a set period. Still, the Ethiopia-Eritrea case shows how fragile such agreements can be.

Start Discussions or Negotiations Early

In virtually no case did this happen because criteria for citizenship are a sovereign right. As a result, it was easy to focus—as in Sudan's case—on the referendum and postpone citizenship until the new sovereign state was created. Yet, again, the situation in Ethiopia and Eritrea is a stark example of the risk of deferring these issues, and Serbia and Montenegro a less dramatic one. Citizenship may be a sovereign right, but the overlap of sovereignties when new states are created can lead to tragedy until agreements are reached.

Immediate Issues on Secession: Sudan as Case Study

If the general principle for citizenship is to start discussions or negotiations early and give people time to decide, the immediate issues can be very pressing. Before the secession vote, Sudan exemplified them. The real concern was that if the South voted for independence, there could be serious repercussions for southerners currently living in the North, among them one to two million IDPs.

Before secession, Sudan operated under an Interim National Constitution (INC). Although the INC demonstrated a fair amount of tolerance for other religions and ethnicities and accorded all citizens equal rights, the government of Sudan (GoS) had not historically shown a similar tolerance, hence the concern that a secession vote would lead to Khartoum using the new constitution to revoke the rights of southerners or other non-Muslims living in the North. This discussion of Sudan's national law, presecession, is less relevant than the discussion of international law that follows. But it does illustrate, graphically, the challenge confronting IDPs during a secession.

Citizenship Rights Under National Law

Despite the INC safeguards, at secession there remained the question of how the GoS would react to a vote for independence in the South. If it chose to react in a vengeful or spiteful manner, there was the possibility that those assurances would be stripped away. On that score, the GoS's record was unpromising notwithstanding the protections that the INC and international law provided: it was a history of discrimination and abuse with regard to southerners and non-Muslims.

Like many well-meaning constitutions, the INC provided that every human being had the rights to life and human dignity, rights to personal liberty and security, freedom from arbitrary arrest and from slavery and torture, equality before the law, rights to a fair trial, litigation, and privacy, freedom of creed or worship, and freedom of assembly and association. The Bill of Rights provided other rights and freedoms only to citizens, including freedom of movement and residence, the rights to own property and to vote, access to public health care and education, and freedom of expression and media.[10] Although the freedom of worship and the freedom of assembly are safeguarded even for noncitizens, the freedom of movement, the freedom of expression, and the right to own property are worrisomely absent.

The INC granted an "inalienable right to enjoy Sudanese nationality and citizenship" to any person born to a Sudanese mother or father. Thus, Sudanese citizenship was not automatically provided to all people born in Sudan, but rather was contingent on having a parent who was a citizen. This, coupled with a new geographical definition of the boundaries of the Republic of Sudan, could mean that many southerners in the North would be considered to no longer have a "Sudanese mother or father" for purposes of nationality and citizenship.

Citizenship was "the basis for equal rights and duties for all Sudanese" according to article 7 of the INC. However, article 22, the "Saving Clause," provided that some INC provisions were not, by themselves, enforceable in a court of law. Given that rights and governmental obligations were derived only through citizenship, the large-scale revoking of citizenship would have serious consequences for southerners living in the North, leaving them without many rights and without the ability to legally enforce the ones they are left with.

Moreover, the rights provided in the INC's Bill of Rights were full of conditional language, granted only if they accorded with and were regulated by "the law," or conditioned upon "morality" or other similarly ambiguous terms. If "morality" is based on the government's idea of Muslim morality, this could be used to discriminate against southerners and non-Muslims. Given that the current northern government had not encouraged tolerance for divergent religions and cultures, despite the fact that the words "religion" and "culture" were plural in the INC, new constitutions for Sudan might not reflect that plurality of belief.

The rights of non-Muslims in Khartoum were dictated and protected through the Non-Muslims Rights Special Commission,[11] which guaranteed the protection of non-Muslims through procedural mechanisms and safeguards. These safeguards included judicial guides for the courts on how to deal with non-Muslims with regard to Sharia law, as well as specialized courts and attorneys to investigate and address any violations of the mandated protections. These safeguards could also be threatened removing the language in the constitution that supports the existence of multiple religions or cultures. Table 1.2 lays out national law and citizenship in Sudan at the time of the secession vote.

Citizenship Rights in International Law

Under international law, several safeguards pertain to the rights of noncitizens. These come in several categories—customary law, refugee law, and international conventions. While the GoS is state party to a number of international laws and conventions, its adherence to those has been limited. Also, the government has not accepted the jurisdiction of any enforcement mechanisms, making it questionable whether rights under the treaties could be enforced in any case.

Under customary international law, two main laws apply to the rights of noncitizens. First, the principle of non-refoulement is binding on all states regardless of their accession to international treaties. This principle prohibits states from deporting noncitizens to a state or territory where they may face serious human rights abuses. Second is the principle of nondiscrimination, which requires all noncitizens to be treated equally. Nondiscrimination is further detailed in the International Covenant on Civil and Political Rights (ICCPR) and the International Convention on the Elimination of All Forms of Racial Discrimination (ICERD), to both of which Sudan is party.

Although the ICERD permits states to make distinctions between noncitizens and citizens, and recognizes that states have the right to determine the laws regulating nationality, it does not permit a state's laws to "discriminate against any particular nationality." Thus, the nondiscrimination clause simply ensures that all noncitizens can be equally repressed. GoS is also a

Table 1.2. National Law and Citizenship in Sudan

Issue	Explanation	Policy approach
Citizenship in original Sudan was conferred on a person who had a mother or father who was a Sudanese citizen.	If South Sudan seceded, it was unclear what would happen to the citizenship of those living in the North. If the North decided to revoke citizenship for individuals and all of their ancestors, then southerners living in the North—including IDPs—could be disenfranchised.	Define the extent to which citizenship will be affected in the case of secession. Potentially change the requirement for citizenship to being born in Sudan.
Rights appeared to be enforceable only for Sudanese citizens.	The INC said citizenship "shall be the basis for equal rights and duties for all Sudanese," suggesting that the GoS was not obliged to provide for or protect the rights and duties provided in the INC to noncitizens.	Even if the GoS did not want to give equal rights to citizens and noncitizens, it should have made all rights enforceable regardless of citizenship status.
Conditional language in the INC provided the opportunity to deny rights to southerners.	Many of the rights in the interim constitution were conditioned on their accordance with the law or with "morality." If, post-independence, "morality" changed to mean morality in accordance with Islam, this could be used to deny southerners or non-Muslims equal rights.	Remove problematic conditional language or, failing that, fully define what is meant by "morality," "except in accordance with the law," and other ambiguous language.

party to the International Covenant on Economic, Social and Cultural Rights (ICESCR), the Convention on the Rights of the Child (CRC), and the Convention Relating to the Status of Refugees (CSR).

Although Sudan is state party to all of these conventions, it has lodged various exceptions to them. For instance, GoS is a party to the CSR but does not recognize the right to movement. Although it has ratified the ICCPR,

Table 1.3. International Law and Citizenship in Sudan

Issue	Explanation	Policy approach
Customary international law requires nondiscrimination and non-refoulement.	International customary law is binding on all states regardless of accession to any international treaties and safeguards nondiscrimination among noncitizens and also bars the deportation of noncitizens to any state where they might face serious human rights violations.	GoS does not have a strong track record of adherence to customary or other international law. Furthermore, these laws don't lessen the opportunity for repression of noncitizens within Sudan, just requires that all be repressed equally.
Sudan is party to ICCPR, ICESCR, ICERD, and CRC.	These international treaties are binding and have been successfully adjudicated in the International Court of Justice (ICJ) (*Georgia v. Russia*).	So long as the GoS has signed an international law without reservations, its provisions should be subject to enforcement by the ICJ.
Sudan is a state party to the Convention Regarding the Status of Refugees.	The CSR should guarantee the rights of refugees living in a host country, so long as they fulfill the definition of a refugee under the definition of the protocol.	GoS signed the CSR with an exception to an article that allows for freedom of movement. In addition, if GoS refused to recognize IDPs as refugees, they could be denied the rights outlined in the CSR and its protocol.

Sudan does not recognize the competence of the Human Rights Committee to hear interstate complaints, nor has it ratified the optional protocol that allows individuals to file communications with the committee. Beyond these state-level disagreements with law, international law supports a state's right to depart from a number of human rights in, for instance, "time of public emergency which threatens the life of a nation" (ICCPR). So there will remain opportunities for the GoS to avoid providing rights to refugees or other South Sudanese living in the North if it so desires.

Following a secession, IDPs living in the "other" state are no longer considered internally displaced but instead may qualify as refugees, stateless persons, or legal or illegal immigrants in the territory. In the Sudan case, the GoS was bound to protect the rights of refugees under the CSR; however, this would be binding only if the IDPs fit the criteria of refugees, postindependence. If they were declared stateless persons or otherwise, they might not be able to access the rights given under CSR. Moreover, Sudan signed the CSR with a reservation to the right of movement for refugees, meaning that they would not have to honor that particular clause.

Two conventions relate to stateless persons—the 1954 Convention Relating to the Status of Stateless Persons and the 1961 Convention on the Reduction of Statelessness, which refer to de jure and de facto (respectively) stateless persons. However, Sudan is not a party to either, and thus they are not directly relevant to the secession, although they may provide theoretical guidance. Sudan is state party to both the 1951 CSR and its 1967 protocol that elaborates the rights, obligations, and consequences for breach of international refugee law. However, if Sudan refused to recognize the status of a refugee, it would not be bound to deliver to them the rights guaranteed in these conventions.

Above all, whether the Sudan will fulfill the rights obligated by international treaties is deeply in question. The GoS has not accepted the jurisdiction of any of the enforcement bodies of these treaties, so individual enforcement of obligations could be difficult or impossible. It is, however, subject to the jurisdiction of the International Court of Justice for infringements of obligations under ICERD and CSR, so there is at least some possibility of redress of discrimination. Table 1.3 summarizes international law and immediate citizenship issues.

Because citizenship is an essence of sovereignty, national discretion is high and international enforcement weak. Indeed, outside parties have difficulty influencing decisions until it is too late, even when national track records are poor, as they were in the case of the GoS. There is also a binary quality to citizenship, though that can be muted through permanent residency and long periods for individual decision making. Yet that binary quality increases the risk that, in a secession, citizenship will become subject to a "drop-dead" date—a deadline that touches off panic, mass migration, and violence.

CHAPTER 2

Refugees and Security

If citizenship is the enduring people issue, refugees and their security will be an acute one in secessions. Even with goodwill on both sides, it will be hard to avoid the perception of drop-dead dates, touching of mass movements of people. Almost any secession will leave some people in limbo. A critical part of that limbo can be citizenship, the issue discussed in the previous chapter.

More immediately, though, secessions are likely to produce refugees, for those who identify with the original state and those who back the breakaway region will not be neatly separated. Indeed, in the 1990s, the world learned anew the horror of "ethnic cleansing" as the former Yugoslavia split apart. Even in less bloody cases, people will often have moved for military service or government employment, or they may have fled from fighting. If the last, they would become internally displaced persons (IDPs) if they remained in the original state. When secession occurs, however, they become refugees if they are not located in the state with which they identify.

After secession, the two states can negotiate separately with third countries into which their citizens may have fled. But Sudan, for instance, had to deal with perhaps two million southerners who lived in the North at the time of secession. Those who seek to move to their country of identity will face security risks, and while they may be welcome in principle in the state with which they identify, that state may be ill prepared to integrate them.

This chapter outlines the major issues related to refugees and secession and makes suggestions based, in particular, on four cases involving breakaway states—India and Pakistan after the partition of British India;

Russia and the breakup of the Soviet Union; Bosnia-Herzegovina after the disintegration of Yugoslavia; and Georgia and Abkhazia after Georgia's independence from the Soviet Union.

Policy Suggestions

Start Early in Improving Public Understanding

It is important to educate the most affected local communities about the implications of a secession well before it happens, and also to give them ample time to digest the new borders. In the India-Pakistan case, in the haste to achieve independence, none of this occurred. In fact, the Radcliffe Line was announced only two days after the two countries declared their independence. This may have added to the uncertainty, fear, and panic in local communities, particularly among religious minorities. In contrast, Sudan had the advantage that division long had been on the agenda, and had occurred de facto to a considerable extent even before the formal secession of South Sudan.

Assess Refugees' Intentions

An assessment of the refugees' intentions can help countries forge more coherent and long-term strategies to quickly integrate them if they so wish. Both Indian and Pakistani leaders simply assumed initially that most of the refugees were there only temporarily. Thus, these governments did not start thinking about integrating refugees until the overcrowding of refugee camps was becoming a problem.

The lessons of Bosnia may be less immediately relevant to a country like Sudan; after all, the returnees to South Sudan were not, in general, returning to places where they were not wanted. In Bosnia, where ethnic conflict was the direct cause of displacement, it was naïve to view returning displaced persons to their homes as undoing the ethnic divides created by war. While multiethnic communities may be desired in principle by national (and international) entities, the rights of displaced persons, including the right not to return to their place of origin, should be paramount.

Make Sure Formal Agreements Are Rooted in Real Agreement

While formal agreements can be valuable for outlining the principles of returning IDPs to their homes, they will prove woefully inadequate if both parties are not committed to the process. The language of such agreements is typically broad enough that either party can stall the process without violating the letter of law. Such was the case between Georgia and Abkhazia; the latter, having achieved an Abhaz ethnic majority in Abkhazia, had little interest in seeing displaced Georgians return.

Prepare for the Returnees

When a nation breaks up, mass population movements of ethnic minorities toward their ethnic home can ensue even in the absence of ethnic persecution and violence. The migrant-receiving country must therefore have adequate institutions and support for potential returnees from the onset. Russia was not well prepared for the migrants when the Soviet Union came apart, and thus many of them wound up feeling disillusioned at best.

Transparency in resettlement benefits is also key, as the Pakistani case showed. Indeed, by favoring Punjabi refugees over Bengali ones, the Pakistani government fueled the tensions between these two groups. In particular, if tensions between different factions are high before partition, it is important to have key institutions like law enforcement functioning well, so as to be able to maintain order if tensions escalate. In India and Pakistan, these institutions were barely functional at partition. If they had been better, many deaths and displacements could have been avoided.

Protect the Returnees

In the event of a partition or secession, even when relations between the two states are acrimonious, it still may be possible to come up with joint solutions to facilitate the evacuation of refugee populations. The establishment of the Military Evacuation Organization by India and Pakistan is a good example. IDPs have frequently been used as political capital to establish or maintain a majority population in an area where political clout falls along ethnic lines—as they were in Bosnia. To combat this, durable solutions for the displaced should be viewed first in humanitarian terms.

Benefit from Third Parties

Third parties, especially UN organizations, can be very helpful both as providers of assistance and as guarantors of agreements. Especially in secessions like Sudan's, where the countries are both poor and inexperienced in dealing with large population inflows, the international community can help the migration and settlement process. It can therefore be helpful for states to work with UN organizations, especially the UN High Commissioner for Refugees (UNHCR), and nongovernmental organizations (NGOs) both to establish needed institutions and to provide direct assistance to the returnees. That lesson emerges strongly in all the cases. In Russia, for instance, the UNHCR and the IOM, along with several NGOs, not only helped the Russian government set up the institutional and legislative framework for dealing with migration, but also provided direct assistance to the migrants themselves, in the forms of both financial support and capacity building, in order to facilitate their integration within Russia.

Those third parties must, however, be truly neutral. The UN Observer Mission in Georgia (UNOMIG), for instance, was composed entirely of Russian troops, and Russia had provided both arms and assistance to Abkhazia. In any case, given the lack of real agreement between Georgia and Abkhazia, UNOMIG has been able to sustain a ceasefire but hardly can guarantee the return of Georgian IDPs or refugees.

Avoid Letting Those Who Do Not Wish to Return Become Bargaining Chips

Georgia-Abkhazia in the mid-1990s was in some respects the mirror image of Sudan in 2010, for ethnic Georgians wished to return to their homes in Abkhazia but could not feel secure enough to do so. In the case of southern

Sudanese in the North, that was not the case. The Georgian government was so focused on repatriating the IDPs that it took years to even begin to seriously try to integrate them in Georgia; they became a bargaining chip. Negotiations should aim to make sure that southern Sudanese or other IDPs who wish to return to the state they identify with do not become a bargaining chip.

Protect Those Who Do Not Wish to Return

A key strategy for migrant-receiving countries in avoiding a sudden flood of migrants is negotiating and advocating for the protection of ethnic minorities in the states where they reside, as Russia did with many of the other newly independent states (NIS). In general, protecting displaced persons' right to return should not be construed by policy makers as a mandate to enforce their return. The freedom of movement—and therefore local integration in a new area—should simultaneously be respected.

Sometimes, even activities to ensure the protection of human rights can be construed as political. The UNHCR provided protection to Bosnian Muslims fleeing their homes in the 1990s and was later accused of being an accomplice to ethnic cleansing. Later, when the UNHCR protected ethnic communities that remained in their place of residence, it was criticized for sparing neighboring countries from receiving floods of refugees. Table 2.1 summarizes the policy suggestions.

Partition of British India

Issue and Outcome

At independence, British India was partitioned into two countries: on August 14 and August 15, 1947, respectively, the Dominion of Pakistan and the Union of India came into being. The former was composed of the two nonadjacent regions of East Pakistan (which is now Bangladesh) and West Pakistan, separated by one thousand miles of Indian territory. The partition derived from a deep religious divide between Muslims and Hindus dating back to the early 1900s, as well as between Muslims and Sikhs, and from the desire of some Muslims to set up a separate state made up of the provinces

Table 2.1. Policy Suggestions for Refugee Issues

Issue	*Policy suggestion*	*Relevant cases*
When to start public education?	Start early—indeed Sudan had the advantage of already having de facto separation.	India-Pakistan as starkest negative example of failure to prepare.
How to understand refugee intentions?	Carefully assess intentions, perhaps in surveys.	Both India and Pakistan thought refugees created by division would be temporary. In Bosnia, too, it was assumed that return would undo ethnic cleansing.
What is the role of formal agreements?	They are important but need to be based on real agreement between the parties; almost all formal agreements can be stalled or evaded.	Formal agreement between Georgia and Abkhazia meant little because there was no real agreement that the IDPs should return to Abkhazia.
How to prepare for the returnees?	This is very important, in terms of not only housing and jobs, but also legal institutions. Transparency is also key.	Russia did little to prepare, and thus returnees were disillusioned. Neither India nor Pakistan was prepared; worse, Pakistan favored Punjabi over Bengali refugees.
How to protect the returnees?	Even given tension between the two states, it is possible to fashion arrangements to protect refugees and returnees.	India-Pakistan Military Evacuation Organization is an example.
What role for third parties?	The strong lesson all the cases is that third parties—especially UN organizations but also NGOs—can be invaluable as honest brokers and as providers of assistance.	Caution: third parties must be impartial. The UN Observer Mission in Georgia (UNOMIG) was composed entirely of Russian troops and thus seen as pro-Abkhazia.

Table 2.1 *(continued)*

Issue	Policy suggestion	Relevant cases
How to avoid refugees as bargaining chips?	This is a key aim for negotiations, so that the right of return for those who wish to return does not become a bargaining chip.	Georgians displaced from Abkhazia became, in effect, hostages to Georgia's determination that they return, and suffered as a result.
How to deal with those who don't wish to return?	Right to return can't become the obligation to do so. Thus, it is critical to protect the rights of those IDPs who want to stay.	Russia was very active in seeking protections for those Russians who wished to remain in other states of the former Soviet Union.

with Muslim-majority populations. They felt the predominantly Hindu leadership in India would not adequately represent their interests.[1]

The run-up to the partition and the immediate aftermath were marked by riots and violence resulting from religious persecution of minorities on both sides. An estimated half million people were killed, and mass displacements of religious minorities in turn touched off mass population movements between the new borders and a major refugee crisis in the border provinces.[2] An estimated seven million Muslims fled India for Pakistan, while some eight million Hindus and Sikhs fled Pakistan for India.[3]

The extent of the violence and the ensuing exodus took both governments by surprise. At independence neither had put in place mechanisms and institutions either to protect minorities or to facilitate their evacuation. Furthermore, the two countries received very little help from the international community, as Western governments did not view the two countries as geopolitically important and the UNHCR did not at the time have any provision for dealing with "partition" refugees. As a result, the massive population movements caused appalling loss of life, rocked both newly established countries, and nearly collapsed state infrastructures.[4]

Nevertheless, after the initial months of chaos, particularly in the western part of the subcontinent, the authorities in the two countries were able to organize the evacuations of religious minorities as well as to provide some security during the migration process through the creation of two joint institutions, the Military Evacuation Organization (MEO) and the Joint

Refugee Council. Yet both countries assumed that the refugees were temporary and would go back to their original homes once the violence had died
down. As such, the formidable challenge of resettling refugees took center
stage only starting in 1948.

Course of the Dispute

While religious tensions had existed in India since at least the early 1900s,
the violence began shortly after the British government decided in 1945 to
grant India its independence. On August 16, 1946, the All India Muslim
League (AIML), a party created in 1906 to promote Muslim interests, called
on Muslims to participate in the "Direct Action Day" to pressure the government to accept the two-nation concept at independence. This however led to
riots in Calcutta, in which over four thousand people died. Over the next
couple of weeks, the unrest spread into other areas, with communal riots in
several other provinces including Bihar and Punjab.[5] These events convinced
the British government that the partition of India was unavoidable, and London's plan for partition was announced on June 3, 1947.

The borders between the two countries, known as the Radcliffe Line, were
announced on August 17 and were determined on the basis of the religious
distribution of the population: provinces with a majority Hindu population
became India and those with a majority Muslim population became Pakistan.[6]
This meant that Pakistan was made up of two nonadjacent enclaves. In the
west, Punjab province was separated into East Punjab, located in India, and
West Punjab, located in Pakistan, and likewise in the east, Bengal province
was divided into West Bengal and East Pakistan, located respectively in India
and Pakistan.[7]

Partition immediately touched off riots and unrest in many cities (Lahore
in Pakistan, Amritsar, Delhi, and Calcutta in India). In the western part of
the former British India, this translated into the persecution of religious
minorities. Many of them fled their homes by foot or by train under very
perilous conditions, risking attacks by opponents who killed and tortured
on a large scale, and raped and abducted women in the migrating convoys.
In sum, within three months of the partition—between August and November
1947—an estimated half million people were killed as 4.5 million Hindus and
Sikhs moved from Pakistan into India and 5.5 million Muslims went the
opposite direction.[8]

In the eastern part of the subcontinent, reactions immediately after independence were calmer. Indeed, while Calcutta experienced some unrest, the two-way population movements were relatively minor and more voluntary, with people moving for socioeconomic reasons rather than fleeing religious persecution. However, in late 1949, riots in East Pakistan led masses of Hindus to migrate from East Pakistan into India. Similarly, communal riots in West Bengal led more than one million Muslim refugees to flee to Pakistan.

The flow of East Pakistani Hindus into West Bengal continued over the next five years as border quarrels between Pakistan and India in the west (in Kashmir) intensified. Uncertainty over proposals to make Urdu the official language of Pakistan (to the detriment of Bengali) and to adopt an Islamic constitution led to increased unease among Hindus living in East Pakistan. This flow was stopped only briefly between 1959 and 1964 when the government of India decided to close all the refugee camps in West Bengal and not provide any assistance to refugees from East Pakistan. It had to reopen them in 1964 when tensions arose in East Pakistan, which eventually led to its secession from Pakistan in 1971, which again resulted in more refugees flocking into India.[9]

At independence, the governments of India and Pakistan did not expect the level of violence and the mass population exodus that the partition induced. As a result, they were ill prepared to deal with the crisis, especially in the western part of the subcontinent, where the bulk of the population movements happened in the first three months. And given that the pace of the movements was so different between the western part (i.e., between East Punjab in India and West Punjab in Pakistan) and the eastern part (i.e., West Bengal in India and East Pakistan), the arrangements that the two governments established to deal with the crises in the west and in the east differed substantially.

In the west, the pressure on the civil administration was such that the military had to take over the evacuation of the endangered religious minorities and to provide them with humanitarian aid. On August 1, 1947, the Boundary Force, an Indian military force of about twenty-five thousand men of "mixed class composition" under the British command, was created as a neutral entity to ensure civil order and protect the religious minorities. However, while the force supported some of the evacuation efforts, it largely failed to prevent the riots and the atrocities that followed. In the end, the Boundary Force was disbanded just a month after it was created.[10]

As the crisis intensified, the two countries formed ministries to handle refugee evacuation and rehabilitation. Both recognized the need to secure

the paths of the refugees during their journey to the border and to protect
them from attacks from opposing groups, so MEO was formed in September 1947 as a joint endeavor to organize the flow of migrants and secure
evacuations by rail, road, and foot. For those traveling by foot, the MEO
prepared a Joint Evacuation Movement Plan to schedule the movement of
large convoys of refugees in order to avoid clashes. In addition, the MEO
acted to secure trains and reduce attacks on them, and was able to organize
sixty mass evacuations by rail in November 1947. The Joint Refugee Council
was also set up by the two governments to provide emergency medical supplies and food at rest stops for the migrating refugees.[11]

Very little by way of resettlement occurred in either country, as authorities in both expected the refugees to go back to their original homes once
the situation stabilized. In India, refugees were accommodated in transit
camps, which were run by provincial governments with financial help from
the central government. In Pakistan, where the situation was more urgent
(one in ten people was a refugee), the new administration had less state infrastructure and experience than its Indian counterpart to deal with the
refugee crisis. The Pakistani government did not come up with a coherent
strategy to deal with refugee settlement until late September 1947. At that
point, refugee camps were set up in West Punjab and an Emergency Committee of the Cabinet was created to manage the distribution of food and
emergency aid to refugees, in conjunction with the Joint Refugee Council.[12]

The rising number of refugees in transit and refugee camps signaled that
the situation was unsustainable and that more needed to be done to reha-
bilitate and integrate refugee populations. In India, the Ministry for Relief
and Rehabilitation was renamed the Ministry of Rehabilitation in 1948 and
took on the mission of preparing the refugees to be resettled in newly constructed townships. Refugees were relocated to more permanent camps, where
they were provided with vocational and technical training; some were given
remunerative employment,[13] and were then gradually dispersed into the new
townships.

In its resettlement strategy, the Pakistani government was more draco-
nian: in August 1948, it declared a state of emergency that gave it the right to
resettle refugees from Punjab in other provinces. There, provisions were made
to provide housing for urban refugees and loans for agricultural land and
inputs for the rural refugees. However, Pakistan tended to be more generous
to the relatively more prosperous—and thus influential—Punjabis than to the
Bengalis, most of whom were poor farmers.

In the eastern part, given the lesser hostility between Hindus and Muslims, the two countries' strategy was to prevent major population movements across the border through bilateral negotiations of rights for religious minorities. In the 1948 Inter-Dominion Conference, the two governments agreed that both would be responsible for protecting the religious minorities who resided in their respective states.

In 1950 the two countries negotiated to remove administrative burdens for those seeking citizenship, and provide guarantees for the rights of religious minorities in their chosen residence. These negotiations culminated in the Nehru-Liaquat Pact, which provided religious minorities in both India and Pakistan "with complete equality of citizenship irrespective of religion; a full sense of security in respect of life, culture, property and personal honor and also guaranteed fundamental human rights of the minorities, such as freedom of movement, speech, occupation and worship."[14] Both countries subsequently established minority commissions to implement the pact.[15]

However, these agreements and negotiations were not enough to prevent some sporadic migration, and the governments had to respond accordingly. For example, as the result of unrest in late 1949, the Indian government was forced to set up refugee camps in West Bengal. It used the same model applied in the Punjab, but because the refugees were mostly rural, the government arranged for loans or grants to enable them to purchase land. Yet the steady stream of refugees arriving from Pakistan was putting more pressure on land, and starting in 1955 the government of India actively sought, albeit unsuccessfully, gradually to close the camps in West Bengal.[16]

Assessment and Possible Lessons

Several important lessons emerge from the India-Pakistan partition:

The case underscores the importance of educating the most affected local communities about the implications of a partition or secession before it happens and giving them plenty of time to digest the new borders. Neither happened in this case, creating fear and panic.

When tensions between different groups are high before partition, it is important to have key institutions, especially law enforcement, in place and functioning well in order to be able to maintain order if tensions escalate. In India and Pakistan, these institutions were barely functional at partition; had they been, many deaths and displacements could have been avoided.

In a secession, the parties can fashion joint solutions to help evacuate refugee populations even if relations between the two states are acrimonious. The establishment of MEO is a good example.

An assessment of the refugees' intentions can help countries carve more coherent and long-term strategies to quickly integrate them if they so wish. Both India and Pakistan simply assumed initially that most of the refugees were there only temporarily and so came late to the need for resettlement.

Transparency in resettlement benefits is key, as the Pakistani case showed. Indeed, by favoring Punjabi refugees over Bengali ones, the government fueled the tensions between these two groups.

The Breakup of the Soviet Union and the Russian Diaspora

Issue and Outcome

When the Soviet Union (hereafter referred to as "former Soviet Union," or FSU) was disbanded in 1991,[17] fifteen new republics were formed and, consequently, an estimated 43.4 million people living outside of their "ethnic homelands" instantly became foreigners in their countries of residence.[18] Russians constituted the majority of this group, with 25.3 million of them living outside the Russian Federation. In the years that followed the disbanding of the FSU, many in this new Russian diaspora immigrated back to Russia: 3.3 million Russians who had previously lived in a different FSU state moved to Russia between 1989 and 2002.[19]

In general, Russians living in the other NIS were not the targets of violence, and thus were not forced to leave. Technically, then, they cannot be considered "forced migrants" or "refugees." Nevertheless, because Russians had acquired dominant positions in the non-Russian states under the Soviet regime, at independence they were in some cases seen as "occupiers" and representatives of the "former colonial power," and their positions were sometimes threatened by the new government policies implemented by the other NIS. Moreover, rising nationalism in some of the NIS made ethnic Russians feel less at home, particularly in the non-Slavic states.[20]

In essence, the Russian migrants were "ethno-migrants," who left their homes in the non-Russian states for various reasons, including anxiety about their future and economic well-being outside Russia. The context of this anxiety was rising violence, even if not directed at them, or of the new states trying to establish a national identity separate from that of the FSU or Russia.[21] The pull of economics also attracted some of the migration: Russia's economy was twice the size of those of all the FSU states combined and was more prosperous than any of them except that of Estonia. Probably for economic reasons, fewer Russians emigrated from the more nationalist (but richer) Baltic states than from other NIS that were formally more welcoming but poorer.

While the Russian federal government set up the Federal Migration Service (FMS), and a number of local governments followed suit with their respective regional organizations, very little state support was accorded to the settlers beyond a small emergency payment. As a result, many of the returnees were confronted with difficulties in finding housing and employment commensurate with their professional qualifications. This resulted in widespread dissatisfaction among them and a sense of instability, as well as a loss of confidence in the state institutions that were supposed to provide them with resettlement support.

The international community, through the UNHCR, IOM, and several NGOs, played a key role in the resettlement process by assisting Russia along two lines. First, the UNHCR and the IOM, in particular, helped the Russian government set up the institutional and legislative framework for dealing with migration. Second, they provided support to the migrants in integrating themselves in Russia, in the forms of both direct assistance and individual capacity building.[22]

Course of the Dispute

Although Russian settlements in non-Russian states on the periphery date back to the sixteenth century, the migration accelerated under more systematic sponsorship of the Soviet region. In a number of these states, the Russian population increased rapidly; by 1989, Russians on average made up 18 percent of the population in non-Russian states and 27 percent in their urban areas. Moreover, a number of ethnically non-Russian Soviets, known as "Russophones," identified themselves with Russia in terms of culture and language.[23] The Russian and Russophone population was not evenly distributed among the various states, ranging from 11 million in Ukraine to 52,000 in Armenia. Kazakhstan had the second largest population of Russians, with 6 million, while Uzbekistan, Belarus, Kyrgyzstan, and Latvia also had large Russian populations, between 900,000 and 1.6 million. In contrast, the rest of the republics had Russian populations of half a million or less.

Russians and Russophones also represented a large proportion of the population in some cases—30 percent in Estonia, 34 percent in Latvia, 22 percent in Ukraine, and 38 percent in Kazakhstan.[24] As a result, over four decades of Soviet rule, the proportion of the population from the titular nationality dropped from 90 to 60 percent in Estonia, and from 75 to 52 percent in Latvia. Russification was less of an issue in the other Baltic state, Lithuania, because the Russian population represented only 9 percent of the total population.[25]

In general, the Russian populations residing in the non-Russian periphery were highly concentrated in urban areas, with the exception of Kazakhstan and to a lesser extent Kyrgyzstan.[26] On the whole, they were also relatively more educated than the titular nationalities, occupied higher-level posts, and had superior socioeconomic status. In some cases, this caused strong anti-Russian sentiment among the titular groups.[27] Partly as a result of this and partly because of strong cultural differences between some of the titular nationalities and ethnic Russians, there was little mixing between the two groups during the Soviet years.

The ethnic Russians formed "isolated ethnic enclaves," except in the Slavic states, where Russians had closer cultural ties with the local populace.[28] Given that Russian was the official language within the Soviet Union, very few Russians learned the local language even if they had lived outside Russia for generations, a practice that further reinforced their isolation from the local populations.[29]

The breakup of the Soviet Union launched a gradual emigration of ethnic Russians and Russophones to the Russian Federation. Net immigration to Russia from the non-Russian states increased from 105,000 in 1991 to a peak of 915,000 in 1994, then fell back to 124,000 in 2001. The extent of the emigration from the various NIS was not uniform. Indeed, the majority of Russians and Russophones residing in the Transcaucasus states and Tajikistan chose to leave, while far fewer of them emigrated from Uzbekistan, Kyrgyzstan, and Turkmenistan (25 percent) and Kazakhstan (22 percent). On the lower end of the spectrum, 10 to 13 percent of the Russians and Russophones residing in the Baltic states and Moldova chose to emigrate, while very few of them left Ukraine and Belarus.[30]

Despite some anti-Russian sentiment, ethnic Russians were not persecuted, nor were they targeted for major ethnic violence. Rather, their decision to emigrate was driven by some combination of more subtle factors. For one, at independence, in order to build a separate identity from the Soviet Union, the other post-Soviet states changed the official language from Russian to the local one and elevated their ethnicity, for instance by ensuring positions in the government administration and greater political representation for local ethnicities.

Some states, notably Estonia and Latvia, took even more drastic steps by restricting citizenship to just titular nationalities. This not only made the Russian/Russophone population uncomfortable but also directly threatened their acquired social and economic status, prompting many of them to leave. So too the level of cultural connections between the Russian/Russophone diaspora and the titular nationalities played a role in determining the level of emigration: the extent of emigration from the other Slavic states was minimal, while in Turkmenistan, growing nationalism as well as the rise of Islam led to increased ethnic Russian emigration.[31]

In other states, emigration was driven by factors unrelated to ethnicity. In Georgia and Tajikistan, for example, instability and violence following independence, while not targeted at the Russian diaspora, led many of its members to leave. Finally, the pull of the Russian economy, twice as large as all the FSU economies combined, appeared to offer better employment opportunities and earning potential.[32]

At the breakup of the Soviet Union, policies toward the Russian diaspora in the post-Soviet states ranged from hostile to accommodating. Some states devised exclusionary policies toward the Russians, while others shaped policies to dissuade them from emigrating, though none was prepared to give the political representation to the Russians on a scale commensurate with their share of the population. At one extreme, the Baltic states, with sizeable Russian populations, feared that the ethnic Russians would overshadow the titular groups and turn the latter into minorities within their own states. As a result, the new governments established very exclusionary citizenship and language laws. Estonia and Latvia denied automatic citizenship to Russian minorities, and in both countries ethnic Russians were considered in theory illegal immigrants, on the argument that the Soviet Union had occupied the two countries since 1940.[33]

In contrast, in the central Asian countries—particularly Kazakhstan and Kyrgyzstan, and initially Turkmenistan—where the ethnic Russians constituted a large proportion of the educated labor force, the governments put in place polices to entice the Russians to stay—for instance, some political representation and dual citizenship in Tajikistan and Turkmenistan. They feared an economic loss if the Russians were to leave en masse.[34]

At independence, the Russian Federation did not have much of a legislative foundation for dealing with mass population movements, nor did it have the institutional experience. Therefore, in the immediate aftermath of the breakup, with the help of the UNHCR and the IOM, the Russian government took a number of steps toward adhering to international migration norms, abolishing the internal passport system and granting its citizens the freedom of movement, as well as acceding to the 1951 United Nations Refugee Convention and Protocol. In February 1992, it also devised its first citizenship law, which was in theory supposed to be ethnically neutral: anyone who was a permanent resident of Russia or who felt "ethnically or emotionally connected to Russia" could apply for citizenship, which essentially meant that all citizens of the FSU were eligible to apply.[35]

In addition, to avoid a mass return of ethnic Russians, the Russian government advocated forcefully for the protection of the rights of ethnic Russians and Russophones living in the other NIS. Moscow pursued a policy of dual citizenship, which was rejected by all but Tajikistan and Turkmenistan lest it weaken their nation-building efforts, and pushed for Russian to be the language of interethnic communication within the FSU.[36] In addition, it pursued a policy of open borders with the other NIS. For example, in October 1992 it signed the Bishkek Accord to allow for free movement among the signatories (Belarus, Armenia, Uzbekistan, Tajikistan, Turkmenistan, Kazakhstan, Kyrgyzstan, and Moldova, in addition to Russia). Georgia joined the accord in 1995.[37] In 1997, Russia negotiated separate bilateral visa-free travel arrangements with Ukraine and Azerbaijan.

In terms of resettlement and integration policies in Russia, there was more rhetoric than concrete support for returnees, due in part to resource constraints. In 1994 a Russian presidential decree promulgated a "Basic Conception of a Programme to Help Compatriots" and an accompanying resolution on "Measures for the Support of Compatriots Abroad." In these pieces of legislation, the Russian government designated the returnees as "forced migrants" or "refugees," entitling them to resettlement and integration support. Institutionally, the FMS was set up in 1992 to manage the migrant resettlement process. It was supplemented by parallel regional organizations across the country—eighty-nine at the height of the in-migration—that were supposed to coordinate with the federal government to provide the needed support.[38]

However, in practice, the level of support for and receptiveness to the returnees varied greatly across the regions, depending on the number of in-migrants to the region and the particular socioeconomic and political environment. In some areas, the returnees were seen as a benefit because they represented either a way to attract more federal resources or a source of labor amid dire demographic trends, high mortality, and low fertility. In others, they were seen as a threat to the socioeconomic stability of the region. In either case, the regional organizations determined their own policies, either encouraging or discouraging in-migration. Some of these policies, particularly those geared toward restricting in-migration, contravened federal directives and international law.[39]

Whether they encouraged or discouraged migration, regions provided at most modest support to migrants. Many received only a small emergency payment but no support for key needs like housing and employment. As a result, a number of the migrants had to take jobs that were far below their qualifications and skills, in the process becoming highly disillusioned by the system.[40]

To some extent, the IOM, the UNHCR, and some international NGOs, including the Danish Refugee Council and Opportunity International, stepped in to fill the void. In 1993, the IOM provided the first set of direct international assistance under its Direct Assistance Programme, which supplied migrant organizations with equipment to help them set up small-scale private enterprises.

Later, the UNHCR, in conjunction with the two NGOs, implemented regional micro-credit projects targeting the resettling migrants with the similar objective of spurring sustainable livelihoods for the settlers. It also organized capacity-building programs to help migrants set up and manage regional associations, which were then provided with grants to enable them to undertake large-scale projects geared toward resettlement and integration of returnees. In addition, to deal with the more immediate needs, the UNHCR provided small-scale loans to those deemed internally displaced to aid them with essential needs such as housing.[41]

Assessment and Possible Lessons

The emigration of the Russian diaspora back to Russia after the fall of the Soviet Union presents lessons that may be relevant for other secessions:

Negotiating and advocating for the protection of ethnic minorities in the states where they reside can be key to a strategy for migrant-receiving countries in avoiding a sudden flood of migrants. Russia did just that with many of the other NIS.

When a nation breaks up, mass population movements of ethnic minorities toward their ethnic home can ensue even in the absence of ethnic persecution and violence. It is therefore important for the migrant-receiving country to at least plan institutions and support for potential returnees from the onset.

The international community can play a positive role in assisting with the migration and settlement process, especially when the secession involves poor and inexperienced states. States should work with UN organizations, especially UNHCR, and NGOs to establish the required institutions as well as to direct support the returnees.

In terms of resettlement in the context of a decentralized state, it is important to align the goals and incentives of federal and regional institutions in order to provide consistent support to the settlers. Otherwise, the resettlement process will be nonuniform across the country, increasing the opaqueness of the process.

Georgia and Abkhazia

Issue and Outcome

Following Georgia's independence from the FSU, two regions demanded independence from Georgia, including Abkhazia in 1992.[42] The fighting that followed displaced more than 250,000 people, mostly ethnic Georgians. In 1994 a four-way agreement for the voluntary return of IDPs and refugees was negotiated among Abkhazia, Georgia, the Russian Federation, and the UNHCR. Over the more than a decade and a half since the conflict began, the UNHCR, the Organization for Security and Cooperation in Europe (OSCE), and other international organizations have been involved in efforts to establish peace in the region and facilitate the safe return of IDPs to their homes in Abkhazia.

Despite the presence of these international organizations, armed conflicts and ethnic cleansing have continued to flare up periodically. Thus, in spite of official agreement to repatriate ethnic Georgians to Abkhazia and participation by multiple international aid organizations, the return of IDPs to Abkhazia has been stymied by the political issues that remain unresolved between Georgia and Abkhazia. Nearly two decades after the conflict began, the vast majority of those who fled Abkhazia remain displaced, too fearful of further targeted violence to return to their homes in Abkhazia.

Course of the Dispute

Abkhazia is small region in the northwest corner of Georgia, bordering the Black Sea and Russia. Its primary economic activities are agriculture and tourism. Of strategic importance, the BTC (Baku-Tbilisi-Ceyhan) oil pipeline traverses Abkhazia en route to Turkey. For decades Abkhazia has been a multiethnic society composed of people of Abkhaz, Georgian, Armenian, Jewish, and Greek descent, among others. During the Soviet era, Abkhazia was an autonomous republic within the Georgian Soviet Socialist Republic. When the Soviet Union dissolved in 1991, Georgia declared its independence and included in its international borders the region of Abkhazia.

Abkhazia declared its own independence from Georgia in the following year, sparking armed conflict between Abkhazia and Georgia, and "ethnic cleansing" between the Abkhaz and Georgian populations in Abkhazia.[43] Ethnic Georgians in particular were targeted because over the previous several decades the demographics of the Abkhazia region had shifted, leaving ethnic Georgians constituting 46 percent of the population, up from 39 percent in 1959.[44] The Abkhaz claim this was the result of deliberate demographic policy by Georgia in an effort to quell the ethnically driven call for Abkhaz independence. As a result of the fighting and persecution, most ethnic Georgians (approximately 250,000 to 280,000 people) fled Abkhazia as refugees.[45] Little is known about those who were internally displaced within Abkhazia.

In 1994 Abkhazia and Georgia reached an agreement to end the armed conflict and repatriate those who had been displaced. The four-way agreement was negotiated; it is formally the Quadripartite Agreement on Voluntary Return of Refugees and Displaced Persons. According to the agreement, the parties "agree to cooperate and to interact in planning and conducting the activities aimed to safeguard and guarantee the safe, secure and dignified return of people who have fled from areas of the conflict zone to the areas of their previous permanent residence."[46] The four parties met periodically to address ongoing issues, but negotiations were often driven by other political issues among them.

In addition to the UNHCR, other international organizations—for instance, the Group of Friends, the OSCE, and the Commonwealth of Independent States Peace Keeping Force—became involved in efforts to restore peace and resettle returning IDPs in Abkhazia. In particular, UNOMIG sent a long-term peacekeeping force whose mission began in 1994. UNOMIG has helped to maintain the formal ceasefire for more than ten years but has not yet established a safe and secure environment to which IDPs might return. This stems largely from the fact that the fundamental disagreement between Abkhazia and Georgia regarding Abkhaz independence has not been resolved.

Demographics have played an important role in the conflict between Georgia and Abkhazia. Since expelling the near-majority ethnic Georgians, the Abkhaz have become the largest ethnic group in Abkhazia. By blocking the return of ethnic Georgians, the Abkhaz hope to hold onto their ethnic majority, thereby solidifying a consensus vote for independence. Demographics have played a part on the Georgian side, too, albeit in a less extreme manner. From 1990 to the mid-2000s, Georgia lost nearly 20 percent of its population to emigration.[47] Thus the loss of Abkhazia would represent a further reduction of the Georgian population, as well as a substantial economic loss.

Given the circumstances, it is unsurprising that very few IDPs have returned to Abkhazia in the fifteen years since the ceasefire. The only notable exception is the Gali region, to which an estimated 45,000 ethnic Georgians have returned. However, those returnees were met by the Abkhaz militias' attacks and efforts to intimidate, despite the presence of monitors from the UNHCR.[48] In contrast, the formal repatriation process to which all parties agreed has resulted in only 311 returnees. Moreover, most settlers fled a second time in 1998 due to recurrent ethnic cleansing.[49]

Nor is it clear that the returnees to Gali are permanent since many ethnic Georgians return there temporarily during the hazelnut harvest out of economic necessity. In fact, what looks like a "success" from the perspective of the government's repatriation agenda may in fact serve as a cautionary tale for ethnic Georgian who fled areas where Georgians were not in the majority. Given the extent to which returnees were terrorized in Gali, where they outnumbered the Abkhaz, there is little hope that smaller groups of returnees would fare better in areas where they were in the minority.

The inability of IDPs to return to Abkhazia means that Georgia has been faced with accommodating more than a quarter of a million IDPs. This represents more than an eighth of the nation's population in a country already struggling with economic hardship. Of the refugees who fled to Georgia, 70 percent settled in urban areas. The region bordering Abkhazia, just across the Induri River, absorbed 38 percent of refugees, especially those who fled from the neighboring Gali region. Tbilisi drew roughly a third of the refugees. The displaced primarily live in private accommodations (typically with family members) or makeshift collective centers (e.g., hotels, schools, and factories that have been taken over by refugee families).

Most IDPs live in extremely precarious circumstances, suffering from poverty, poor health, unemployment, psychological stress, and social alienation. Most of the communal centers lack adequate basic accommodations and are in urgent need of repair.[50] IDPs are entitled to social support benefits similar to those provided to vulnerable Georgian residents, conditional on being registered with the Georgian Ministry of Refugees and Accommodation (MRA), which was established in 1996 to address the specific needs of IDPs in Georgia. Registered IDPs who live in private residences are entitled to US$8.00 per month, while those in collective centers receive US$6.50 plus free public utilities (e.g., water, electricity). The registry was updated in 2004, and the status of 210,000 IDPs from Abkhazia was verified ten years after the end of armed conflict.[51] In 2006 the MRA launched a program that allows IDPs to register the titles to their land in Abkhazia in a state inventory to protect property and inheritance rights of ethnic Georgians.[52] This could become a bargaining chip with Abkhazia should the parties restart negotiations over the rights of refugee to their property (as protected by international law).

In 2007 the Georgian government developed a new national strategy on IDPs. It again emphasized their right to return but made more explicit that integration into Georgian society need not hinder future return to their place of origin (including Abkhazia).[53] The reemergence of armed conflict between Georgia and South Ossetia (another breakaway region) highlights the need for the swift implementation of measures to address IDPs' short- and long-term needs, whether through repatriation or resettlement and integration in Georgia proper.

Assessment and Possible Lessons

Abkhazia, while formally agreeing to repatriation, has hindered the return of refugees both officially and unofficially for more than fifteen years. In 1995 the de facto authorities of Abkhazia offered to accept two hundred returnees per week, which observers argued was too few given the number of IDPs in Georgia.[54] More recently Abkhaz officials claimed that resettlement to areas outside of Gali was "impossible now."[55] Unofficially, Abkhaz militias continue to terrorize ethnic Georgians who do return, while others expropriate the property of those who do not. Their actions continue to deter any substantial resettlement of IDPs in their homeland. The authorities have little incentive to combat these activities since the longer Abkhazia can keep returnees at bay, the greater the opportunity to cultivate an Abkhaz-centric society to which Georgian refugees would not wish to return if permitted.

For its part, Georgia has single-mindedly pursued the goal of resettling IDPs in Abkhazia. Critics claim that the needs of IDPs have been secondary to the issue of territorial control.[56] Georgia has drawn criticism for being so committed to the right of IDPs to return to their homes in Abkhazia that it effectively denied IDPs other rights, such as legal rights to vote, own property, or work. Georgia has also failed to provide adequate humanitarian assistance to those who return of their own accord and denied displaced persons the full rights of citizens in Georgia.

In more recent years Georgia has taken steps to integrate IDPs into political and economic life, while taking precautions that these do not preclude their right to return. For example, IDPs were granted the right to acquire property in Georgia while maintaining their IDP status (and thus the right to return to and reclaim their property in Abkhazia). As yet there is no change in Georgia's official policy toward Abkhazia, which is of course the most significant determinant of IDPs' prospects for return.

Russia's role has continually been a complicating factor. Initially, Russia refused to recognize Abkhazia's independence for fear that it would be used to legitimate Chechnya's calls for independence. However, Russia supplied weapons to Abkhazia and passports and pensions to its citizens, and imposed economic sanctions on Georgia at various times since 1994.[57] Given that Russia had clearly taken sides in the conflict, it was an inappropriate choice to be the sole supplier of peacekeeping forces in the UNOMIG operation. This, no doubt, harmed relations between Georgia and Abkhazia.

So long as no political solution to the conflict between Georgia and Abkhazia is in sight, there remains little hope for the peaceful return of many ethnic Georgian IDPs to their homes in Abkhazia. Moreover, in recent years the Georgian government has begun to recognize that many IDPs may prefer not to return to Abkhazia, given their safety concerns. Thus, a durable solution may take the form of resettlement in Georgia rather than repatriation, regardless of how the territorial dispute is resolved. The Gali region may be an exception, as both Georgia and Abkhazia benefit from reversing the decline in agricultural production, which would involve restoring ethnic Georgian farmers to their land. Outside of this one area, there are no immediate prospects for the return of the remaining 220,000 to 250,000 Georgians to Abkhazia.[58]

Many national and international forces were marshaled to resolve the conflict between Abkhazia and Georgia in such a way that those who fled their homes could return without fear of recurrent violence. However, the best agreements and outside assistance could not overcome the discord between parties, both of which have used the IDPs for political gain. This case study provides a cautionary tale of the importance of addressing the root cause of the dispute. The following are several lessons from the experience of Georgia and Abkhazia that may have broader relevance:

While formal agreements can be valuable for outlining the principles of returning IDPs to their homes, they are woefully inadequate if both parties are not committed to the process. The language of such agreements is typically broad enough that either party can stall the process without violating the letter of the law. In short, formal agreements are a necessary condition for resettling IDPs but not a sufficient one.

Without peace, repatriation is infeasible. The ethnic divide that caused the conflict between neighbors in the first place will reemerge if efforts to resolve the underlying issues are not successful. This was made apparent when, in 1998, the homes, schools, and farms of Georgian returnees to Gali, which had been rebuilt with international donor assistance and under international monitoring, were decimated by partisan attacks once again. In a matter of days, 40,000 people fled the renewed violence.[59]

Prolonged periods of displacement may make either eventual return or integration into the receiving country more difficult as IDPs' lives remain fractured. Evidence collected from interviews with IDPs in communal centers in Georgia suggests that living as IDPs without integrating into Georgian society encourages many to relive the memory of the ethnic conflict in Abkhazia, thus hardening their outlook. They become less able to reconcile with the ethnic Abkhaz in their homeland and remain isolated from fellow ethnic Georgians in Georgia.[60]

IDPs can be used as a political bargaining chip, thus slowing progress on repatriation or other forms of settlement. It is important to understand what stake each party to the negotiations has in the outcome. The commitment to returning displaced persons to their homes can inadvertently lead to further disadvantaging them in the meantime. Granting the legal rights to vote, purchase property, and make a living is vital to the well-being of IDPs, and this can be pursued without abandoning efforts to return them to their homes.

The details of the conflict are critical to determining what will and will not be feasible solutions. For example, it has been argued that the solution offered by Georgia, namely that Abkhazia become a largely autonomous region within the Republic of Georgia, is dismissed out of hand by Abkhaz leaders because it is likened to the "autonomy" former Soviet republics had under Soviet rule, which was a fig leaf.[61] Thus, improving the communication and trust between parties is critical to overcoming such semantic debates and developing a resolution to the conflict.

Bosnia and Herzegovina

Issue and Outcome

In 1992, after the collapse of Yugoslavia and declaration of independence by Bosnia and Herzegovina (BiH), Bosnian Serb leaders, especially, embarked on armed conflict and ethnic cleansing.[62] During the three-year conflict that ensued, more than one million people were driven out of the country and an equal number were internally displaced. In December 1995 the Dayton Peace Agreement (DPA) was signed, ending the conflict and establishing BiH as a federal republic made up of two "entities," divided largely along ethnic lines. The DPA outlined a path to peace and provided for the return of displaced peoples, with involvement from NATO and the UNHCR. The Office of the High Representative was established to oversee the civilian implementation of the DPA.

In the decade following the DPA, refugees and IDPs have steadily returned to BiH, many under a registration program run by the Ministry of Human Rights and Refugees to monitor and assist resettlement, including through reconstruction assistance. Although half of the displaced seem to have returned, the drive for ethnically "pure" areas that drove ethnic cleansing in the early 1990s continues to threaten the recovery of returnees and the long-term displaced alike.

Course of the Dispute

For three years immediately after the dissolution of Yugoslavia, BiH was plagued by the atrocities of ethnic cleansing, primarily carried out by Bosnian Serbs. By the time the war ended with the signing of the DPA in December 1995, more than half of the 4.4 million people of BiH had been hounded from their homes. Approximately 1.3 million people were internally displaced, and nearly the same number fled the country. In addition to calling a ceasefire, the DPA established the framework for the transition to peace and democracy. BiH was split into two "entities"—the mainly Serb Republika Srpska (RS) and the predominantly Croat and Muslim Federation of Bosnia and Herzegovina (FBiH). Initially, each entity had its own government while progress toward national integration was being made.

The DPA outlined pivotal roles for NATO peacekeeping forces and for the Office of the High Representative (OHR), which was in charge of civilian affairs. The 1997 Bonn Conference conferred upon the OHR the power to guide the reconciliation process. The so-called Bonn powers included the authority to remove public officials and ban legislation that violated the DPA or otherwise hindered progress toward peace and reconciliation. Under this arrangement many roadblocks were eliminated, but the formation of a fully functioning, integrated political system is still to be accomplished.

The DPA also made explicit provisions for the rights of displaced people to return to the areas from which they fled (Annex VII).[63] Underlying the emphasis on return was the "moral and political imperative to reverse 'ethnic cleansing.' "[64] To accomplish the objective of a speedy return, the DPA designated the UNHCR as the lead international agency to oversee the return of refugees and IDPs. The Ministry of Human Rights and Refugees (MHRR) coordinated return efforts at the national level, while both "entities"—RS and FBiH—also maintained their own ministry for refugees.[65] A registry was established by the MHRR to monitor and assist resettlement, and to provide reconstruction assistance, when applicable.

As is the case in other instances of ethnically motivated displacements, the return of displaced persons to the communities they fled can be used to fan fresh ethnic tensions. Depending on their ethnicity, returnees will bolster a majority group or weaken its numbers. Thus, vested interests in who returns, where, can result in a patchwork of de facto local policies, a pattern that played out in BiH. Many displaced people returned before the ink was dry on the DPA. However, in the first two years returnees were predominantly "majority returns"—that is, displaced people who returned to areas in which they belonged to the ethnic majority. Minority returns followed later once additional guarantees were in place.

Not until the early 2000s did minority and other returns gather momentum again. Several factors are credited with this development, including improved security, reconstruction, and property restitution. With the coordinated efforts of the OSCE, UNHCR, and OHR, ethnic violence declined, and many felt comfortable returning to the areas they had fled. Massive housing projects rebuilt at least some of the housing that was destroyed during the war. Perhaps the most important factor in these later flows of returnees was the provisions to reclaim or receive compensation for property abandoned during the war.[66]

The DPA affirmed that all refugees have the right to reclaim their homes or be compensated for lost or destroyed property. To accomplish this goal, the DPA created the Commission for Real Property Claims of Displaced Persons and Refugees (CRPC). The CRPC's mandate called for the commission to "receive and decide any claims for real property in BiH, where the property has not voluntarily been sold or otherwise transferred since April 1, 1992, and where the claimant does not now enjoy possession of that property."[67] Although the CRPC's decisions were final, it was not vested with the power to directly enforce its decisions, and the domestic institutions that did have such power lacked the will to enforce the rulings.

The commission remained largely ineffective and was ultimately replaced by Property Law Implementation Plan (PLIP) in 1999. The PLIP was organized by the OHR, NATO, and the UNHCR to enforce new legislation governing the resolution of property claims. Compared to its predecessor, the PLIP was well funded and supported by the international community. It was also more flexible and capable of handling emerging needs, such as the claims to occupancy rights in socially owned apartment properties. It has been very effective. Of the 200,000 claims received, 93 percent had been resolved by mid-2005, making this the first successful case of large-scale property restitution in a postconflict setting.[68]

As time has passed, the MHRR has come to recognize that return is not the universally appropriate solution to displacement. Many of those who remain as registered IDPs within BiH are vulnerable—the elderly, the mentally and physically handicapped, individuals traumatized by war, all of whom are unable or unwilling to return to the communities they fled. Thus, the MHRR and the international community have increased funding for efforts to support IDPs where they have now settled. In addition, the MHRR's 2008 revision of the National Strategy for Implementation of Annex VII acknowledged the need to provide means for compensating the displaced for their lost property, in addition to enabling restitution for those who want to return to their homes.[69]

Assessment and Possible Lessons

Perhaps the most obvious means of assessing the success of dealing with displaced people is by measuring the extent to which they have returned to the areas they fled. According to UNHCR and MHRR estimates, more than one million refugees and IDPs combined (slightly more IDPs than refugees) had returned to their prewar residence in BiH by June 2008. However, this estimate may undercount those who have returned to the area but not the residence in which they lived and overcount IDPs who returned only to leave again.[70]

Returning has proven to be difficult for a number of reasons. Rural areas, in particular, have had high unemployment rates following the war. Thus, many young IDPs and refugees from the countryside have chosen to remain in larger cities and towns or indeed abroad, where they have greater access to education and jobs. Some return only to reclaim their property and subsequently sell or rent it while continuing to live elsewhere. Still others return with plans to resettle permanently but find it daunting to do so. There are fewer economic opportunities after the devastation. In addition, those who returned to their former communities as ethnic minorities have experienced discrimination in employment and access to health services and ethnocentric curricula in local schools.[71] Thus, while significant progress has been made, the goal of returning the displaced to their homes amid safety, security, and dignity remains only partially fulfilled.

Officially the armed conflict between ethnic groups in BiH ended many years ago, and while a stable unified government has yet to be achieved, the government has held together. Yet ethnicity continues to cleave BiH society. So long as that is the case, the issue of displaced people cannot fully be put to rest, though many may have found a place to settle. The following are several lessons from the experience of BiH that may have broader relevance:

When ethnic conflict is the direct cause of displacement, it can be naïve to think that returning displaced persons to their homes undoes the ethnic divides created by war. While multiethnic communities may be desired in principle by national (and international) entities, the rights of displaced persons, including the right not to return to their place of origin, should be respected.

IDPs have frequently been used as political capital to establish or maintain a majority population in an area where political clout falls along ethnic lines. To combat this, durable solutions for the displaced must be viewed first in humanitarian terms.[72]

The protection of displaced persons' right to return should not be construed by policy makers as a mandate to enforce their return. The freedom of movement—and therefore local integration in a new area—must simultaneously be respected.

Even activities to ensure the protection of human rights will be construed as political. The UNHCR protected Bosnian Muslims fleeing their homes and so was later accused of being an accomplice to ethnic cleansing. When the UNHCR protected communities that remained in their place of residence, it was criticized for sparing neighboring countries from receiving floods of refugees.[73]

Without peace and security, and without the establishment of power-sharing politics that defend the rights of minority communities, return is not a durable solution, regardless of the humanitarian aid that is provided. As one UNHCR report put it, "Providing material aid while ignoring the fact that the displaced are being beaten, raped or killed too often leads to the tragic description of the victims as the 'well-fed dead.'"[74] Premature resettlement of the displaced in BiH and other conflict-affected areas has led to the reemergence of violence even after the ceasefire takes effect. Addressing the root cause of the conflict that caused displacement is essential.

The contrast with the Russian case underscores the point. While Russians in the other NIS were subject to various forms of discrimination and while Russian regions varied is their eagerness to host returnees, the ethnic tensions between Russians and other groups in the FSU were mild by comparison to tensions in Georgia and Bosnia. Politicians in many of the NIS sought to increase the weight of their titular nationality, but none resorted to violence and ethnic cleansing.

CHAPTER 3

Pastoralists

The third of the people issues in secessions—how to deal with pastoralist populations who migrate seasonally in search of pasture and water but who, with secession, will now have to cross international borders—probably will be an issue only in African secessions. But it is likely to be an issue there, all the more so as global warming and desertification increase the length of seasonal migrations. It was crucial issue for Sudan. Indeed, the cycle of the civil war often turned on the migration cycle: when the pastoralists, especially the Misseriyya, were in the south, there was no war, and war came only after they returned with their cattle to the north. However, other secession cases will also have to deal with migration cycles, internal to the original state but international once secession occurs.

This chapter is slightly different from the others. It draws on cases—the Sámi people in the Nordic region, and Native Americans who migrate across both the U.S.-Canada border and the U.S.-Mexico border—where people move but the borders do not. These are not cases of secession involving poor or shattered states but of migration involving relatively prosperous ones; they are cases that shed light on issues posed by secession, not cases of secession itself.

Those best documented cases about how to handle pastoralists deal with wealthy, stable countries and perhaps are not easily adaptable to other, poorer contexts. Nonetheless, some useful lessons and ideas can be identified on key elements of any potential mechanism. These include questions of citizenship, taxation, and administration. Because published information is in short supply, the chapter's policy suggestions also draw on conversations and correspondence with a number of specialists and on a review of what experience has been recorded, especially in dealing with pastoralist issues in other regions that bear some resemblance to Sudan.

Policy Suggestions

Sámi of Norway, Sweden, Finland, and Russia

The Sámi (aka Saami, Lapps, Sápmi) are an indigenous reindeer-herding people living in Scandinavia. The 1751 Lapp Codicil, signed between Dano-Norway and Sweden, officially recognized the need for the Sámi to retain access to land and their right to cross borders during seasonal migrations. It gave them citizenship rights in one home country, where they also pay taxes. Thus cross-border rights are granted without extending new citizenship rights, and Sámi are taxed only once by their home country. Problems have emerged in modern times, as the divergence between modern state practice and traditional livelihoods has grown. The Sámi concept of territoriality is essentially communal, and has been difficult to account for or incorporate into law. Today there are Sámi Parliaments in Norway, Sweden, and Finland, which hold administrative powers and seem largely concerned with issues of cultural preservation. However, they do provide a valuable voice for incorporating Sámi perspectives into state policy.

Native American Tribes of the United States and Canada

The 1794 Jay Treaty between the United States and Britain (later Canada) allowed for Native American indigenous peoples living along the border free passage across the U.S.-Canada border without paying duties on personal goods and granted the right to engage in commerce. U.S. and Canadian Native Indians are given government-issued identification cards that are used for cross-border movements. However, Washington and Ottawa disagree over aspects of the legal interpretation of the agreement, differences that have caused continuous problems with implementation.

In addition, the two governments hold different legal interpretations of who is covered by the treaty, and what rights and responsibilities accrue to visiting indigenous peoples. For example, the United States recognizes all Indian tribes in Canada and provides public benefits—for instance, health care, food stamps, and disability insurance. The Canadian government requires that U.S.-based Indian groups prove they descend from persons the Canadian government recognizes as members of an Indian tribe in Canada. If they do, they receive grants equal to those of a Canadian citizen. Ottawa has generally held a higher threshold to grant claims to free passage than has Washington.

Native Americans of the United States and Mexico

Two tribes, the Tohono O'odham and the Texas band of Kickapoo Indians, reside in Mexico yet retain the right of free passage into the United States. The U.S.-Mexico border was set by a series of treaties and agreements in the 1800s, and it cut through the land of the tribes. The O'odham traditionally moved across the border frequently and with ease, but growing U.S. security concerns since the 1980s have made this more difficult. Traditional crossing points have not meshed easily with the new international border, making the process for crossing burdensome for the O'odham. Efforts to grant the O'odham U.S. citizenship have not yet succeeded.

The Kickapoo fled south from the northeastern United States as a result of colonization, with some resettling in Mexico. Beginning in the 1940s, Kickapoo began migrating to the United States as seasonal labor, a practice that has become solidified over time. In 1983, U.S. legislation granted Kickapoos the right to enter and work in the United States using government-issued tribal membership cards. It also granted Kickapoos the option of gaining U.S. citizenship and receiving permanent border crossing rights.

The lack of much formal experience in dealing with migratory populations across international borders is striking. As one expert summed up tersely, "If the migrating group is strong enough, or the recipient state weak enough, it simply moves across the border; if it isn't, it doesn't." This chapter is based on the proposition that this terse guidance cannot be the last word. What is striking about such accounts of experience as have been documented is how varied the responses to pastoral populations have been—from nonresponse, basically letting local dynamics take their course, to the use of considerable force to coerce or repress pastoral populations

The cases, along with experience in Africa, suggest a few touchstones for policy:

Sponsor Face-to-Face Talks

This may not be as easy as it sounds, for the questions of how and among whom arise. In the words of one recent study of Sudan, "Traditional mechanisms for conflict resolution can no longer be relied upon in negotiating with the Dinka for access to the South. With the Native Administration so politicized, the old ways would now require the involvement of senior NCP [National Congress Party, the governing party in Khartoum] and GoSS [government of South Sudan] representatives. The Native Administration would not be accepted as a credible mediator."[1]

Or as a close observer put it,

> Whatever the customary patterns of north-south migration may have been, and whatever the customary institutions which regulated those migrations, they will have been [irrevocably] changed by the war and the raiding. The only hope the northerners have of regaining the sorts of passage and grazing rights they used to have would be through face to face negotiation with the traditional southern receiving populations, pastoralists or farmers. This is something that could be facilitated for them by outsiders, but in the end they will have to do it themselves.

The challenge for governments is to play that facilitating role, while letting the populations talk face-to-face. In effect, the government would set up a forum where pastoralists and those affected by them could negotiate a new set of rights and conflict-resolution mechanisms based on the old ones but reflecting the new realities. Specifically, there would need to be discussion of livestock routes, watering places, resting places, normal grazing areas, reserve grazing areas, as well as emergency routes and grazing areas. These provisions should be negotiated specific subclan area by specific subclan area.

Imagine Several Agreements

If the peoples concerned negotiate face-to-face, agreements may well differ somewhat from one locality to another, reflecting differences in context and relations between pastoralists and receiving populations. In principle, some variation is to be expected, as a reflection of differing local circumstances. To be sure, though, if agreements are very different, the relatively "generous" ones may spur grievances from those on both sides who came out far less well. The key is lots of talks to try to defuse the sense that "referendum day" or "arbitration day" is a day of doom, another form of a drop-dead date. What might be possible to negotiate at the local level becomes harder when national politics interferes, frightening local groups or manipulating them.

Gather Data

One relatively unthreatening way to start would be to begin by collecting data. What are the numbers of migrants at various stages in the migration process? That data gathering might become a simple survey, trying to determine how many people would like to migrate but didn't, why or why not, and the like. It would also ask about the adequacy of services as various stages in the migratory process. It would be important to structure the data gathering as participatory, involving both the pastoralists and the receiving populations.

Think Hard About Whether Pastoralists Should Be Allowed to Arm

This is a very sensitive issue, and one about which it is hard to construct general rules. On one hand, more arms mean more wherewithal for violent conflict, all the more so because the pastoralists and the receiving peoples will have very similar security concerns, hence incentives to arm. On the other, small arms play a vital role in pastoralist communities by (1) protecting livestock from rustlers, (2) protecting individuals from crime and predation, (3) arming the community for self-defense, and (4) deterring hostile groups from attack.[2] It is also likely that pastoralists will not trust the "protection" of local security forces in the receiving areas; indeed they may have been fighting those same forces within recent memory.

Here the best approach probably is agreement on general principles, such as that fewer arms is the goal, along with some flexibility in specific discussions. Over time, the hope at least is that the pastoralists will come to have more confidence in the security forces of the recipient areas, and thus will feel less need to arms themselves.

Consider Access Points, Migration Time Periods, and Identification Cards

States naturally want to control their borders, and a seceding state will want to do so. That argues for designated crossing points as well as time limits on migration—that is, no entry to x pasture before y date. It would also be important that agreements include conflict resolution measures agreed in advance—and agreed by the parties themselves. Again, how specific agreements work out in reality will depend on local circumstances and capabilities. In some areas, the border simply may be too unpopulated to police, in which case there could be some system for pastoralists checking at various point along the trails.

So, too, identification cards seem a good idea in principle, as a means of documenting flows and, perhaps, assisting with conflict resolution. Use of such cards elsewhere, as in West Africa or the Horn, has also illustrated some of the practical difficulties, ranging from the unreliability of ID cards among mostly illiterate populations, to concern that applying for cards will open the applicant to pressure or danger (a risk with checkpoints as well.)

The Economic Community of West African States (ECOWAS), which was agreed in 1975 and modified in 1986, includes a Protocol on Free Movement of People Among Member States that allows citizens of ECOWAS member states to establish residency in sister states for up to ninety days. Doing so requires only the presentation of "valid travel documents" and a health certificate.[3] Pastoralists have been issued explicit sets of "livestock passports," "international transhuman certificates," and "handbooks of travel" since at least 2000.[4]

Yet the problems are real and serious. Migrants are often subject to extortion (or worse) by border agents, who refuse the right of entry if bribes are not forthcoming. Second, different official languages at various border crossings impede the movement of people due to either outright problems in communicating intentions or the inability to comprehend authorizing documents. Third, conditions in member states impose their own limits. That is, if the receiving state is very poor, migrants are often evicted in order to free up limited resources.

Finally, many migrant and pastoral communities lack the requisite documents both because authorizing institutions do not have a presence in the pertinent areas and because many people in the communities lack, for instance, birth certificates necessary to obtain the documents. The documents themselves, meanwhile, are easily falsified, which makes for both poor regulation and a black market in false documents.[5]

The net result suggests the need for a broad approach toward pastoral regulation. Regulation without enforcement and enforcement without stakeholder buy-in seem prone to failure. Effectively regulating the movement of pastoral peoples requires addressing an interlocking network of economic, political, governance, and social factors that any *single* policy appears unlikely to resolve.

Pay Close Attention to Taxes and Public Goods/Services

Taxes and public goods are two sides of the same coin. In principle, pastoralists both impose costs and produce benefits for the regions into which they migrate. The direct costs are consuming water and feed; indirect costs might include the costs of possible conflict. The benefits range from "purchasing" local goods and services, especially labor, to the natural fertilization provided by cattle. Research into the economic productivity of pastoralist communities in East Africa and Mongolia indicates that while pastoralists have moved beyond subsistence farming and toward profit-generating activity, their ability to do so is highly contingent on market prices and environmental conditions.[6] As a result, in principle, any taxing of pastoralist access to land access would require both flexible rates and attention to broader market conditions lest the system collapse.

As a practical matter, such careful calibration is probably beyond reach. What governments might try to do is provide some consistency and transparency to the "taxes" migrants pay. Migrants often find themselves being taxed several times during the migration; who taxes often depends on who has the force of arms. If that process could be somewhat more regular, it might be seen as fairer all around. If locals tax migrants a cow or two, as occurs at present, that is probably acceptable as long as the process is not repeated over and over by any armed group.

The principle should be that any taxes generated should benefit, first, the recipient populations and, second, the pastoralists themselves in terms of services, like schooling. This is all the more important because studies have found that, for understandable reasons, state efforts to provide public goods in pastoral areas may lag those in other parts of the country—thus penalizing both local populations and the migrants.[7]

Sámi of Norway, Sweden, Finland, and Russia

Issue and Outcome

When the Nordic states sought to define their boundaries, in the 1751 Strömstad Treaty between Dano-Norway and Sweden, an addendum to the treaty, the Lapp Codicil, accounted for the migratory Sámi people and has been referred to as the Sámi Magna Carta.[8] The Lapp Codicil officially recognized the need for the Sámi to retain access to the land and the ability to cross the defined borders during seasonal migrations. It protected the pastoralists from being taxed by both states, instead mandating they choose a country of citizenship.[9]

State interactions with the Sámi people have long been hindered by a lack of understanding of the Sámi concept of territoriality. Often state policies have treated the Sámi as if they do not possess land but rather blindly follow their herds. Sámi herders do have a complex conception of territoriality based on collective ownership. Sámi villages (or *Siidas*) formed the basis for governance. Siidas owned the rights to the land and were responsible for determining allocation of land resources to herders.[10]

The challenge in the modern era is that changing state-to-state politics in the region and, especially, continuing economic development have undermined the Lapp Codicil. Working out arrangements to protect the Sámi has become uneven across the region, more a state-by-state task than a regional one.

Course of the Dispute

The Sámi are indigenous people of a region in Northern Europe encompassing Norway, Sweden, Finland, and Russia. Sámi settlement in the region is thought to have occurred during the Bronze Age.[11] In the 800s, as Nordic states expanded influence into Sámi regions, the Sámi engaged in trade with them.[12] By the sixteenth century, as they traded with the Nordic peoples moving into their region, they had evolved from hunting, gathering, and fishing to migratory reindeer husbandry, which became a central aspect of their cultural identity.[13] Expanded state activities pushed the Sámi farther north; the Sámi ceded territory without conflict. The Sámi became accustomed to paying taxes to the Nordic states they inhabited. Because seasonal migration routes sometimes crossed national borders, they could be required to pay taxes to both states. The Lapp Codicil was intended to rectify that problem.

The influence of the Lapp Codicil seems to have diminished over time. In the early 1800s Sweden lost control of Finland to Russia in the Finnish War. Attempts to develop an agreement between Russia and Norway regarding transborder herding failed, and migration across the Norway-Finland border ceased after 1852.[14] In addition, state development of these lands for farming and forestry encroached on the Sámi herding in the region. In 1854 Norway passed the Reindeer Husbandry Act to limit Sámi grazing rights on private land.[15] In 1933, Norway passed a second Reindeer Husbandry Act that redrew reindeer herding districts, effectively ending Siida involvement in land management.[16] The continued economic development (e.g., mining, hydroelectric power) of these frontier lands in concert with a protracted Norwegian policy to promote assimilation threatened traditional Sámi culture and economy into the twentieth century.[17] Reindeer herding in particular was viewed as an economically primitive activity and not in the best interest of the state.

Today three Sámi Parliaments represent the Sámi populations in Norway, Sweden, and Finland. The Sámi Parliaments do not have much power over national policies but instead primarily play an advisory role, with some administrative responsibilities. That lack of power has led Sámi leaders to fear that state policies with a direct impact on Sámi well-being are being implemented without sufficient consideration of effects on the Sámi.[18]

Since the 1970s, a series of efforts has sought to ensure that Sámi rights are considered in state policy and cultural preservation, yet those have faced challenges and have not been pursued uniformly across the Nordic countries. In 2002 the ministers in charge of Sámi relations for Norway, Finland, and Sweden, together with the heads of the Sámi Parliaments in each country, appointed an expert group to create a Nordic Sámi Convention. In 2005 the expert group submitted a draft Nordic Sámi Convention to the three states and the Sámi Parliaments. Each state and Sámi Parliament must approve the convention for it to take effect, which would establish the Sámi people's right to self-determination.[19] However, state talks regarding the Nordic Sámi Convention have been slow to progress.

Current management of Sámi reindeer herding, including crossing international borders, is managed individually by the states. Recent policies have been increasingly geared toward cultural preservation and eliminating discrimination. While the Sámi have become more sedentary, the increase in herding in the 1970s through 1991 was unsustainable; thus reindeer herding has been decreasing among Sámi.[20] In addition, implementation of new technologies to assist in reindeer herd management (e.g., snowmobiles), while increasing efficiency, has increased the costs of herding.[21] Herders have also been adversely affected by increasing village connections to world markets, causing prices to fluctuate. One herder noted, "It is not enough to simply be a good herder anymore. Now we have to be experts in a number of other things as well, like marketing, in which we don't really have much experience."[22]

Norway has acted to incorporate Sámi perspectives into policy. The Sámi Parliament of Norway was activated in 1989. In 2006 the Finnmark Act removed control of natural resources in Finnmark County from a state-owned company. The act created a Finnmark Estate to manage land resources. The estate consists of six members, three of them elected exclusively by the Sámi.[23] In 2006 Norway began dispersing funds to Sámi elders who were determined to have been harmed (e.g., higher illiteracy rates) by government assimilation policies preventing them from speaking in their native language.[24]

The Sámi Parliament of Sweden was activated in 1993. In 2007 it was given responsibility to manage reindeer husbandry, previously carried out by the Swedish Board of Agriculture. However, most of these responsibilities were considered to be administrative in nature. County Administrative Boards maintain responsibility for allocation of land and resources.[25] In 2007 tensions surfaced in Troms County in Norway. A convention between Sweden and Norway in 1919 prevented Swedish Sámi from using grazing land on Norwegian territory. Norway later allowed other Sámi people to utilize this land, and the Sámi people who originally used the land wanted to reclaim the ability to use it. Sweden and Norway are attempting to generate a resolution, but no progress has been evident to date.[26]

The 1990 Finnish Reindeer Herding Act created a new administrative system for the management of reindeer herding. The system further diminishes the previous Siida management authority. The act enables non-Sámi people to participate in reindeer herding on traditional Sámi land.[27] This has increased competition for scarce pasture resources. In addition, the act has been criticized for failing to recognize differences in herding practices by traditional Sámi herders and non-Sámi industrialized modern practices.[28] The Sámi Parliament of Finland was activated in 1996. Finland appears to be more widely criticized for policies regarding the Sámi people.

Assessments and Possible Lessons

Although the results of Sámi-state interactions have been uneven, some general lessons emerge from this case.

Sámi people have a fundamentally different conception of territoriality than nation-states. Sámi people view land as collectively owned and managed through local administrative units (i.e., Siidas). This dynamic perspective of land rights was not always appreciated in state policies regarding Sámi people.

Sámi people were often disenfranchised by state policies. States pursued policies to decrease participation in Sámi culture and traditions. Land management policies were sometimes developed without the participation of the Sámi people. When states did consider Sámi perspectives, they sometimes did so by assuming that Sámi economic activity was backward and inefficient. Incorporating the Sámi people into governmental mechanisms (e.g., Sámi Parliaments) provides a structure to enable Sámi perspectives to be considered in state policy.

Economic development in the Sámi region has been a critical challenge to maintaining traditional practices. Consultation with Sámi people prior to development activities has enabled some improvement in Sámi perspectives on development. In addition, courts have sometimes awarded compensation to the Sámi people affected by activities.

Sámi-state interactions have typically occurred between a single state and the Sámi people within its borders. There have been fewer cases of multilateral state-Sámi agreements.

Native American Tribes of the United States and Canada

Issue and Outcome

Since time immemorial,[29] Native American tribes have crossed what is now the U.S.-Canadian border.[30] Following the end of the American Revolution, the United States and Britain signed the Treaty of Amity, Commerce, and Navigation (commonly referred to as the Jay Treaty) in 1794. John Jay was chief negotiator of the treaty, which was intended to settle compensation, border, debt, and trade issues, and also allowed, in Article III, Native American indigenous peoples free passage across the U.S.-Canadian border without paying duties on personal goods and allowed indigenous peoples to engage in commercial activities during such visits.[31] The Jay Treaty was met with overwhelming public hostility because its terms provided little benefit for the United States. However, it was eventually supported by George Washington and was viewed as a means to maintain peace with Britain.[32]

In one view, the right of free passage of indigenous peoples between the United States and Canada was reaffirmed by the signing of the Treaty of Ghent, which ended the War of 1812.[33] During the negotiations over the Treaty of Ghent, the British attempted to create a separate Indian territory to act as a buffer zone. However, the U.S. commissioners rejected what was regarded as unreasonable cession of territory. Instead, the Treaty of Ghent simply sought to restore the rights and privileges as they existed in 1811.[34]

Course of the Dispute

For over one hundred years after the Treaty of Ghent indigenous peoples on either side of the U.S.-Canadian border did indeed enjoy free passage. However, the U.S. Immigration Act of 1924, as it was interpreted, placed increased restrictions on immigrants.[35] Legislation enacted in 1928 clarified that the 1924 act was not meant to place restrictions on indigenous peoples. In 1952 the Immigration and Nationality Act restricted free passage rights only to those who met a 50-percent Indian blood requirement. The 1990 Immigration and Nationality Act changed this to allow anyone with 50-percent Indian blood or anyone recognized as an Indian by the Canadian government or by a Canadian tribe to enjoy free passage.[36]

The continued relevance of Article III of the Jay Treaty in both countries has been a difficult issue for the courts to resolve, all the more so because the United States has continued to pass new laws, while the Canadian government has chosen to address issues relating to free passage of indigenous peoples with common law, letting its courts interpret previous law and action. At the core of the confusion over whether the Jay Treaty terms of free passage for indigenous peoples continue to apply today is a debate over whether the War of 1812 abrogated the Jay Treaty and, if so, whether the Treaty of Ghent properly reinstated free passage rights. However, the Treaty of Ghent was not self-executing and thus required additional legislation to reenact that right.[37]

Still, many Native American indigenous peoples continue to claim that the Jay Treaty provides them the right of free passage between the United States and Canada. While the courts have tended to rule in favor of providing free passage to Native American indigenous peoples, they have not provided consistent explanations for their decisions, as suggested by the following descriptions of some of the primary cases in U.S. courts.

UNITED STATES: *DIABO V. MCCANDLESS*

The first U.S. case interpreting the Jay Treaty was *Diabo v. McCandless* in 1927. Paul Diabo was an Iroquois born in Canada. He was arrested in 1925 for not complying with immigration laws. Diabo claimed he was free to cross the border, citing free passage rights under the Jay Treaty. The district court judged that Diabo should be afforded free passage; however, it justified this with a much stronger claim—that indigenous peoples had an aboriginal right to free passage regardless of any such treaties. The court stated, "We do not see that the rights of the Indians are in any way affected by the [Jay] [T]reaty, whether now existent or not. The reference to them was merely the recognition of their right, which was wholly unaffected by the treaty, except that the contracting parties agreed with each other that each would recognize it. The right of the Indians remained, whether the agreement continued or was ended."[38]

An appellate court subsequently agreed that Diabo did have a right to free passage, but it did not ground its ruling in aboriginal rights. Instead, its decision was based on the continued validity of rights granted to indigenous peoples through the Jay Treaty. The court noted that the indigenous peoples were not signatories to the Jay Treaty but third-party beneficiaries. Thus, the War of 1812 should not abrogate portions of the treaty related to free passage rights, which the court considered unaffected by the War of 1812.[39] This point remains controversial, as scholars often point out that Indian tribes (including Diabo's tribe) fought in the war.[40]

UNITED STATES: *KARNUTH V. UNITED STATES*

In 1927, a British citizen and a Canadian citizen were arrested for illegally crossing the border from Canada into the United States. They claimed the free passage right from the Jay Treaty allowed them to enter the United States for temporary employment. A lower court ruled that they were allowed entry to the United States under the Jay Treaty as long as they did not intend to remain in the United States.[41] However, the Supreme Court overturned this decision, ruling that Article III of the Jay Treaty had been abrogated by the War of 1812 and had not been reinstated by any subsequent treaty. They explained that treaty rights of free border passage would have been inconsistent with hostilities between the signatories. In addition, the Supreme Court stated unambiguously that free passage was not an inherent right of indigenous peoples.[42]

UNITED STATES: GOODWIN V. KARNUTH

Dorothy Karnuth was a full-blooded Canadian Indian woman who was detained and ordered to be deported to Canada after crossing the border without the proper documentation required for immigration in 1946. The court ruled that Goodwin was legally allowed free passage of the border but cited the free passage statute and explicitly stated that the decision was not made on the basis of the Jay Treaty.[43] In addition, the court decided that Goodwin's marriage to a non-Indian did not change her status as an Indian.

Assessments and Possible Lessons

Indigenous peoples were not included in the design of treaties determining the rights to be afforded to Native Americans. They were simply beneficiaries of the treaties rather than parties to them. This caused difficulties in determining the continued validity of the Jay Treaty after the War of 1812.

In 1988 a Regional Border Rights Meeting attempted to develop a more organized approach to address issues regarding Indian passage rights. Held in Idaho with tribes from the United States and Canada, the meeting issued a policy statement, but no subsequent action was taken.[44]

Several lessons from the issue of Native American free passage rights may be more generally applicable:

First, policies regarding aboriginal peoples should be explicit in order to enable clear, consistent judicial treatment. Indigenous peoples continue to cite the Jay Treaty as the source of their free passage right. In one case an Indian even chose to address the matter by carrying a copy of the Jay Treaty with him to display to border authorities.[45] While the right of free passage may trace its roots back to the Jay Treaty, subsequent U.S. statutes have superseded that authority. In addition, statutes gave the U.S. government more freedom in designing policies, and as a result Canadian indigenous peoples entering the U.S. have rights afforded to them that go beyond those included in the Jay Treaty (e.g., more inclusive definition of Indian, access to government services such as Medicaid and social security).[46]

Some judicial authorities have supported free passage as an aboriginal right. They claim the subsequent policy tools serve as recognition of a basic aboriginal right. Other judicial authorities have not supported the idea of aboriginal rights to free passage. Policy must determine how to incorporate any rights of aboriginal people that will be recognized. Stakeholders should consider how these rights should evolve as groups may change customs and cultures as a result of contact with non-aboriginal cultures. In addition, policy makers should incorporate aboriginal stakeholders in the policy process. Some indigenous peoples expressed contempt for their traditional rights being litigated by a colonizing entity.[47]

Second, stakeholders must be mindful of potential costs imposed on migrants while ensuring compliance with policies. Indigenous peoples have complained of extended and unpredictable wait times at border crossings. In addition, ritually significant materials have not always been handled in accord with Indian tradition or have even been confiscated on the suspicion of being used for drug activity.[48]

Finally, addressing aboriginal issues uniformly between bordering nations reduces potential for cross-border disparities.[49] Canadian indigenous peoples have access to greater government benefits in the United States than U.S. indigenous peoples have access to in Canada. More importantly, Canadian courts have tended to hold a higher threshold to grant claims to free passage rights. U.S. indigenous peoples seeking free passage to Canada must prove a "nexus" relationship to Canada. This puts the burden on the Indian individuals to prove historical and continuing nexus to Canada for stated purposes.[50]

Native Americans of the United States and Mexico

Issue and Outcome

Similar to the situation with the U.S.-Canadian border, Native Americans have historically crossed what is now the U.S.-Mexico border.[51] The

U.S.-Mexico border was defined by the Treaty of Guadalupe Hidalgo in 1848 and the Gadsden Purchase in 1853. These transactions split several Native American tribes. While these treaties recognized that they were defining a border through territories occupied by Native Americans, they did not explicitly contain any components to address passage rights. Instead, the agreements obligated the United States to respect the rights of those tribes and refrain from removing them.

Course of the Dispute
TOHONO O'ODHAM

One of the tribes split by the U.S.-Mexico border is the Tohono O'odham. Movement of O'odham people across the border was not regulated initially. For example, federal school buses transported O'odham children from Mexico to the United States until the late 1970s.[52] By the 1980s, security had significantly increased and Native Americans found their cross-border movements greatly restricted by policies designed to curtail drug trafficking.[53] There have been efforts to pass legislation in the U.S. Congress to offer all O'odham tribal members U.S. citizenship, though thus far such efforts have been unsuccessful.[54] Many are now frustrated in obtaining U.S. citizenship because they are unable to prove birth in the United States or were born in Mexico on O'odham territory.[55] O'odham tribes depend on cross-border movements to preserve cultural practices because those living in Mexico have tended to retain language and ritual traditions. In addition, border agents have sometimes confiscated items of religious significance.[56]

THE TEXAS BAND OF KICKAPOO INDIANS

The Kickapoo originated from the Great Lakes region. Many resisted colonization and fled south to Kansas and Oklahoma. As a result of hostilities in the United States, some of these Kickapoo subsequently moved to Mexico. After drought and industrialization of surrounding lands in the 1940s, some Kickapoo in Mexico began to migrate to Texas to work on farms from April through October.[57] In the 1950s, the U.S. Immigration and Naturalization Service granted parole status to the Kickapoo. This enabled them to use tribal identification cards to freely cross the U.S.-Mexico border. These cards had to be reissued every year and did not ensure permanent crossing rights.

In 1983, the Kickapoo Act was passed, which allowed tribal membership cards to be used for crossing the border. In addition, it allowed Kickapoo members to elect to become U.S. citizens and receive permanent border-crossing rights.[58] Currently, members of the Kickapoo Band of Texas and Tribe of Oklahoma are able to cross the border if they present a Form I-872 American Indian Card (this includes members who reside in Mexico).[59] The U.S. Department of Homeland Security plans to continue to issue I-872 cards after the Western Hemisphere Travel Initiative is fully implemented.

Assessments and Possible Lessons

Existence of traditional routes may pose hurdles for implementing border-crossing arrangements. For example, the Kickapoo Indians were not native to territories in which they resided in Oklahoma, Texas, or Mexico. As a result, lacking traditional crossing points, the Kickapoo were more willing to accept alternate points to cross the border. This was not the case for the O'odham people, who wished to use only traditional crossing points, which were more remote. Some O'odham people would have to travel over a hundred miles out of their way to cross at a legal border crossing point.

Goods that are of religious or ritual significance need to be handled respectfully. Native Americans have been offended when such materials have not been handled in accordance with their traditions.

Policies should be designed with thought given to potential unintended consequences. For example, some Native Americans have been prevented from receiving health services on their territories because accessing them would have required crossing the border.

Many proposed policies were challenged because Native Americans did not have adequate records of all members. This made it difficult to prove, for example, place of birth. As these cases attest, even rich countries have had difficulty coming to grips with traditional peoples whose migration takes them across national borders. Records are problems for those countries too, and regulations vary across countries. Yet the cases do demonstrate that arrangements can be constructed, ones that work tolerably well, and they also suggest principles that can serve as the basis for those arrangements.

PART II

Natural Resources

CHAPTER 4

Oil and Infrastructure

Many countries, including rich ones, endowed with valuable natural resources have learned to their chagrin that those assets can be more curse than blessing. Not for nothing does the literature speak of the "resource curse" or the "Dutch disease," after the Netherlands' experience when it became a major natural gas exporter. When a nation has resources that can be extracted and sold in global commodity markets, it is all too tempting to develop the economy around that industry. Large resource exports drive up the value of the nation's currency and drive out other economic activity, all the more so when the resource becomes valuable immediately after extraction, as is the case with oil, diamonds, and other mineral deposits.

The curse is compounded for poor, unstable, and seceding states. Resources, especially newly discovered ones, will become something over which to fight. They will become objects of conflict, not means of development. Resources may be a special curse of secession. A state that has long relied on a given pool of natural wealth abruptly finds it on the other side of a border, generating ill will and even outright conflict. On the other sides of that new border, national leaders may encourage exaggerated expectations of the gains the new state will reap.

And oil and gas pose special challenges. But for the fact of Sudan's oil, most of which is located in the south, South Sudan's secession surely would have been far less contested. Mineral resources could, as a starting point, be allocated to the state in which they reside. But the locations of oil and gas wells may be contested or imprecisely defined (offshore, for instance). Moreover, oil requires elaborate infrastructure to move, and that infrastructure, especially pipelines, may pass through what will become, after secession, a foreign country.

The cases in this chapter shed light on two clusters of issues in the oil sector. The first is pipelines and arrangements for, in effect, sharing revenues through fees to countries through which pipelines pass. On that score the chapter looks at two models of such arrangements—the Chad-Cameroon Petroleum Development and Pipeline project (CCPP) and the TransMed Pipeline. The second cluster is joint development of oil territory. There, the cases include three different examples of joint development arrangements—two offshore joint developments (United Kingdom–Norway, Timor-Leste–Australia) and one onshore joint development (Saudi Arabia–Kuwait Neutral Zone).

None of the cases, save Timor-Leste, involve a secession. Rather they illustrate ways that pairs or groups of states have found to cooperate for mutual gain in extracting natural resources and transporting them to market. In some cases, they have been able to do so even when borders were undefined, relations between the states were less than amicable, or one or another state experienced bouts of instability.

Policy Suggestions

Both models of pipelines were relatively successful. CCPP, financed and negotiated with heavy involvement from the World Bank, was seen as a new model for the petroleum of the developing world in the twenty-first century. Though the international component of the CCPP ultimately failed—the Chadian government broke its earlier commitments to target oil revenue primarily for social services in order to spend more on security, and the World Bank pulled out completely in 2008, five years after the project began operating—the Chad-Cameroon arrangements have worked well. The oil fields lie entirely in Chad, and the concessions are entirely owned by the oil companies. Cameroon receives transit fees for oil passing through the pipeline ($0.41 per barrel). Both Chad and Cameroon own a small stake in their respective national oil transportation companies, and benefit from taxes and other related revenue streams.

The TransMed Pipeline connects Algeria, Tunisia, and Italy, and serves primarily as a way of transporting Algerian natural gas to the Italian and European markets. Negotiated, built, and jointly owned by the Algerian parastatal Sonatrach and the Italian state energy enterprise ENI, the TransMed is a good example of how important it is for participating nations to see the project as a win-win situation. Tunisia hosts part of the pipeline, for which it receives 5.625 percent of the gas shipment as a transit fee. Sonatrach and ENI both benefit from shared transportation revenue.

The joint development cases include ones in which the border was already demarcated and ones where the border was contested yet oil development was still able to proceed. The three commonly used models are a joint venture structure, with the interstate border almost surely known and agreed upon and with each state retaining the right to licensing in its portion of the joint development zone; a joint authority structure managing resources on behalf or with direct representation of both states under an agreed revenue sharing ratio, even if there is no agreement on borders; and a single state structure, with one state managing the development of the resources on behalf of both under an agreed revenue sharing ratio.

The Saudi Arabia–Kuwait Neutral Zone was left unresolved by the 1922 boundary agreement and led to an early territorial dispute between Saudi Arabia and Kuwait. Both countries began granting oil concessions in 1948 and 1949 on their respective sides of the Neutral Zone, while sharing administrative rights. The zone was formally divided in 1969, with national sovereignty applying to each country's respective side of the border. However, on- and offshore development of oil in the Neutral Zone is carried out through a joint development arrangement. A joint company, funded and staffed by the Kuwait Gulf Oil Company and Saudi Arabia Chevron (representing the Saudi government), manages all oil and gas exploration and production. Revenue is split fifty-fifty between the two companies. This Saudi-Kuwaiti cooperation has led to high levels of productivity across the six oil fields, thanks in part to greater economies of scale and fewer coordination challenges.

When Timor-Leste became independent following a 2002 referendum, it inherited Indonesia's revenue sharing arrangements with Australia and oil contracts. The Timor-Leste government largely maintained the oil contracts but challenged the 1991 Timor Gap Treaty with Australia. Using the Law of the Sea Treaty as a basis, Timor-Leste sought to alter the boundaries, and with them, the sharing ratios. A new agreement signed in 2002 created three new districts in the Timor Sea between Timor-Leste and Australia—one belonging to Timor-Leste, one belonging to Australia, and a third called the Joint Petroleum Development Area (JPDA). The JPDA is jointly managed, with revenue split ninety-ten in favor of Timor-Leste. This is widely considered a generous deal for Australia, since the international maritime boundary almost certainly put this area within Timor-Leste's borders. However, the Timor-Leste government gave up potential longer-term revenue in return for a stable partnership with Australia, which has played a key peacekeeping and diplomatic function in Timor-Leste, and immediate access to much needed oil revenue.

Arrangements between the United Kingdom and Norway for jointly exploiting North Sea oil are also a successful model. Following several decades of ad hoc joint development efforts in the North Sea between the U.K. and Norwegian governments, in 2002, the two began develop a more consistent and streamlined approach to cross-border offshore oil exports. Following the recommendations of a three-year joint working group, the governments agreed in 2005 to the Framework Agreement Concerning Cross-Boundary Petroleum Co-Operation. While the boundary between the two nations' waters was not disputed, the Framework Agreement established common rules for cross-border projects, a shift from the earlier case-by-case approach. Establishing common ground rules increased the level of commercial cooperation between the two countries by reducing extraction costs of new developments and eliminating the oil industry's perception that the border was a barrier to developing transboundary fields.

The Framework Agreement's core principles included treating transboundary fields as a single unit, appointing a unit operator for each transboundary field (agreed upon by the governments), and giving each government the right to grant sublicenses in its territory. The revenue sharing arrangements follow the boundary split for any given field.

A half dozen lessons emerge from the cases:

First, trust between the parties is necessary for successful cross-border cooperation. When trust is low, transparency in decision making becomes even more important, and third-party involvement and oversight can help allay fears and act as a guarantor for an agreement.

Second, cross-border cooperation in the oil sector has significant economic benefits for both parties, removing otherwise significant barriers to development, including the oil industry's negative perception about cross-border projects. All too often resource issues are seen as a zero-sum game, so the challenge is reframing the issues to produce a positive-sum outcome—for instance by reducing uncertainty, thus increasing outside investment, and planning new joint projects. Ensuring that all parties have an incentive to see the project succeed is a crucial element for the success and sustainability of any cross-border cooperation.

Third, demarcated borders are important for successful cross-border development but are not absolutely necessary. As the Saudi Arabia–Kuwait Neutral Zone case indicates, the lack of a fully demarcated border need not prevent development. By agreeing on the revenue sharing ratio for the general area (or field) in question, it is possible to decouple oil from the border. Oil development and production can continue uninterrupted and in parallel to any border demarcation process.

Fourth, some compromise in principle can be wise if it produces important side benefits, such as quicker access to a stable revenue source, diplomatic or political capital, or improved relations with a key partner. That seemed apparent in Timor-Leste's approach to Australia. It was prepared to concede Australia a larger share of revenues than it might have for reasons both economic and diplomatic: it wanted projects, hence revenue flow, to begin quickly, and it was prepared to be generous with a powerful neighbor.

Last, if capacity is lacking, a country's interests in a joint development scheme can be represented by an experienced private sector partner, such as Chevron Saudi Arabia in the Saudi Arabia–Kuwait case. Table 4.1 summarizes the policy suggestions that emerge from the cases. The chapter then turns to more detailed presentations of the cases outlined above.

Chad-Cameroon

Issue and Outcome

CCPP,[1] a US$4.2 billion venture, is one of the largest infrastructure investment projects ever undertaken on the African continent.[2] It is the first public-private partnership of its kind involving an oil consortium, two national governments, and a major multinational organization. When it began operating in 2003, the CCPP was viewed as a model for future oil and natural resource exploitation in poor countries looking to use newly generated income to reduce poverty and pursue long-term economic growth.[3]

The main aim of the CCPP was to develop three oil fields in the Doba Basin located in southern Chad, and, because Chad is a landlocked country,

Table 4.1. Policy Suggestions for Oil

Issue	Policy suggestion	Relevant cases
How important is trust in pipeline arrangements?	Very important, but transparency and third parties can help.	Chad-Cameroon and TransMed were successes, despite regional instability in Chad.
What is the key to joint development?	Projects need to be framed as win–win, not zero sum, to facilitate investment and give all parties an incentive.	Saudi Arabia–Kuwait; Norway–United Kingdom; Timor-Leste–Australia
Are there different models for joint development?	Yes. Most common is joint development with an agreed split of the oil revenues.	Saudi Arabia–Kuwait; Timor-Leste
	Another possibility is separate development with an agreed boundary and agreed sharing of transboundary field.	Norway–United Kingdom
Is it imperative that the boundary be full delineated?	No, with shares agreed, development can occur even absent a delineated boundary.	Saudi Arabia–Kuwait
Are there special considerations?	Weaker partners may benefit from generosity in getting project under way faster or reaping political benefits.	Timor-Leste with regard to Australia
What are the keys to national petroleum funds?	More transparency in rules, functions, decision making, and expenditures.	

build a pipeline 760 millimeters (30 inches) in diameter and 1,070 kilometers in length crossing through Cameroon to transport the extracted oil offshore to the Atlantic coast.[4] Over its projected lifetime of twenty-five years, the CCPP was expected to yield US$2 billion and US$500 million in direct government revenue for Chad and Cameroon, respectively, in addition to new employment opportunities and other project-related economic activities (such as local procurement of goods and services).[5]

The project has met considerable success; the pipeline and the associated infrastructure came into operation a year ahead of schedule and have generated higher than expected revenues for the government of Chad. However, the CCPP has not entirely escaped the "resource curse." Poverty reduction goals have not been achieved; in fact, since 2003, when the new oil money started flowing in, Chad's economy has deteriorated, and poverty has worsened.[6] In addition, the simple presence of the new petroleum resources has spurred greed and strife, and the country has suffered more internal dissident activity, including military insurgencies and new rebel groups fighting for control of oil resources, as well as increased tension with Sudan as the Darfur conflict has spilled into Chad.[7]

Course of the Discussions

Oil was discovered in the Doba Basin in Chad in the 1970s, but because of political instability and civil war, the resources remained underexplored and unexploited until the late 1980s, when the country regained relative stability and the government implemented new laws to improve the investment climate. In 1988 Chad granted a ten-year permit (later extended) for exploration and a thirty-year lease to develop and export crude oil from three oil fields—Miandoum, Bolobo, and Kome, in the Doba Basin in southern Chad—to a consortium initially composed of ExxonMobil, Shell, and Elf.[8]

In addition, given Chad's landlocked status, feasibility studies were undertaken in 1985 and 1994 to determine the best way to export Chadian oil. These studies suggested building a pipeline from the oil fields in Chad to the Atlantic coast of Cameroon. In 1996 the governments of Chad and Cameroon signed a treaty agreeing on the procedures and rules for the construction and operation of such a pipeline (and the related infrastructure). The treaty covered regulations related to land acquisition, revenue entitlements of Cameroon as a transit country, and environmental and social safeguards.[9]

Shortly thereafter, the oil consortium, led by ExxonMobil (through its subsidiary Esso Exploration & Production Chad, also known as Esso Chad) and including ChevronTexaco and Petronas, proposed the CCPP project. It involved developing the three oil fields in southern Chad, drilling approximately three hundred wells, and constructing a pipeline with an estimated capacity of 225,000 barrels per day, buried a meter deep, from the oil fields in Chad to the Atlantic coast of Cameroon at the Kribi port. The project also included three pumping stations, ancillary facilities, and the installation of an offshore floating storage, an offloading vessel, and an eleven-kilometer submarine pipeline from the Atlantic coastline to the vessel.[10]

The project confronted daunting obstacles, especially its very high cost and high risk given Chad's history of political instability, corruption, and weak institutions. As a result, in 1994 the oil consortium sought the World Bank's involvement. The World Bank's participation was considered crucial, for it would not only provide some financing, but also signal that the project, while risky, could be developed responsibly. In a sense, the World Bank's backing would serve as a guarantee or insurance policy, thus helping to mitigate some of the hesitation from private lenders.[11]

The World Bank's Board of Directors approved the institution's participation in June 2000. The bank saw the project as an opportunity for oil revenues to bolster economic growth and poverty reduction, and so agreed to become involved on the condition that Chad use the oil revenues to strengthen the country's social sectors. In 1998, the Chadian government and the World Bank agreed on the Petroleum Revenue Management Law (Law 001), which stipulated that the government put 10 percent of the generated revenues into a Future Generations Fund and allocate 80 percent of royalties and 85 percent of dividends to "priority poverty-reduction" sectors, as well as 5 percent of royalties to regional development in oil-producing regions.[12] The two entities also agreed to set up an Oversight Committee on the Management of Petroleum Resources (Collège de Contrôle et de Surveillance des Ressources Pétrolières, also known as the Collège), a government institution that would authorize the allocation of the revenues.[13]

In owning and operating the CCPP, the oil consortium led by Esso Chad would fully own the exploration and the development rights of the oil fields, while two companies, the Cameroon Oil Transportation Company (COTCO) and the Tchad Oil Transportation Company (TOTCO), jointly owned by the oil consortium and Cameroon and Chad, would be set up to manage the construction and operation of the pipeline. Effectively, the oil consortium would own 80 percent of the shares of both COTCO and TOTCO,[14] the government of Chad would own 3 percent of COTCO and 8 percent of TOTCO, and the government of Cameroon would own 5 percent of COTCO.[15]

The oil consortium would provide 85 percent of the US$4.2 billion, and one percent came from a loan from the European Investment Bank (US$22.5 and US$39.7 million to Chad and Cameroon, respectively, and US$97.7 million to the consortium).[16] The World Bank lent US$37.2 million and US$53.4 million to Chad and Cameroon, respectively, to finance their minority stakes in COTCO and TOTCO. Furthermore, the International Finance Corporation, the World Bank's more commercial arm, provided loans of US$100 million each to COTCO and TOTCO from its own account and mobilized a further US$100 million each from private lenders.[17]

Under these arrangements, the governments of Cameroon and Chad stood to earn revenues from their equity participation in the oil transportation companies and from taxes, as well as from royalties for Chad and transit fees set at US$0.41 per barrel for Cameroon. Cameroon's revenue flows from the CCPP were intended to be dependent on the crude volumes of oil shipped through the pipeline. The direct revenue gains over the twenty-five years of expected lifetime of the pipeline were estimated at US$500 million and US$2 billion for Cameroon and Chad, respectively.[18]

Assessment and Possible Lessons

The construction of the pipeline and the related infrastructure began in 2001 and was completed in July 2003, a year ahead of schedule.[19] While actual production of oil from the three fields ended up approximately 17 percent lower in volume than anticipated, Chad has derived great benefit, not only through increased revenues from oil, but also through increased investments in Chad's oil industry.[20] Indeed, in its first five years in operation, the Chad-Cameroon oil pipeline transported a total of 266 million barrels of oil to world markets, yielding over US$3 billion in direct revenues for Chad.[21] Furthermore, two additional fields, Nya and Moundouli,

are being exploited, and there are now 449 active production wells in the
Doba Basin.[22]

However, the new oil revenues were accompanied by new instability
within the country, as well as increased tensions with neighboring Sudan as
the Darfur conflict spilled over into Chad. As a result, the Chadian government breached its agreement with the World Bank and used the bulk of the
oil revenues to buy weapons and strengthen its army. In response, the World
Bank suspended disbursements to active projects in Chad but did agree
to a renegotiation. In an interim accord in April 2006, Chad agreed to
spend 70 percent of the direct oil revenues on priority sectors, excluding
security.[23] However, by mid-2008, Chad had again failed to comply with
the new arrangements, resulting in the World Bank's demand for repayment of all loans related to the financing of the CCPP. In September, Chad
fully repaid the loans and the World Bank officially disengaged from the
project.[24]

The withdrawal of World Bank raised concerns that the government of
Chad would divert more revenues toward the security sector. This may in
turn fuel the internal instability. For example, there were allegations that
the government used the oil income to fund militias to fight some of the
rebel groups.[25] Moreover, while Esso Chad, TOTCO, and COTCO continued to extract oil from Chad and operate the pipeline, with the government
and in particular the presidency holding most of the power, Chad's oil policies became increasingly become unpredictable. For instance, in 2006 it
threatened to nationalize the oil resources, and that same year it temporarily expelled ChevronTexaco and Petronas, claiming that they had tried to
evade US$500 million in taxes.[26]

In sum, while the economic rationale for the CCPP was sound, the political safeguards, as well as World Bank participation, proved too limited to
escape the resource curse. Indeed, exploiting oil resources actually ampli-
fied the country's instability, not only by encouraging new dissident groups
but also by providing new financial resources to procure weapons.

The weak institutional capacity of the Chadian government also contributed to the project's sorry outcome. Chad was unable to build the strong
and independent institutions needed to implement a complex revenue management scheme (such as the one outlined in Law 001) and provide oversight. Very little capacity building accompanied Law 001. Worse, Chad's
autocratic government and lack of accountability made its oil policies er-
ratic. With power concentrated in the presidency, decisions with regard to

oil exploitation and management of revenues were increasingly made uni-laterally.

TransMed Pipeline

Issue and Outcome

The TransMed Pipeline (renamed the Enrico Mattei Pipeline) transports natural gas from fields in Algeria to customers in mainland Italy.[27] The pipeline traverses Algeria, Tunisia, the Mediterranean Sea, Sicily, and the Sicilian Channel before it reaches Italy, where it connects with a national gas distribution system. Despite involving three nations whose interests are at times at odds, the TransMed pipeline remains one of the oldest and most successful underwater pipelines. The arrangement among the parties has succeeded in aligning the interests of each in such a way that all have an incentive to ensure supply continuity.

Yet a look at the detailed history of the development of the TransMed pipeline reveals that the process was nearly derailed several times. Its ultimate success is due to the fact that at each juncture, parties to the dispute had an incentive to strike a deal given that they each benefited more from compromising than from abandoning the arrangement. It thus is a model for seceding stats that will be required to cooperate with another state in transporting oil or gas.

Course of the Discussions

Algeria is among the top ten largest natural gas producers in the world, and is second (after Iran) among OPEC countries.[28] This is largely due to the HassiR'Mel gas field, which was discovered in 1956 and is one of the world's largest gas fields. Recent estimates of the proven reserves suggest it contains approximately 85 trillion cubic feet of gas. Production in the HassiR'Mel field began five years after discovery, and the gas was initially supplied to Algerian cities and power plants.

In 1962, after a violent war against colonial ruler France, Algeria gained its independence. Eighteen months later Algeria's first state enterprise, the Societé Nationale pour le Transport de la Commercialisation des Hydrocarbures

(Sonatrach), was created to manage gas and oil production and sale. By 1971 Sonatrach had established control over the entire energy sector in Algeria. Since the enterprise's creation, domestic energy consumption had grown little, but President Houari Boumediene recognized the strategic importance of the nation's energy supply. He aggressively developed the sector and insisted on state control over it to support his burgeoning nation as it left colonial rule behind.[29]

At the same time, Western European countries had begun searching for new energy supply sources. During World War II Italy had discovered gas in its north, which led to the development of pipelines connecting the reservoirs to major factories. As a result, Italy came earlier to natural gas than the rest of Western Europe, but it also recognized the need for foreign suppliers starting in the 1950s. In 1955, Enrico Mattei, in his capacity as the leader of the state energy enterprise Ente Nazionale Idrocarboni (ENI), set out to establish supply arrangements with various North African nations, garnering support by favoring their independence movements.[30] Though Mattei died before the pipeline that was ultimately named for him could even be conceived, his knack for forging partnerships in the region paved the way for future negotiations between Italy and Algeria.

Throughout the 1960s, Algeria exported liquefied natural gas to Italy via tanker. The high transport costs led both sides to begin to consider building a pipeline that would run under the Mediterranean, the first of its kind. In October 1973 the state energy companies of the two nations agreed to build a 2,500-kilometer pipeline from HassiR'Mel to La Spezia, Italy. Two months later, ENI signed an agreement with Tunisia to build the portion of the pipeline from the Algerian border to the Mediterranean Sea. ENI would operate the Tunisian and Italian sections of the pipeline, while Sonatrach would operate the Algerian portion.

Progress on the pipeline stalled several times. In 1977, after the contract had been agreed, Tunisia introduced untenable demands for its participation. The project was temporarily canceled but resumed after two months of negotiations between ENI and Tunisia. When the pipeline was completed in 1981, deliveries were delayed by disagreements between Algeria and ENI over the pricing scheme. According to the 1977 contract, the price of the gas was indexed to a basket of fuel oil and gas oil. But the second global oil shock usurped the earlier contract, spurring Algeria to hike its prices.

In October 1982 Algeria and ENI agreed that the gas price would be indexed to the price of crude oil (a competing fuel), substantially increasing the prevailing price. A critical component of the arrangement was the provision that the Italian government would provide a subsidy worth roughly 10 percent of the gas price.[31] This was a political maneuver. The export of dry natural gas from Algeria to Italy, via Tunisia, finally began in 1983, and it, along with the pricing scheme agreed in 1982, has been maintained ever since.

Since Tunisia is merely a link in the transport chain, its arrangement with respect to the pipeline is quite different from that of the other parties. Tunisia receives royalties for the gas transported across its territory in the form of a 5.625 percent share of gas shipments as a transit fee.[32] Tunisia was offered the option of taking its fee in cash or in gas, and it chose the latter, which gave it a vested interest in preventing any interference with the flow of gas, another factor in the ultimate success of the pipeline.[33]

Particular aspects of the institutional arrangement have been critical to the success of the pipeline over the years. For instance, since Tunisia and Algeria have a tense history, they agreed not to be partners in any part of the three-party pipeline operation. Thus, upon crossing over from Algeria to Tunisia, the gas derived from the HassiR'Mel field is determined to be Italian property. The Tunisian portion of the pipeline is operated by a subsidiary of ENI. Under this arrangement, anything that occurs within Tunisia is a matter to be resolved between the Tunisians and Italians.

In its pursuit to become competitive with Mobil and BP, ENI set out to develop its own capacity to build the unprecedentedly long and deep pipeline. Thus, ENI could have built and operated the underwater portion of the TransMed pipeline without the assistance of Sonatrach. However, to increase the latter's stake in the pipeline, ENI and Sonatrach established the Trans-Mediterranean Pipeline Company Ltd (TMPC) to finance, construct, and operate the portion of the pipeline that traversed the Sicilian Channel. Sonatrach and ENI each maintain a 50 percent stake in the pipeline company. Portions of the gas transported to Italy through the TransMed pipeline belong to ENI on the basis of its stake in Algerian production, while additional volumes of gas are procured through long-term natural gas sale agreements between Sonatrach and several larger gas purchasers in Italy.[34]

The tariff ENI pays the TransMed Pipeline Company for transporting gas is regulated such that return on invested capital is ensured.[35] Apart from this provision, ENI bears nearly all of the risk.[36] It has provided most of the financing, and the country relies on the TransMed pipeline for nearly a third of its gas consumption.[37] This is likely not an ideal arrangement for most gas importers, but the particulars of the pipeline's history have made this situation tenable.

Another factor that is credited with the success of the pipeline is the involvement of state-owned enterprises, ones representing the interests of the nation rather than those of a particular company. Those enterprises drove the negotiations, and they had the backing of their respective governments, which provided a guarantee of the political will and necessary funds to realize the pipeline.[38]

Assessments and Possible Lessons

Beyond doubt, TransMed has been a successful transborder pipeline project.[39] This is apparent from the quarter-century history of reliable gas flow from Algeria to Italy, through Tunisia. In addition, Italy and Algeria have agreed to add three subsequent pipelines to the TransMed system since its initial construction. More plans are in the works to increase the capacity yet again. But success was never a foregone conclusion.

The attempt Tunisia made early on to hijack the project provides an important lesson. With a relatively small stake in the capital investment of the project as a whole, Tunisia was in a position to strong-arm the other two parties that had much more at stake. This is a common problem with infrastructure projects that require long-term investments. The issue is exacerbated in the case of energy projects in which the underlying commodity to be sold experiences substantial price volatility, since it is difficult to establish a transparent and mutually acceptable pricing scheme in advance that will cover the capital costs of the initial investment.

Energy pricing has evolved since the 1970s to account for this, and the pricing arrangements for gas supplied to Tunisia and Italy from the TransMed pipeline are now much less contentious. Trust in the pricing scheme is evidenced by the fact that in July 2007 Algeria agreed to eliminate destination clauses that restricted the resale of gas from Italy to other EU member states.[40]

The TransMed pipeline has weathered tumultuous times since its inception. It has withstood political and social turmoil in both Algeria and Tunisia, including the Tunisian revolution of 2011, along with energy crises that dramatically shifted the balance of power between energy producers and importers. All the while, Algeria and Tunisia have remained less-than-friendly neighbors. Despite that fact, in its decades-long history the TransMed pipeline has experienced no supply interruptions due to sabotage or disputes.[41] The lesson for seceding states is that contractual arrangements can align parties' incentives, which is critical to the success of an agreement between countries that would otherwise have had little reason to cooperate.

Timor-Leste–Australia

Issue and Outcome

When Timor-Leste finally became independent in 2002, it inherited arrangements for sharing revenues from its oil resources that had been negotiated over its head between its postcolonial occupier, Indonesia, and its neighbor, Australia, and in a treaty agreed to share revenues fifty-fifty.[42] Timor-Leste sought to renegotiate the treaty because, by customary rules for drawing maritime boundaries, virtually all of the oil lay beneath Timorese waters. Australia resisted, and in 2002 Timor-Leste agreed to a regime that is relatively generous to Australia. Timor-Leste had other stakes in its bilateral relationship with Australia: Australia has repeatedly provided much-needed peacekeeping forces to stabilize the fledgling democracy. Timor-Leste's maritime neighbor also provided substantial foreign aid to help rebuild Timor-Leste's infrastructure, nearly all of which was destroyed by Indonesia.[43] Whether Timorese generosity over resource revenues reflected its wise recognition of national stakes or Australia's ability to intimidate a small, fragile neighbor is a matter of contention.[44] What is uncontested is that the agreement allowed the oil and the revenue for Timor-Leste to flow quickly.

Course of the Dispute

Timor-Leste, East Timor in English, is an oil-rich independent nation with a population of around one million. A Portuguese colony, it became independent in 1976 but was immediately occupied by Indonesia. The UN Commission on Human Rights affirmed East Timor's right to independence and self-governance in 1983, but the Australian government officially recognized

Indonesia's annexation of East Timor in 1985. This set up the tensions that would later arise between Australia and an independent Timor-Leste over offshore oil reserves.

The departure of Indonesia's General Suharto in 1998 ushered in a new era for Timor-Leste, and the following year Indonesia agreed to allow the UN Mission on East Timor to conduct a national poll to determine whether the populace preferred to remain part of Indonesia with increased political autonomy or to become an independent state. That announcement was met by violence from anti-independence militias backed by Indonesia. The violence and anarchy continued until arrival of Australian peacekeeping forces and eventually the UN Transitional Administration in East Timor. The latter oversaw the administration of East Timor after the referendum resulted in a 78.5 percent vote for independence, and Timor-Leste was internationally recognized as independent on May 20, 2002.[45]

Significant offshore petroleum resources lay in the waters between Timor-Leste and Australia in a disputed region called the Timor Gap, the result of an unresolved maritime boundary between Australia and Portugal.[46] Under Indonesia's rule, it agreed with Australia on the Timor Gap Treaty in 1991, under which Australia and Indonesia shared royalties from the resource reserves on a fifty-fifty basis. When it became independent, Timor-Leste inherited Indonesia's side of the treaty, along with exploration and production contracts with international oil companies. It upheld the latter in their existing form, presumably to ensure that it would receive the much-needed tax revenue from ongoing oil activities.[47]

In contrast, Timor-Leste requested a complete renegotiation of the treaty. Since the UN had never officially recognized the legitimacy of Indonesian occupation of Timor-Leste, it considered the earlier treaty to be without legal standing. This meant that Timor-Leste was not bound to accept the terms to which Indonesia had agreed. Thus, Australia and Timor-Leste entered a prolonged period of negotiations over the disputed territorial boundaries governing rights to the underwater oil reserves in the Timor Sea. The boundary recognized by UN Convention on the Law of the Sea (i.e., the midpoint between the shores of each country) would have allocated 90 to 100 percent of the oil resources to Timor-Leste. Australia vigorously objected, though it had agreed to the same midpoint principle in its contemporaneous negotiations with New Zealand over maritime boundaries.

After lengthy negotiations, the two countries signed a new Timor Sea Treaty in 2002 to govern the commercial exploration of offshore oil and gas reserves in the Timor Gap. The treaty redrew territorial boundaries, creating three distinct areas—one under the jurisdiction of Timor-Leste, another under Australia's, and a third, referred to as the Joint Petroleum Development Area (JPDA), in which both countries retained underwater rights.

In accordance with the treaty, Australia and Timor-Leste were to jointly manage and pursue exploration and exploitation of petroleum resources within the JPDA. Activities in the JPDA were to be coordinated by a three-tiered administrative structure composed of a Designated Authority, a Joint Commission, and a Ministerial Council. The Designated Authority was given responsibility for day-to-day regulations. It reports to the Joint Commission, which is charged with establishing overall policies and regulations for activities in the JPDA. The Joint Commission is, in turn, overseen by the Ministerial Council. Each layer of administrative structure includes representatives from Australia and Timor-Leste.[48]

The treaty also stipulated that revenues from oil and gas extracted from the JPDA were to be shared between Timor-Leste and Australia in a ninety-ten split. The government of Timor-Leste receives two revenue streams from the JPDA agreement, one from taxes levied on companies operating in the JPDA and another from royalties on the sale of petroleum (conducted by companies on behalf of the government).[49] While this appears to be a very favorable arrangement for Timor-Leste, it is widely considered to be biased in Australia's favor, considering where the actual international boundary should be delineated and the substantial downstream revenue that will accrue to Australia.[50]

In January 2006, Timor-Leste and Australia signed a subsequent treaty to resolve the ongoing boundary dispute regarding the Sunrise and Troubadour fields within the JPDA region. After years of acrimonious negotiations, Timor-Leste proposed a "creative solution" to the impasse that entitled both parties to an equitable share of the revenues generated from oil and gas exploration in the fields without demarcating the border.[51] This allowed progress to continue in the region, specifically on the Greater Sunrise Project, which is worth an estimated US$10 billion in taxes and royalties, even though the boundary dispute was not resolved under the treaty. Agreement on the maritime boundary was postponed for another fifty years.[52] In addition, the 2006 treaty—which took effect in 2007—established the Timor-Leste/Australia Maritime Commission, a bilateral committee responsible for consulting on boundary, security, and other maritime issues related to the JPDA.[53]

Once the revenue sharing agreements became effective, income started to flow to Timor-Leste. In response, it enacted the Petroleum Fund law in August 2005, which established the Timor-Leste Petroleum Fund (TLPF) to accumulate the nation's share of oil revenue. It was modeled in part on the Norway Pension Fund (formerly the Norway Petroleum Fund), recognized as one of the best oil revenue funds. The primary objectives of the TLPF are to provide a permanent source of funds for much-needed government investments to rebuild the nation and to provide savings for future generations after the oil supply has been exhausted.

The fund is operationally managed by the Banking and Payments Authority (BPA). The BPA maintains reserves and a balance sheet for the fund, separate from its own. The TLPF is fully integrated into the budget process, operating as a government account rather than a separate entity.[54] Support is provided by foreign investment advisors and the investments themselves are foreign, but TLPF remains under local control, reflecting the objective of building domestic capacity so that the fund can eventually be run completely independently.

Another requirement of the TLPF is that its asset allocation be fairly conservative. For the first five years the TLPF was required to invest nine-tenths of its money in qualifying sovereign bonds that were benchmarked against the Merrill Lynch zero- to five-year U.S. government bond index; the remaining 10 percent of assets could be used for other investments. As of February 2007 the funds were entirely invested in U.S. government bonds and passively managed. This strategy is typical of other smaller oil-producing countries, especially when first starting out. As the TLPF and the capacity of BPA grow over time, the investment strategy will be broadened to incorporate slightly more aggressive investments.[55]

Assessment and Possible Lessons

Timor-Leste stopped short of demanding a maritime boundary at the median line in part to keep the peace with its powerful southern neighbor, but perhaps more important to ensure the earliest possible flow of revenue from the oil and gas reserves.[56] Thus, the revenue sharing agreement with Australia is a compromise, but it represents Timor-Leste's strategic approach to ensuring a stable future as new nation in a volatile region. As a newly independent democratic state with a lot of resource revenue at stake, the first years of sovereignty have been tumultuous, but the government of Timor-Leste has very successfully managed the oil wealth derived from its agreements with Australia. The first substantial stream of tax and royalty revenue came from the Bayu-Undan field in 2004 and resulted in a 40 percent jump in gross national income per capita.[57] In 2007, oil and gas revenues were estimated to be US$1.3 billion, representing 331 percent of non-oil GDP.

Over the next twenty years, the net present value of revenues from oil and gas production in currently operating fields is projected to be more than US$9 billion (although this estimate is extremely sensitive to oil price fluctuations). Since 2004 the government has received around US$3 billion in taxes and royalties. During that time the rate of government spending tripled, but savings remained aggressive.[58] As of mid-2008, the value of the TLPF value was approximately US$3.2 billion.[59]

The 2007 IMF Country Report on Timor-Leste was quick to point out the opportunity cost of having such a conservative investment strategy. However, the lack of local capacity to fully manage the fund, coupled with

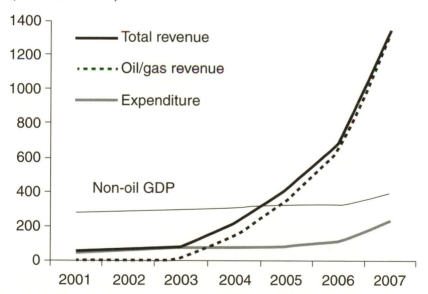

Figure 4.1. Timor-Leste: Government revenue and expenditure.
Source: International Monetary Fund, "Democratic Republic of Timor-Leste: Selected Issues and Statistical Appendix" (Country Report 05/250).

the inadequacy of the Timorese legal, financial, and support service infrastructure poses grave challenges to replicating the more sophisticated funds administered elsewhere, in Norway or Alaska, for instance.[60]

On balance, the consensus seems to be that if Timor-Leste continues to administer the TLPF according to its guiding principles, it bodes fair to avoid the "resource curse" that plagues so many oil-wealthy countries and be able to rely on a stable, permanent flow of budgetary resources to fund public investment, all derived from its oil and gas revenue in the Timor Sea.[61]

United Kingdom–Norway

Issue and Outcome

Five countries, Denmark, Germany, the Netherlands, the United Kingdom, and Norway, have been involved in offshore oil production licensing in the North Sea, with the Norwegian and British sections having the largest petroleum reserves.[62] A number of oil and gas fields span the maritime boundaries of the two countries, but until very recently, these had remained underexplored because transboundary ventures had foundered on the different laws and institutions of two different countries, as well as the challenge of setting up commercial agreements between the two.[63]

The two had, though, negotiated a number of case-by-case treaties since the 1970s to facilitate the joint development of specific cross-border oil and gas resources and to promote the efficient use of infrastructure for exploiting and transporting these resources.[64] However, in 2002, recognizing the inefficiencies of the case-by-case approach, the two governments set up a joint work group comprising representatives from the oil industry, contractors, and policy makers from each country to look into the potential gains from a more comprehensive agreement that would outline general principles for cross-border hydrocarbon development,[65] and would effectively remove the need to negotiate an individual treaty for every project.[66]

On April 4, 2005, the efforts of the work group culminated in the Framework Agreement Concerning Cross-Boundary Petroleum Co-Operation between the United Kingdom and Norway.[67] As envisioned, the treaty covers a wide range of cross-border projects, including any future development of oil and gas reservoirs, and the construction and optimal use of pipelines, installations, and other infrastructure.[68] The treaty has encouraged the development of cross-border projects, including the development of oil fields. Indeed, the agreement immediately prompted the start of the exploitation of two transboundary fields, Enoch and Blane, both of which were discovered in the mid- to late 1980s,[69] but remained undeveloped due to the perceived risks associated with the exploitation of cross-boundary resources.[70]

Course of the Discussions

The U.K.-Norway Co-Operation Workgroup was established with the overarching goal of increasing the level of commercial cooperation in oil and gas between the United Kingdom and Norway. In effect, the work group was assigned three short-term objectives: (1) "developing a greater level of understanding at government, industry and contractor level of how cross-border co-operation can enable the optimum development of the North Sea," (2) developing a better "understanding of any barriers acting to inhibit the optimum development of the UK-Norway North Sea," and (3) "Making practical recommendations to address any such barriers, including the sponsorship of joint activities."[71]

In August 2002, the joint work group released its first report, whose main recommendation was that the two governments negotiate a more comprehensive agreement that would remove the need to negotiate a new treaty each time an oil or gas project was proposed.[72] The work group argued that such a comprehensive treaty would increase the incentive to exploit cross-border resources not only by reducing extraction costs of new developments (and therefore increasing the expected value of exploration) but also by eliminating the oil industry's perception that the border was a barrier to developing transboundary fields. As such, a more comprehensive treaty would encourage the industry to deploy more resources into formerly underexplored and underexploited areas and would therefore accelerate cross-border development plans.[73] All in all, the work group estimated that the total potential monetary gains from such an extensive cooperation could amount to US$2 billion by 2010, with up to US$1 billion coming from the accelerated development of shared hydrocarbon resources.[74]

Both governments endorsed the report and embarked on the negotiation of key principles for regulating potential cross-border hydrocarbon-related projects.[75] The negotiations were completed in April 2005, with the signing of the Framework Agreement, which was described by the negotiators as the "most comprehensive energy co-operation agreement yet between the two countries."[76] Indeed, the ensuing agreement contains detailed directives on a number of areas related to gas and oil projects in cross-boundary fields and in those neighboring the border delimitation—jointly exploiting transboundary reservoirs as a unit, constructing, operating, and securing access to pipelines, and installing and using other infrastructure, along with dispute settlement procedures.[77]

The Framework Agreement set up clear guidelines on the obligations of each government and the requirements that their respective licensees need to fulfill in order to exploit transboundary resource as a single unit. As per the agreement, both the governments of the United Kingdom and Norway have to approve the definition of a transboundary reservoir and the proposal for exploiting it. To that effect, both governments are required to enter into a Licensees' Agreement with their respective licensees, an agreement that defines the transboundary reservoir to be exploited, both geographically and geologically, the total amount of the reserves to be exploited, and the distribution of the reserves between the licensees of each government.[78]

In addition, the Framework Agreement stipulates that a unit operator, which acts as a joint agent for the exploitation of the reservoir, is to be appointed by agreement of all the licensees and the two governments. The unit operator in turn is responsible for submitting a development plan for approval to both governments and is also required to seek their approval if it wants to make any amendments to the plan.[79]

In the event that one of the governments does not approve a proposal for the determination (or redetermination) of the distribution of the reserves between the licensees, it is required to notify the other government and the unit operator within sixty days of the submission of the proposal. The different parties would negotiate to resolve the issue, and if an impasse occurred, a single expert would be appointed by the different parties to independently determine the issue.[80]

Assessment and Possible Lessons

As foreseen by the work group, the signing of the agreement encouraged the development of cross-border oil and gas reservoirs. Indeed, shortly after the deal between the two countries was announced, the development of two cross-border oil fields was approved by the two governments. The Enoch and Blane fields, with estimated reserves of 3.4 million and 5.1 million standard cubic meters of oil equivalents, respectively, became the first transboundary developments to be approved under the new agreement.[81]

The fields straddle the offshore boundary between the United Kingdom and Norway, with the bulk of each of the fields located on the U.K. side of the border delimitation. Accordingly, the interests in the Enoch field have been split 80 to 20 percent between the United Kingdom and Norway, and Blane 82 to 18 percent.[82]

Paladin Resources, a U.K.-based independent oil company, was appointed as the unit operator for both fields.[83] The other licensees in the case of Enoch include Dyas, Roc Oil, Bow Valley Petroleum, Dana Petroleum, and Petro-Canada UK on the U.K. side, and Lundin North Sea, Statoil, Total Norge AS, Detnorskeoljeselskap AS, and DONG Norge AS on the Norwegian side. In the case of Blane, the other licensees are MOC Exploration, ENI UK, Roc Oil, and Bow Valley Petroleum on the U.K. side, and ENI ULX Limited, and Talisman Energy Norge AS on the Norwegian side.[84]

Both the Enoch and Blane fields started production in 2007, and are each expected to reach between twelve thousand and fourteen thousand barrels of oil per day in production. In terms of infrastructure supporting the production and transmission of the oil, the Enoch field is tied back to Marathon's Brae platform on the U.K. side for processing and then transported through the Forties pipeline system. As for the Blane field, it is tied back to the Ula platform on the Norwegian side and then transported via pipeline to the Teeside Oil Terminal in the United Kingdom.[85]

In sum, three lessons emerge from the cooperation of the United Kingdom and Norway in North Sea hydrocarbon-related projects:

First, the Framework Agreement reached in 2005 removed the perceived barriers to developing cross-border projects. Indeed, the extensive and comprehensive nature of the agreement helped to motivate the oil industry to develop previously underexploited oil fields.

Second, in order to reach an agreement as extensive as the one between Norway and the United Kingdom, having a long history of cooperation helps: since the 1970s, the two countries have cooperated closely with respect to hydrocarbon-related projects in the North Sea, signing a total of six treaties to govern the joint oil- and gas-related projects. This may mute the value of the U.K.-Norway case for poorer or newly seceded states with no history of cooperation.

Third, the establishment of the U.K.-Norway North Sea Co-Operation Workgroup, with representation from all relevant parties, was key to determining the course of the agreement and ultimately to its successful implementation. Indeed, the work group played a key role in understanding the issues around transboundary petroleum projects and in identifying the barriers to their development, as well as in recommending practical steps for both governments to pursue.

Saudi Arabia–Kuwait Neutral Zone

Issue and Outcome

The Saudi-Kuwaiti Neutral Zone is a five-thousand-square-kilometer area between Saudi Arabia and Kuwait.[86] The region evolved from a territorial dispute in the early part of the twentieth century. Once oil was discovered in the region, establishing claims to the land became imperative. In the 1960s, Saudi Arabia and Kuwait agreed to partition the land for administrative purposes but to maintain joint rights over the natural resources contained there. By all accounts the joint development of the oil fields in the Neutral Zone has been very successful. With rare exceptions, relations between the neighbors have remained constructive (and very lucrative) despite the high stakes.

Course of the Dispute

The 1922 Uqair Convention established the first formal boundaries between Kuwait and Saudi Arabia. According to the agreement, a region between Kuwait and Saudi Arabia, which was later named the "Neutral Zone," was to be shared by both nations until a partitioning of the territory could be agreed. For decades the border remained unresolved, though that was never the intention of the convention's authors. Until oil was discovered near the Neutral Zone in 1938 there was little need to negotiate the exact boundary across the desert between Saudi Arabia and Kuwait. Furthermore, to the nomadic tribes that inhabited the shared region, national borders were largely meaningless.[87] As one scholar at the time characterized it, "With goodwill on both sides, an indeterminate frontier with a definite understanding regarding the proper allegiance of the various tribes concerned would be better than a line which no tribes could possibly be expected to recognize on the spot."[88] Thus formal division of the territory was postponed.

In 1948 and 1949 Kuwait and Saudi Arabia, respectively, granted oil concessions that permitted private companies to explore for and produce oil in the Neutral Zone. These contracts served as the basis for property rights in the region, while administrative rights remained shared between Saudi Arabia and Kuwait.[89] Joint administration of the Neutral Zone was required at that time to ensure coordination of taxation, laws governing foreign workers, and other factors related to the production of oil.[90]

In 1960 the leaders of Saudi Arabia and Kuwait agreed that the Neutral Zone should be formally divided. The agreement took effect in 1969. Under the arrangement, which has remained in effect ever since, the Neutral Zone is partitioned between the two. National sovereignty applies, and the countries administer their half of the Neutral Zone as an integrated part of their national territory. Despite administrative separation, the development of oil production remains undivided for both on- and offshore oil fields.[91] The joint economic development arrangement represented a strategic decision on the part of Saudi Arabia and Kuwait to settle on a compromise that would allow oil production to proceed without the disruption that would have accompanied a territorial dispute. Agreement was easier because the Neutral Zone was relatively uninhabited, thus there were virtually no land claims from local groups.[92]

In the early days after the discovery of oil, Saudi Arabia and Kuwait pursued their onshore oil development separately through separate concessions. More recently, onshore field operations have been conducted jointly. A company was established to engage in oil and gas exploration and production in the Neutral Zone. The so-called Joint Operations is funded and staffed equally by Saudi Arabia Chevron and Kuwait Gulf Oil Company, which represent each country's 50 percent stake in the Neutral Zone oil production.[93]

Currently, Chevron is the only foreign corporation that maintains significant involvement in oil production within the Neutral Zone. In the 1970s, much of the Saudi oil industry was nationalized, and Kuwait took over oil operations in the Neutral Zone from a foreign company in 1977. Now, Chevron has a thirty-year concession (renewed in July 2008) to operate on behalf of Saudi interests, while the national oil company does so for Kuwait. Chevron retains an unusually high 40 percent share of oil production,[94] while the remainder is remitted to Saudi Arabia in the form of royalties and other taxes.[95] Chevron also provides technical assistance to the Kuwait National Petroleum Company.[96] While, like Kuwait, Saudi Arabia could have taken over operations of its share of oil production, the benefits of Chevron's advanced technical experience are considered to be of strategic importance for the long-term development of Neutral Zone oil reserves.

The development of oil production in the offshore fields has been somewhat different. For forty years, Japan's Arabian Oil Company (AOC) held the concession to operate the two offshore oil fields within the Neutral Zone on behalf of both Kuwait and Saudi Arabia. Under the concession contract AOC was entitled to 80 percent of revenues, while Saudi Arabia and Kuwait each received 10 percent, in line with their respective ownership stakes in AOC. In 2000 AOC lost the renewal of its concession when Japan refused to invest in selected development projects in Saudi Arabia. The Arabian American Oil Company (Saudi Arabia's Aramco) assumed operations in the offshore fields on behalf of Kuwait and Saudi Arabia.[97]

Currently the Neutral Zone contains approximately five billion barrels of proven oil reserves. Saudi Arabia and Kuwait are entitled to equal shares of the oil reserves and production. Recent oil production averages about 600,000 barrels per day, with onshore and offshore reserves accounting for roughly equal portions of the production.[98] Onshore oil fields in the Neutral Zone include Wafra, South Fawaris, South Umm Gudair, and Humma (which is under evaluation); the offshore fields are Hout and Khafji. The high level of productivity of the six oil fields is due in large part to the unique arrangement between Saudi Arabia and Kuwait that allows for greater economies of scale and fewer coordination challenges.

Assessment and Possible Lessons

The Neutral Zone is politically divided between Saudi Arabia and Kuwait but economically shared. By all accounts the arrangement has been very successful. The administrative partitioning of the zone has worked smoothly since it took effect in 1970. Oil production in the Neutral Zone has been extremely high. Moreover, Saudi Arabia and Kuwait have been able to pursue different institutional arrangements with respect to the field operation (i.e., issuing an operating concession to a foreign corporation and operating its own national oil company, respectively) without disrupting the operating agreement between nations. For sixty years Saudi Arabia and Kuwait have successfully negotiated sharing the rights to oil reserves and production in the Neutral Zone to which they both lay claim. The results and longevity suggest that this arrangement has been a success.

The countries in this chapter's cases were mostly neither poor nor seceding. Yet the cases do illustrate principles that could undergird policies in sharing, transporting, and saving resources in secessions—that joint development of natural resources is possible even if boundaries are not precisely demarcated, that a tradition of cooperation helps but that joint transborder exploitation and transport of resources can persist even through political instability in the parties.

CHAPTER 5

Resource Revenue Funds

A critical part of avoiding the resource curse is wisely managing the revenues from natural resources to promote broader national interests. A critical part of that management can be funds to stabilize government revenues during the ups and downs of resource prices and to save revenue to promote long-term economic growth. Typically, these funds call for a predetermined contribution (as a percentage of revenues or above a certain benchmark) of all government revenue from oil or another resource.

Rules for the funds often prescribe strict investment and expenditure guidelines, in order to accomplish three purposes: shoring up government budgets when other revenue or the price of oil drops, saving from nonrenewable resources for future generations, and benefiting the population directly. These funds also can help avoid the macroeconomic instability that can result when a flood of money suddenly hits a relatively small economy.

The "prime standard" example of state petroleum funds is the Norwegian Pension Fund. However, the Norwegian model is not easily applicable to developing country contexts with less advanced bureaucracies and less generous natural resources. Other successful models include Alaska's oil fund and Botswana's diamond fund. What distinguishes them is greater transparency in rules, functions, decision making, and expenditures. The Timor-Leste Petroleum Fund is another positive example. The Kuwait, Oman, and Kazakhstan funds all share some positive attributes but suffer from a lack of both transparency and consistency in applying rules, and as a result have not necessarily succeeded in their stated role.

Policy Suggestions

In the past three decades or so, countries producing natural resources have sought to avoid the worst effect of the resource curse by establishing resource revenue funds. The first goal of such funds is usually to stabilize fiscal resources. For nations that depend on a single commodity for a large portion of their income, shifts in the market can mean huge budget surpluses and shortfalls. Overspending in surplus years can stimulate inflation in the domestic economy, which is then exacerbated by rising currency values. Stabilization funds typically aim to smooth government spending, to prevent inflation and budget deficits, and to hedge against currency fluctuations by holding financial assets in foreign currencies.

A second common goal of natural resource funds is to save resource revenues for future generations. This objective rests on both a sense of intergenerational equity and a desire to convert natural resources into a sustainable source of financial resources that can fund public needs in the future. Typically these funds are invested for long-term growth. Some countries maintain separate funds for their stabilization and savings goals, while others combine them in one fund.

The cases presented below provide a sense of the range of options that countries might employ, including countries newly enriched by resources, perhaps by secession. Resource revenue funds from six locales (five countries and one U.S. state) are profiled. The discussion begins with Norway's fund for petroleum revenue, which is generally held as the most successful, in part due to its strict adherence to the principles of transparency and accountability. Two other success stories—the funds in Alaska and Botswana, which manage revenue from oil and diamonds, respectively—are presented next.

Finally, the chapter describes the oil funds in Kuwait, Oman, and Kazakhstan. These three funds have been relatively successful at accumulating and investing their oil wealth, but they demonstrate scant transparency or accountability. As a result, they may not be sustainable, and their procedures and institutional structures are best avoided.

The Prime Standard: Norwegian Pension Fund–Global

Following the discovery of oil in the North Sea, Norway experienced the economic turbulence that accompanied drastic shifts in world oil prices in the 1970s and 1980s. In response, Norway established a fund to cushion itself against the impact of market fluctuations and save for the future when the oil had been exhausted. Today the Norwegian Pension Fund–Global (NPFG, formerly known as the Norwegian Petroleum Fund) is perhaps the best such fund in the world. Policy makers from around the globe have studied Norway's example.[1] Norway's NPFG represents the current best practice in natural resource revenue management.

Norway's NPFG was established by a Parliamentary Act in 1990 and the first deposits were made in 1995. The objective of the fund is twofold—to save for the future and to stabilize fiscal resources. Norway's population is aging, and its pay-as-you-go pension system simply will not be adequate in the future.[2] In addition, Norway's oil reserves will eventually be exhausted. Thus, Norway now has a window of opportunity to accumulate excess oil revenue and invest it for future fiscal requirements—in effect, to replace the nation's oil wealth with financial wealth. The more immediate goal of the fund is to provide the resources to smooth government spending despite volatile revenue streams.

Oil revenues accrue first to the national budget. Each year Parliament decides how much to spend and how much to save. The rule of thumb is that only the real return on investments (approximately 4 percent) may be used for budgetary purposes.[3] This disciplined approach to government spending also has a countercyclical component. When oil prices rise, the budget is tightened, which both reins in inflation and currency escalation, and swells the fund's coffers. When oil prices decline, the fund can be tapped to address a budget deficit. As Figure 5.1 illustrates, historical spending has been relatively smooth compared to revenue. Contributions are made to the NPFG only if there is a budget surplus, and withdrawals from the fund are not restricted. In another setting this would likely lead to depletion of the fund over time, but the transparency of the fund ensures that the government will protect the people's interests by exercising restraint.

While Parliament determines the transfers to and from the NPFG, the Ministry of Finance is responsible for overseeing the investment of the assets. In accordance with parliamentary guidelines on fund management and approved investment choices, the Ministry of Finance establishes the investment guidelines, the target rate of return, and a benchmark portfolio to monitor the investment performance of NPFG holdings.[4] The ministry also establishes the acceptable level of exposure to risk. Any changes to the

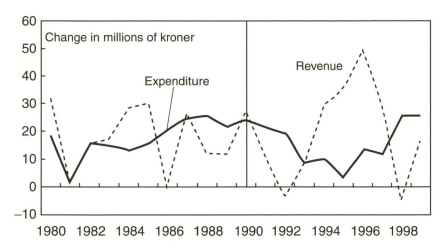

Figure 5.1. Norway's central government fiscal indicators, 1980–1999.
Source: U. G. O. Fasano, "Review of the Experience with Oil Stabilization and Savings Funds in Selected Countries" (International Monetary Fund Working Paper 00/112, 2000).

NPFG's management, including those regarding transfers and investment, must be approved by Parliament.[5]

Norges Bank, Norway's central bank, is responsible for the operational asset management of the fund. Based on a management agreement with the Ministry of Finance, the central bank, through Norges Bank Investment Management, manages separate operations for equities and fixed-income investments.[6] In an effort to reduce portfolio risk and avoid the temptation for political maneuvering, investments are highly diversified. The fund holds positions in approximately 3,500 companies, with an ownership stake of less than one percent of available shares from any individual company. It has made equity investments in forty-two developed and emerging markets and fixed-income investments in thirty-one currencies.[7] From 1998 to 2007, the average annual return on invested assets was more than 7.5 percent. The NPFG was estimated to be worth US$370 billion as of September 2008.[8]

The separation of power within the system governing the NPFG, as illustrated in Figure 5.2, establishes effective layers of accountability. This is bolstered by a high degree of transparency. Norges Bank prepares quarterly and annual reports that provide information on transfers to and from the budget, investment holdings and returns, exposure to risk, and other

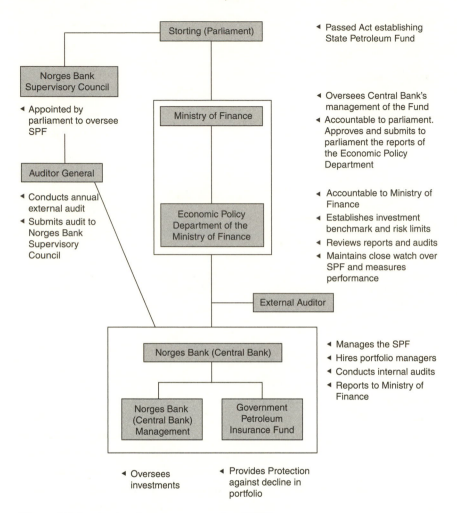

Figure 5.2. Institutional struture governing NPFG.
Source: S. Tsalik, R. E. Ebel, and C. R. Watch, "Caspian Oil Windfalls: Who Will Benefit?" (Open Society Institute, Central Eurasia Project, 2003).

operational details. All such reports are made publicly available on the Internet. In addition, an external auditor is engaged to verify the reported information.[9]

Despite the broad public and political support for the fund and its conservative management, from time to time Norwegians debate its appropriate use.[10] Given the range of possible uses of such resources, if this or another similar fund is to be sustained, it is critical to have mechanisms in place to conduct such discussions in front of or including the public—the ultimate stakeholders of the fund. This feature is one of the elements that sets Norway's fund apart from most other oil revenue funds. It is, however, one that is not easily replicated as it relies on a national culture of openness and public participation in governance. The NPFG is not designed per se to be a transparent and accountable organization; rather, it reflects those features in the governance of Norway itself.

For this reason many experts doubt that the Norwegian model would work in developing countries. But many of the practices used to safeguard the NPFG can in fact be replicated in other countries, even when Norwegian-style openness in government is not the norm. In fact, nations with less transparent governments arguably need more measures to protect the fund from political maneuvering, not fewer.

Other Successful Models
ALASKA

Alaska maintains two separate funds for oil resources, one for savings and the other for fiscal stability. The Constitutional Budget Reserve Fund (CBR), established in 1990, is used to smooth budgetary resources and finance needed public projects. In practice it has mostly been used to address budget shortfalls. The fund assets may be tapped provided there is three-fourths approval in each house of the legislature. Transfers from the CBR represent a loan to the budget that must be repaid out of future fiscal surpluses. Unlike for the savings fund, contributions to the CBR are derived from legal settlements relating to earlier tax and royalties disputes.[11]

By contrast, the purpose of the Alaska Permanent Fund (APF) is to share the wealth derived from oil reserves with current and future generations of Alaskans. Established in 1976, the APF is one of the oldest natural resource savings funds. It is based on the principle that the state's residents are the ultimate owners of any resources within the territorial boundaries. By constitutional provision, 25 percent of all mineral lease rentals, royalties, royalty sale proceeds, federal mineral revenue sharing payments, and bonuses received by the state must be deposited into the APF.

The funds are invested in bonds, U.S. and foreign equities, and real estate. The target rate of return is 4 percent, but actual returns have been significantly higher. By 2003 the APF had generated US$20 billion in net income since its inception.[12] The principal in the fund is now worth nearly US$28 billion.[13] Virtually all information about the fund—including annual reports, audited financial statements, investment earnings, and performance against goals—is publicly available, with the exception of the list of companies in which the APF is a shareholder, which is kept confidential.[14]

The invested principal in the APF may not be spent without amending the state constitution, which requires a majority vote by the Alaskan population. However, a portion of the investment income may be spent each year. The most notable expenditure from the fund is a dividend program that issues a check to all qualified Alaskan residents. This is the fund's most visible demonstration of the philosophy that the oil wealth belongs to the people.

A unique feature of the APF is its organizational design. In 1978 the Alaska Permanent Fund Corporation (APFC) was established to manage the fund resources independently and shielded from political influence. The APFC is accountable to the government and citizens of Alaska, and is overseen by an independent board of trustees. The board is composed of four governor-appointed members of the public, the commissioner of revenue, and another member of the governor's administration. The chair rotates each year among the four members of the public, who are appointed for staggered four-year terms. The state legislature in turn has a final say over the board's proposals.[15] The multitiered management structure of the APF resembles that of Norway, but has the distinct feature of including citizen-stakeholders on the oversight committee. This, too, reflects the philosophy of public ownership of, and responsibility for, the state's natural resources.

BOTSWANA

Botswana is endowed with many natural resources, most notably diamonds. The gems account for three-quarters of Botswana's exports and more than half of government revenue.[16] But revenue from diamonds, as from other natural resources, can vary. Given Botswana's level of dependence on diamond revenue, having no strategy to counteract the destabilizing effect of such shifts on the economy could be devastating.[17] To that end, the government established two foreign exchange reserve funds to achieve short- and medium-term stability and long-term savings.

A portion of the government's diamond revenue is allocated to the Liquidity Portfolio in order to meet the economy's short-term needs for liquidity and foreign currency. Its investment portfolio includes foreign currencies, bills, and securities. The fund is managed by the central bank, the Bank of

Botswana. A larger portion of diamond revenue is set aside for long-term savings in the Pula Fund. It, too, is managed by the Bank of Botswana, and its holdings include foreign equity and fixed-income investments for long-term growth. These positions typically have a longer investment horizon than do those in the Liquidity Portfolio.[18] The Pula Fund is currently worth an estimated US$6.9 billion.[19]

Both funds are successful. They are managed with a degree of transparency that is uncharacteristic of Africa, though Botswana is relatively well off by regional standards. Disbursements made from the fund are usually done in coordination with medium-term national development plans, five-year fiscal policy instruments that help to allocate diamond revenues to needed capital investments.[20] Spending fund money on development projects is conditional on the projects being able to recover long-term operating costs and generate returns on par with alternative investment opportunities. The objectives of avoiding external debt, stabilizing growth, and diversifying the economy also guide economic decision making.[21] Thanks to its generally good governance and appropriate management and use of the resource revenue funds, Botswana has achieved steady economic growth over the past few decades. Still a relatively poor country by global standards, Botswana has successfully avoided the resource curse while harnessing the potential of its resources.[22]

Cautionary Examples: Kuwait, Oman, Kazakhstan

Kuwait

If Norway, Alaska, and Botswana suggest models to emulate as nations seek to stabilize and save natural resource earnings, the experiences of these four countries are more cautionary. Kuwait maintains two oil revenue funds. The General Reserve Fund (GRF), established in 1960, serves as a stabilization fund. The fund allows government spending to run countercyclical to oil revenues, providing for a more stable fiscal environment.[23] While the use of funds has historically been rather conservative, there are no specific provisions guiding the transfers to or from the fund. Contributions come from the profits and income generated by state-owned enterprises and the sale of assets. Unlike with other funds, there is no mechanism for accumulating savings during peak oil prices.[24]

Kuwait also maintains a savings fund called the Reserve Fund for Future Generations (RFFG), which it established in 1976 to provide an income stream for future generations. Ten percent of all petroleum revenues are remitted to the RFFG each year by law.[25] The funds are invested in foreign capital markets, but details of the fund's holdings are not made publicly available, reportedly to avoid political interference. To sustain the fund, it is governed by stricter rules about contributions and withdrawals than is the stabilization fund. The Kuwait Investment Authority, an independent legal entity, is responsible for the investment of RFFG and GRF funds. In recent years investment income from the funds has been Kuwait's second largest source of government income, after oil.[26]

Looking at the pattern of government spending and saving, Kuwait's GRF and RFFG would appear to be relatively good models for resource revenue management. However, their complete lack of transparency and accountability runs counter to the recommendations of international organizations such as the IMF, the World Bank, and the Extractive Industries Transparency Initiative. Little is known about the funds' values or holdings. In fact, the RFFG began as a secret account held by the Kuwaiti finance minister. When the fund became public, that discovery led to its formal establishment, but it remains highly secretive. In several instances that also became public, funds were used for dubious political purposes, rather than economic ones.[27] Thus, while the outcome of the fund, in terms of investment performance and relatively smooth fiscal streams, appears positive, this success cannot be attributed to the institutional design of the fund. Failing to incorporate best practices in the design of the fund runs the risk that longevity of the fund is subject to the whims of government. Without rules to govern withdrawals, the resources could be used to fund pet projects or generate public support in times of political upheaval. While such opportunities may be useful for the government to maintain power, they are not the most effective in ensuring the sustainability of stabilization funds such as the Kuwaiti GRF.

Oman

Oman's oil reserves are less than half Kuwait's and are expected to run out in the next decade or two. As a result, Oman has a greater incentive not to waste oil wealth. The State General Reserve Fund (SGRF) has much stricter guidelines governing transfers to and from the fund to ensure that the nation takes full advantage of the opportunity to accumulate wealth needed to sustain its economy in the future. Contributions are made to the SGRF when the price of oil exceeds a specified reference price (e.g., US$15 a barrel in 2004), and withdrawals may be made when the price falls below. Assets that accrue to the fund are managed by the Ministry of Finance. Short-term investments with a two-year horizon are made in one account, while a long-term fund is maintained for higher-return investments.[28]

While the SGRF was originally designed as a savings fund for future generations, it has been used mostly as a stabilization fund. Discretionary use of SGRF assets requires approval by the Council of Ministers, which is advised by the Financial Affairs and Energy Resources Council.[29] Despite the mechanism in place to maintain countercyclical spending and saving, it remains the case that withdrawals to cover budget deficits have been frequent. Due to the lack of fiscal restraint, analysts now believe the fund will run out of money before Oman runs out of oil.[30]

Moreover, as in Kuwait, Oman's SGRF is extremely secretive. While regular audits, reporting, and performance reviews are the norm, the information is not made publicly available. Thus, while the SGRF has some of the trappings of a well-designed fund, they do not serve to improve transparency or accountability. As in Kuwait, the superpresidential system governing Oman's SGRF allows leaders to change fund rules, making the funds akin to secondary budgets rather than highly disciplined savings schemes.

Kazakhstan

As in Kuwait, Kazakhstan's national fund for oil revenues originated from a secret account linked to the sitting president and became official only under the subsequent president. The National Fund (NF) serves as a savings, stabilization, and development fund. Previously, contributions to the fund were tied to a reference price of oil, but as of 2006 all oil-related revenues are remitted to the NF and subsequently a share is made available to the national budget.

Portions of NF resources are managed by the Central Bank and by international investment institutions. The latter manage roughly 60 percent of the resources, spread across several institutions with the Dutch financial group, ABN AMRO, acting as the overall custodian of the accounts. Investments are made in U.S. Treasury bills and equities and government bonds from other OECD countries. In the first quarter of 2007, the value of the NF was estimated to be US$15.9 billion.[31]

Several government entities are involved in the operation of the NF. The Ministry of Finance is responsible for the transfer of funds to and from the NF, while the central bank, the National Bank of Kazakhstan, oversees the investment of the funds. An oversight council exists to monitor transfers and investments, but it includes representatives from the agencies under monitoring. Ultimately the power to govern the NF lies solely in the hands of the president. There are no caps on fund withdrawals and no rules governing reporting.[32]

In 2005 Kazakhstan joined the Extractive Industries Transparency Initiative in an effort to address the apparent institutional shortcomings, particularly as they relate to transparency and accountability.[33] It remains to be seen whether this development will result in a move toward best practice. To date, very little detailed information is available on the investment management contracts. Furthermore, until Kazakhstan adopts rules governing the use of funds, there is little hope that reliance on fiscal restraint alone will be sufficient to ensure the sustainability of funds.

The countries in this chapter's cases, as in the previous chapter's cases, were not seceding and were for the most part not poor. Yet they too illustrate the importance of a principle—in this case, transparency is key to the success of funds for stabilizing resource revenues and saving a portion for long-term growth.

CHAPTER 6

Water

For many seceding states, especially those in Africa, water is their lifeblood. Division is likely to mean that existing water resources, most often a river basin, will also have to be divided. That probably will entail starting with current usage of the basin by the unified state, then negotiating a division of that usage between the two or more new states, along with mechanisms for preventing abuses, especially by the upriver state, and for handling disputes.

This chapter outlines the issues and draws lessons based on four suggestive cases—the Nile Waters arrangements themselves, plus negotiated arrangements for the Indus, Jordan, and Mekong Rivers. Only one of the cases involves a secession. Yet all of them suggest ways to allocate and manage water resources even in unpromising political circumstances that are all too typical of secessions.

Policy Suggestions

Here, drawn from the cases below, are some preliminary suggestions for policy makers to consider when grappling with cases of secession.

Think Hard About Whether to Open Basic Agreements with States Beyond Those in Immediate Question

The changing status of international sovereignty brought about by secessions can thrust current agreements or disputes into an international context, making the agreements or disputes more difficult to manage. For the Indus, as India gained increased autonomy from Britain, resolving disputes over water resources became more complex. When India became independent and was subsequently partitioned, these disputes over water resources became international issues. In the case of the Nile, the upstream countries have long regarded the arrangements as unfair and sought changes. Incorporating all stakeholders into the decision-making process can help avert future disputes. However, when large numbers of countries pursue cooperative arrangements the results can be slow to materialize. Potential for internal political instabilities in participating countries can also complicate the pursuit of cooperative arrangements.

In Negotiations Among Dividing States, Focus Less on Historic Claims to Water Rights Than on Needs-Based Claims

Arguments for water rights based on history tend to become occasions to reiterate nationalist chest-thumping. By contrast, arguments based on population ratios or irrigable land areas are more concrete and tend to produce more favorable progress between disputing parties. This has been the case for both the Nile and the Indus.

Mechanisms can be designed to account for projected capabilities of a country. For example, the 1959 agreement allowed Sudan to loan water resources to Egypt until Sudan developed the capacity to exploit those resources. Arrangements can be designed to allocate a baseline of resources and then divide potential variations through a separate calculus. This might be especially useful when determining how to divide potential future gains from joint development projects.

Groundwater should be explicitly taken into account in water agreements. The negotiations over the Jordan River focused purely on surface water, which neglected the hydrological connections between surface and groundwater. This connection has long been ignored in water-planning processes, but many within the hydrological community now emphasize this connection, which can often be lost in water negotiations that are too political.

Include Relevant Stakeholders

All riparians in a watershed should be involved if cooperative management structures are to succeed. Excluding watershed members breeds uncertainty about intentions and development plans, which can lead to trouble down the road if their plans conflict with overall watershed health. That has been the experience along the Mekong, where arrangements exclude upstream countries China and Burma. In the case of the Jordan River Basin, all countries were included in talks in the 1950s and but not in the most recent talks, which actually produced some formal agreement. Today, Syria and Lebanon are both left out of the water management bodies, resulting in significant uncertainty regarding their actions and intentions, making integrated basin governance difficult.

Approach Resolving Water Disputes as Positive-Sum Games

Resolution of water disputes can result in water resource development projects for both sides. The Indus Water Treaty created a significant expansion in new development projects in both India and Pakistan. Promise of benefits from potential projects upon settlement of disputes can be an incentive to resolve issues.

In particular, upstream countries often find transboundary agreements particularly constraining because more restrictions on use are present upstream. India has found that any development project it pursues has some impact on Pakistan, whereas Pakistani projects do not always have a similar impact in India. In some disputes, Pakistan has suggested alternative projects in India that would have less impact on Pakistan's water resources but that would be economically inefficient for India.

Don't Focus Too Narrowly on Water

If water negotiations are held separately from other political discussions, which will almost certainly be the case if traditional water experts are in charge of the process, the issue may hit a dead end because of the inherently political nature of the power that water ownership or control confers on riparian nations. The negotiations on the Jordan River watershed failed whenever they were looked at in a purely technical light because in fact the obstacles were political: parties were loath to agree to water distributions that might be seen to give power to other riparian nations that, at a political level, were in conflict with each other.

Moreover, as the Mekong demonstrated, despite the inclinations of traditional water managers, water management agreements need to take into account social and cultural aspects of water rights, rather than adopting a strictly engineering/economic view. If an organizational structure similar to the Mekong's were created, it might be beneficial for people with expertise in social or cultural issues to be included in the secretariat or the expert advisory council to help bring these nontraditional dimensions to the table.

However, once an agreement is reached, the water coordination committee formed should have the power or political backing to make decisions based on scientific review. If a committee's expert findings can be negated by a political decision, then political contentions in water committees will block progress. In the case of Israel and Palestine, Palestinian farmers were sometimes told that they were not allowed to dig wells. Israel cited hydrological issues in these cases, but some insiders acknowledged political reasons for the denials. Such political intrusion into the water decision-making process is to be avoided if at all possible.

Financial Incentives Can Act as a Catalyst in Negotiating Settlements

In water negotiations between India and Pakistan, progress was stalled due to disagreements regarding whether financial responsibility of specific projects was justified. Instead of coming to agreement on these details, momentum was rekindled by settling on a bottom line that India and the international community would provide as financial compensation to Pakistan. Pakistan was then able to pursue projects as it saw fit and India had a predetermined financial commitment. In the case of the Jordan, in the 1990s the United States conditioned some aid on *all* the riparians coming to agreement.

Consider Temporary Agreements and Transition Periods

Temporary agreements may be expedited if it is explicitly stated that the actions do not represent a new precedent. India was willing to resume the flow of water to Pakistan after the Standstill Agreement expired but in doing so made it clear that this was not to be interpreted as a new precedent. Instead, India's resumption of water flows to Pakistan tempered the immediate heat of the dispute without loss of negotiation leverage and helped create an environment in which negotiations for a longer-term settlement could be attempted. So, too, new arrangements can be implemented over a transition period. The Indus Water Treaty required Pakistan to pursue many replacement facilities to exploit new sources of water. The arrangements supported Pakistan's water needs during this transition until new capabilities could be realized.

Make Use of Third Parties

It often is very helpful to have a disinterested third party doing the planning for the water agreement. In countries that do not have the internal resources to plan and build a large-scale international cooperative water management structure, having a third party (or several parties) lend their expertise and resources to the process was invaluable. In the case of the Mekong, the basis for an agreement was laid by the United Nations Economic Commission for Asia and the Far East (ECAFE) and other reports published by the UN in 1958 and by the Ford Foundation in 1962. In the cases of the Jordan, the Working Group on Water Resources was headed by the United States, which was acceptable to all the parties. Egypt was also included in the proceedings despite not really being part of the watershed. Nevertheless, its role as bridge in the negotiations between Israelis and Arabs was invaluable in achieving the measure of consensus that met those early plans.

That said, dependence on third parties for expertise and funding can prove a double-edged sword if the assistance ends. For instance, in 1975 the United States cut off its funding for the Lower Mekong River Commission, which had formerly been 12 percent of the total. While the funding was later reinstated, it was renewed at much lower levels. Despite rising international understanding of the challenge of global warming, water is still often not a very high priority topic, so while parties can benefit from third-party assistance, they probably cannot count on that assistance being permanent. These policy suggestions are summarized in Table 6.1.

Table 6.1. Policy Suggestions for Water Issues

Issue	Policy suggestion	Relevant cases
Should the new states seek to reopen broader basin negotiations with other states?	The likely answer is no, though other state parties will use secession as an opportunity to reopen.	The histories of the Nile and Indus both suggest changes in sovereignty will complicate negotiations.
What should be the focus of negotiations in secession?	Better to focus on needs, rather than historic claims. But also consider groundwater.	As both the Nile and the Indus suggest, agreement based on historic claims is elusive. Needs are more concrete.
Who should be included?	All relevant stakeholder groups in all new states should be included.	Mekong arrangements exclude upstream countries China and Burma. Unilateral Chinese projects have been a particular problem.
How should negotiations be approached?	Resolving water disputes should be approached as a positive-sum endeavor.	Indus agreement opened way for valuable projects in both India and Pakistan.
How tightly should the focus be on water?	Negotiations should consider wider social and political factors. However, once agreement is reached, implementation should be technical, not influenced by politics.	Palestinians feel that Israeli denials of rights to drill wells are politically driven.
Is there a role for financial incentives?	Yes, to be sure.	Indus agreement was facilitated by compensation to Pakistan, and U.S. aid to the Jordan riparians was conditioned on agreement.
What role for third parties?	In addition to providing aid, third parties can be useful in framing and mediating agreements. Yet managing agreements can be complicated if third parties change their minds about aid.	United Nations Economic Commission for Asia and the Far East (ECAFE) set the framework for the Mekong agreement, the U.S. headed the Working Group on Water Resources for the Jordan, and Egypt was also included in the discussion as a bridge between Israel and the Arabs.

Nile Waters Agreements

Issue and Outcome

The Nile River Basin is shared by ten countries, but Egypt has historically dominated the use of Nile water resources.[1] Various agreements designed to ensure downstream flows were signed by colonial powers in the late nineteenth and early twentieth centuries. By the early twentieth century, Britain encouraged increased cotton production in Egypt and Sudan, which necessitated development of irrigation systems along the Nile. That entailed disputes regarding the best placement of development projects, upstream or downstream.

In 1920, the Egyptian government appointed the Nile Projects Commission, which was composed of three independent hydrologic engineers from India, the United Kingdom, and the United States, to analyze potential water projects that would affect Egypt and Sudan.[2] Potential impacts on other Nile Basin riparians were not explicitly included. The commission's report estimated the Nile's average flow to be 84 billion cubic meters per year (BCM/year). Egyptian needs were estimated to be 58 BCM/year and Sudan was projected to be able to meet irrigation needs solely from the Blue Nile.[3] The commission stated that Egypt's rights to irrigation should be limited to the maximum potential irrigated land since the completion of the Aswan Dam. In addition, the commission recommended any surplus or shortfall in water flow be shared equally between Egypt and Sudan.

Also in 1920, a British engineer, Sir Murdoch MacDonald, developed the Century Storage Scheme for a comprehensive series of dams in the upper Nile to enable greater control through periods of drought and flood.[4] However, the plans were highly controversial in Egypt because they proposed controlling waters from beyond Egypt's borders. Some Egyptians worried this was an attempt by the British to leverage control over Egypt in the event they gained independence.[5] In 1925, Egypt formed the Nile Waters Commission to issue new recommendations based on the 1920 Nile Projects Commission's report. The Nile Waters Commission was led by a Dutch engineer, with British and Egyptian engineers as members.[6] The recommendations issued by the commission were used as the basis for the 1929 Nile Waters Agreement. The 1929 agreement allocated 48 BCM/year to Egypt and 4 BCM/year to Sudan. Sudan's flow was restricted to the winter months, which limited cotton cultivation. Egypt was also allowed to have on-site inspectors at the Sennar Dam. In addition, Egypt was guaranteed that no development projects could be pursued in the Nile Basin that might jeopardize Egyptian interests.

Course of the Dispute

In 1952, Egypt proposed the Aswan High Dam. Sudan was not included in planning activities until 1954 as the Egyptian government debated whether the project—which had become a bone of contention between the United States and the Soviet Union, contending for influence in Egypt—should be pursued jointly or unilaterally. When Sudan was approached about the High Dam, it saw the plan masquerading as a joint endeavor but in fact entirely dedicated to Egypt's self-interest. Subsequent Sudanese delegations focused negotiations on the division of Nile waters based upon relative population ratios and size of irrigable lands between the two countries.

These negotiations continued despite occasional escalations in tensions. In late 1958, a pro-Egyptian military regime took power in Sudan, and the new regime was eager to reconcile relationships with Egypt in order to maintain power. Coming to a resolution over the Aswan High Dam plans became a top priority. Previous consideration of population ratios and irrigable land areas was abandoned.[7]

The 1959 Nile Waters Agreement estimated the average annual flow to be 84 BCM/year with 10 BCM/year lost to evaporation, leaving a balance of 74 BCM/year to be divided between the two sides. Based on historical usage, Egypt was allocated 48 BCM/year and Sudan 4 BCM/year. The remaining water resources were divided giving 7.5 BCM/year to Egypt and 14.5 BCM/year to Sudan. These allocations totaled 55.5 BCM/year for Egypt and 18.5 BCM/year for Sudan.[8] Increases in annual flows would be divided equally.

Both the funding for new projects after the High Dam and the benefits of those projects were to be shared equally. Reallocations due to decreases in annual flows would be determined by a Permanent Joint Technical Committee. In 1959, Sudan could not use its entire allocation, so the agreement allowed Sudan to loan water to Egypt. In addition, Egypt agreed to pay compensation for the displacement of people in the Wadi Halfa District resulting from the Aswan High Dam. The water resource allocations stemming from the 1959 Nile Waters Agreement have continued to the present.

From 1967 to 1992, the United Nations Development Programme (UNDP) and the World Meteorological Organization supported a hydrometeorological project (Hydromet) to gather information regarding water levels in Lake Victoria, which would have an impact on potential regulations. Ethiopia did not participate in the efforts, which were led by officials from Sudan and Egypt.[9] In 1993, the Technical Committee for the Promotion of the Development and Environmental Protection of the Nile Basin (TECCONILE) was formed. Ethiopia served as an observer but not as a full member partly due to Egyptian influence in TECCONILE.[10] However, Egypt and Ethiopia did agree that each country would not pursue any development projects that would adversely affect the other.[11]

In 1999, all of the Nile riparian countries joined in the formation of the Nile Basin Initiative (NBI) to coordinate development and management of water resources in the Nile Basin in a sustainable and equitable fashion to promote economic development and security.[12] NBI policy initiatives are guided by the Council of Ministers of Water Affairs of the Nile Basin States (Nile-COM). The Nile Technical Advisory Committee (Nile-TAC) consists of two technical experts from each member country who oversee joint programs and projects and advise Nile-COM.[13] NBI has two components to develop and implement plans—the Shared Vision Program (SVP) and the Subsidiary Action Program (SAP). SVP provides a forum for dialogue between member countries and encourages stakeholder participation.

SAP implements the SVP plans. SAP is organized into two regions, the Eastern Nile and the Nile Equatorial Lakes. SAP is also tasked with identifying and implementing joint projects that are mutually beneficial for all countries involved.[14] While the accomplishments of the NBI are encouraging, concerns remain. For instance, Ethiopia has expressed concern that downstream countries (i.e., Sudan and Egypt) receive disproportionate consideration. So, too, there are debates regarding whether prior agreements should continue to be recognized.[15]

Since the 1959 agreement, Sudan has not fully used its allotment. However, plans to reach the agreement quota are under way with the Merowe and Siteit Dams. Merowe Dam was inaugurated in March 2009 with plans to be fully operational by the end of the year. These dams are intended to produce both hydroelectric power and reservoirs for irrigation. Egypt has supported these construction projects because they will reduce sediment at High Aswan Dam and increase Sudan's potential to use hydropower to extract groundwater.[16]

An analysis of treaties over water resources suggests that needs-based allocations tend to resolve conflicts more often than rights- or efficiency-based approaches.[17] Thus, any division of Sudan's quota between North and South Sudan, for instance, should be determined through a needs-based approach. The Helsinki Rules on the Uses of the Waters of International Rivers provide a framework for determining equitable water allocations based on needs.[18] These rules, adopted by the International Law Association in 1966, are really a statement of general principles for states sharing a water basin. They provide definitions and cover equitable utilization, pollution, navigation, timber floating, and dispute resolution. Subsequent supplementary rules cover related and additional items.

Assessment and Possible Lessons

To recapitulate, five initial lessons can be drawn from the Nile Waters Agreements:

One is that negotiations tended to be more productive when dialogue shifted from historic claims to water rights to needs-based claims to water rights. Arguments for water rights based on historic usage tend toward ideology, while arguments based on population ratios or irrigable land areas are more negotiable and likely to produce more progress.

Second, the changing status of international sovereignty can thrust current agreements or disputes into an international context. This can make the agreements or disputes more difficult to manage.

Third, incorporating all stakeholders into the decision-making process can avert future reclamas. The downside, though, is that more parties can make progress slow and also increase the chances that internal political instabilities in participating countries will complicate pursuit of cooperative arrangements.

Fourth, mechanisms can be designed to account for projected capabilities and needs, not just current ones. For example, the 1959 agreement allowed Sudan to loan water resources to Egypt until it developed the capacity to exploit those resources.

Finally, arrangements can be designed to allocate a baseline of resources and then divide potential variations in a separate way—perhaps especially useful when determining how to divide potential future gains from joint development projects.

Indus Water Treaty

Issue and Outcome

Irrigation systems have been present along the Indus River for centuries but were extensively developed under British rule.[19] With independence, disputes over management of water resources became an international issue between India and Pakistan. After decades of negotiations, the two sides agreed to the Indus Water Treaty, which specifies water allocations and compensation to Pakistan for new development projects that are necessary to meet water needs. It also established mechanisms to implement the agreement and resolve conflicts.

Course of the Dispute

Irrigation systems were extensively developed under British authority in the Indus Basin, and disputes over water resources could be swiftly resolved by British authorities. The 1935 Government of India Act granted greater autonomy to the provinces of India, including jurisdiction over water resources. Provincial disputes ensued over water development projects, particularly between Punjab and Sind, and in 1942 Britain organized a commission to examine the disputes over development plans between the two.[20] The commission, including technical experts from both sides, recommended an integrated management plan for the Indus River Basin. Punjab and Sind opposed the commission's recommendations, and the matter was sent to Britain for final decision.

However, before a decision could be rendered, colonial rule ended, and the dispute became international between the newly independent India and Pakistan. As in other policy areas, transboundary water resource issues in the Indus Basin were not adequately planned for in the partition. Joint control and management of water resources was envisioned, but no tangible steps were taken to toward their implementation. Engineers from India and Pakistan negotiated a Standstill Agreement, which maintained water allocations to Pakistan. In 1948, immediately upon expiration of the Standstill Agreement, India ceased the flow of Indus waters to Pakistan at key locations. Flows were reestablished less than a month later, but the incident highlighted Pakistan's vulnerability to India's control of the Indus waters.[21]

The terms of the resumption of water deliveries emphasized Pakistan's lack of rights to the water resources. India maintained that Pakistan recognized India's rights to the waters by agreeing to make payments for water delivery under the Standstill Agreement. While a longer term resolution was sought, the two sides signed the Delhi Agreement, which assured Pakistan water resources or at least adequate time to complete projects for new sources of water before ceasing water supplies. After signing it, Pakistan almost immediately issued an official complaint about the Delhi Agreement, calling instead for third-party administration of equitable water resource allocations.

The World Bank proposed a resolution of the dispute with the eventual goal of joint management of the Indus River Basin, and both India and Pakistan agreed to participate. They made progress in establishing data sharing and verification arrangements but remained unable to come to within reach of an agreed division of Indus water resources. The World Bank ultimately abandoned joint management goals, instead proposing that India be allocated the entire flow of the eastern rivers and Pakistan the entire flow of the western rivers. India would be allowed some use of the western rivers; however, such use would be tightly controlled by the terms of treaty so as not to hinder flow to Pakistan (Article III). One crucial aspect of the proposal was allowing a transition period so that Pakistan could complete development projects for alternate water sources.

The proposal was hardly perfect but was probably the best that could be done in the political circumstances.[22] Further negotiations focused on determining whether particular development projects would be identified as "replacement" or "development." India would be financially responsible for replacement facilities but not for development facilities. Recognizing that resolving disputes on a project-by-project basis could be a serious roadblock, World Bank representatives shifted focus from assessing financial responsibility for specific projects to determining a total financial responsibility for India.[23] India agreed to financial responsibilities of US$174 million, and the international community raised almost US$900 million.

In 1960, the Indus Water Treaty was signed by both parties and subsequently ratified. The treaty provided a ten-year transition period in which Pakistan was able to continue using prior water sources until development of new sources was completed. After the transition period, the allocations established by the treaty would take full effect. In addition, the treaty created the Permanent Indus Commission, composed of one commissioner from each country, which is responsible for the implementation of the treaty and resolution of issues.[24] If a difference cannot be resolved between the two commissioners, a neutral expert, a highly qualified engineer chosen jointly by the two governments, is appointed to decide the matter.[25]

Alternatively, if one month passes from the time of the initial request without an appointment, the World Bank may appoint a neutral expert after consulting with both parties. If the neutral expert cannot decide the difference, it is considered a dispute, and both governments can dispatch negotiators to try to resolve the dispute. If a resolution is still not reached, the dispute is considered by a Court of Arbitration. The Court of Arbitration is composed of seven members—two appointed by each party, in addition to a chairperson, an engineer, and an international law expert.[26]

Assessments and Possible Lessons

Several lessons from the Indus Water Treaty may be more generally applicable to transboundary water agreements, including those occasioned by secessions:

Financial incentives can act as a catalyst in negotiating settlements. In negotiations between India and Pakistan, progress was stalled due to disagreements regarding whether financial responsibility of specific projects was justified. Instead of coming to agreement on these details, the issue was reframed by settling on a bottom line that India and the international community would provide as financial compensation to Pakistan. Pakistan was then able to pursue projects as it saw fit, and India had only a predetermined financial commitment.

There can be a transition period when new arrangements are implemented. The Indus Water Treaty required Pakistan to pursue many replacement facilities to exploit new sources of water. The arrangements supported Pakistan's water needs during this transition until new capabilities could be realized.

Temporary agreements may be expedited if it is explicitly stated that the actions do not represent a new precedent. India was willing to resume flow of water to Pakistan after the Standstill Agreement expired. However, India made it clear that this was not to be interpreted as a new precedent. Instead, India's resumption of water flows to Pakistan tempered the immediate impact of the dispute without losing leverage for India, and allowed an environment in which negotiations for a longer-term settlement could be attempted.

Resolving water disputes can result in water resource development projects for both sides. The Indus Water Treaty created a significant expansion in new development projects in both India and Pakistan.[27] Promise of benefits from potential projects upon settlement of disputes can be an incentive to resolve issues.

Upstream riparians can find transboundary agreements particularly constraining because more restrictions on use are present upstream. India has found that any development project it pursues will have some impact on Pakistan, while Pakistani projects do not always have a similar impact in India. In some disputes, Pakistan has suggested alternative projects in India that would have less impact on Pakistan's water resources but that would be economically inefficient for India.

Changing sovereignties can make resolution of water resource issues more challenging. As India gained increased autonomy from Britain, resolving disputes over water resources became more complex. When India became independent and was subsequently partitioned, these disputes over water resources became international issues. Negotiations tended to make more progress when they centered on new approaches to meet water needs rather than arguing claims based on historic rights to water resources.

Often negotiations between disputing sides begin with one or both sides claiming an absolute right to water resources based on hydrography (e.g., where the water source originates or the proportion that falls within one's territory) or historic use of water resources. However, in most cases that were successfully resolved, negotiations shifted to a needs-based perspective.[28] Disputing states are more likely to reach a resolution when the issues are cast in terms of area of irrigable land or population sizes, not just "rights."

The Jordan's Joint Water Committee

Issue and Outcome

The Jordan River Basin lies in a parched, perilous setting shared today by Israel, the Palestinian Authority, Jordan, Lebanon, and Syria.[29] In the early

1950s, the basin seemed to be escalating toward violence as one nation after another announced unilateral plans for water use and development along the river and its tributaries. In 1955 President Eisenhower assigned Eric Johnston as special U.S. envoy to oversee negotiations among the riparians. Israel accepted his plan and so did President Nasser of Egypt. However, the Arab states refused to legally ratify it, leading to the failure of negotiations. Several other attempts were made at water negotiations over the next two decades, but none successfully produced a joint water management body until Arab-Israeli peace negotiations in the early 1990s, which led to the creation of two joint water committees, one between Israel and Jordan and one between Israel and the Palestinians. Observers say that it was the discussion of water rights in relation to broader political negotiations that helped to finally solve the impasse that had met previous rounds of talks. And while these agreements are a success in some terms, the river does not have a basin-wide management agreement including all the riparian nations.

Course of the Dispute

Almost all preliminary negotiations among riparians in the Jordan River Basin focused on the Sea of Galilee as the main water storage reservoir for the region. The sea is under Israeli control, and that control became the Arab complaint. The Johnston negotiations included some storage farther upriver on the Yarmuk to appease Arab concerns. Discussions of damming the Yarmuk River lapsed after the Johnston negotiations but picked back up in 1957 as part of the Soviet-Syrian Aid Agreement and later at the First Arab Summit in Cairo in 1964. Arab nations even began construction of a dam at Mukheiba, but when the Golan Heights dam site came under Israeli control in the 1967 Arab-Israeli war, the project was abandoned.[30] The idea was once again renewed in 1977, but a shift in Israeli leadership led once again to the sidelining of the dam project at Mukheiba.

In 1980, after the signing of the Camp David Accords between Israeli and Egypt, U.S. president Jimmy Carter pledged a US$9 million loan toward another low dam at Maqarin, and Congress approved an additional US$150 million provided *all* riparians agreed to the plan. The scheme proposed this time involved Syria receiving all the hydropower generated by the Maqarin dam and Jordan receiving 75 percent of the water. Israel was skeptical about this dam and other development by Syria in the headwaters of the Yarmuk, regarding the Sea of Galilee as the main regional reservoir.

Still, by the fall of 1990, an agreement seemed to be taking shape as Israel agreed to the concept of the dam, and discussions on a formal document and winter flow allocations could continue during construction, estimated for more than five years. Two issues held up any agreement. First, the lack of Syrian input left questions of the future of the river unresolved, a point noted by both sides during the mediations. Second, the outbreak of the Gulf War in 1991 overwhelmed other regional issues, finally preempting talks on the Yarmuk. The issue was not discussed again for nearly a decade, emerging only in the context of the Arab-Israeli peace negotiations.[31]

In 1992, multilateral peace talks were held in Moscow featuring the Working Group on Water Resources, headed by the United States, which addressed water supply, demand, and institutions among the riparian nations. The process was designed to attempt to close the gap between political issues and regional development and perhaps create a "positive feedback loop" between the two. The multilateral working groups aimed to be open forums in which the state parties could get to know one another and build mutual confidence in the processes of building peace and development.

Decisions of the Working Group on Water Resources were meant to be made by consensus, but in practice the group dealt less with specific political or technical issues of water than with building relationships between working group members.[32] These multilateral talks gave way to two bilateral water agreements in the context of sweeping peace accords—the Israel-Jordan Treaty of Peace of 1994 and the Interim Agreements Between Israel and the Palestinians (1993 and 1995).

Decisions to implement the second set of Israeli-Palestinian Interim Agreements are carried out by the Joint Water Committee, under the political leadership of the Israel and the Palestinian National Authority. "This means that when a sensitive water issue of political importance surfaces in the JWC it is passed up to a higher political level."[33] And politics is hardly absent: Palestinian officials maintain that they have had problems getting wells approved by the committee due to unjustified Israeli objections, while Israelis maintain that they have hydrological reasons for denying Palestinian wells.[34]

Another problem with implementing the Interim Agreement is that all protocols, minutes, and other issuances produced by the Joint Water Committee have to be signed by all four members of the committee (two Israelis and two Palestinians), which can lead to significant delays in finalizing any decisions. While it is important to get consensus on water policies, it allows individual members to withhold their signature as a political tool. After the most recent intifada began in 2000, JWC's implementation of its plans became much more limited, despite a joint statement of January 31, 2001, from the Israeli and the Palestinian heads of the JWC reaffirming their commitment to continue their cooperation.

Like the Israeli-Palestinian agreements, the peace treaty between Israel and Jordan also stipulates the formation of a Joint Water Committee made up of six individuals, three from each side. As this Israeli-Jordanian JWC is part of a formal peace treaty, its pace of decision making has moved along faster than that of the Israeli-Palestinian JWC, which is only part of an interim agreement between two nations engaged in ongoing hostilities.

Two other water problems face the region. First, none of these agreements mandate any rules about groundwater, and, second, the agreements reached have not included all riparian states. Neither Syria nor Lebanon has a formal agreement with Israel, as that would acknowledge Israel's legitimacy as a state. In the period after the 1967 war, Syria began increasing its diversion of the flow of the Yarmuk and groundwater sources over the amount allocated under the Johnston Plan, which was the informal agreement functioning in the basin in the absence of bilateral or multilateral agreements with Syria.[35]

Assessment and Possible Lessons

Again, to recapitulate, several lessons can be drawn from the Joint Water Committees in the Jordan River Basin experience that could be relevant to the planning of transboundary water agreements in other politically contentious states:

It is important to put water negotiations in a broader political context. If water negotiations are held separately from other political discussions, which will almost certainly be the case if traditional water experts are in charge of the process, the issue may hit a dead end because of the inherently political nature of the power that water ownership/control gives riparian nations. The negotiations in the Jordan River watershed failed whenever they were looked at in a purely technical light, a reminder that no issue is ever truly technical in the midst of a raging territorial conflict.

Once an agreement is reached, the water coordination committee formed must have the power or political backing to make decisions based on scientific review. If a committee's expert findings can be negated by a political decision, then in contentious settings, such water committees will be stalled. In the case of Israel and Palestine, Palestinian farmers were sometimes told that they were not allowed to dig wells. Israel cited hydrological issues in these cases, but some insiders acknowledged political reasons for the denials. If possible, such political intrusion into the water decision-making process should be avoided.

All riparian nations should be included in talks and agreements. In the case of the Jordan River Basin, all countries were included in talks in the 1950s and later, but not in the most recent talks, which actually produced some formal agreement. Despite that, the fact that Syria and Lebanon are both left out of the water management bodies creates uncertainty about their actions and intentions, and makes integrated basin governance difficult. In the obverse case, Egypt was included in the Johnston negotiations. Nevertheless, its role as bridge in the negotiations between Israelis and Arabs was invaluable in achieving the measure of consensus that met those early plans.

Groundwater should be explicitly taken into account in water agreements. In the Jordan case, discussions purely focused on surface water, which neglected the hydrological connections between surface and groundwater. This connection has long been ignored in water planning processes, but there is a recent move within the hydrological community to emphasize this connection, which can often be lost in water negotiations that are too political.

Mekong

Issue and Outcome

The Mekong River, the tenth longest and seventh largest in discharge in the world, runs through six riparian nations, starting in China and flowing finally through Vietnam to reach the South China Sea.[36] The vast majority of the 60 million basin inhabitants—80 to 85 percent—engage in subsistence agriculture, whose largest product is rice, a water-intensive crop.[37] The basin has huge potential for development; it already produces US$1.45 billion a year in fishing, has large stores of mineral resources, and, according to some studies, has the possibility for 30,000 annual megawatts of hydropower.[38]

In 1957 the countries along the lower Mekong River Basin formed the Committee for Coordination of Investigations of the Lower Mekong Basin, known as the Mekong River Committee (MRC), in order to manage development along the river to best serve all riparian nations' interests. The groundwork for the agreement and cooperative management mechanism was set up in 1957 by the ECAFE and other reports published by the UN in 1958 and by the Ford Foundation in 1962.[39]

The Mekong system has plentiful water, and so the agreement was not forced upon the riparian nations through some particular incident but rather was suggested by the UN in a moment of forward thinking and embraced by the four lower riparian nations—Vietnam, Laos, Thailand, and Cambodia. The agreement signed by the four mandated cooperation "in all fields of sustainable development, utilization, management and conversion of the water and related resources of the Mekong River Basin including, but not limited to irrigation, hydro-power, navigation, flood control, fisheries, timber floating, recreation and tourism."[40] To date, the Mekong River has been one of the most successful and comprehensive jointly managed rivers in the world, despite being located in a relatively poor region with plenty of sources of conflict within and among its parties.

Course of the Dispute

When the ECAFE first made its recommendations to create a joint development organization for the Mekong Basin, data on flows or patterns of water use were unavailable, and so the MRC first took on the task of collecting data. It did so with the aid of the international community. A wide range of countries—Japan, the United States, New Zealand, Australia, India, many European nations—as well as international organizations like the UN contributed to the river mapping and geological and hydrographic surveys, while the Mekong Committee prepared its development priorities for the basin. These first years produced the fastest progress toward achieving basin goals. Progress in more recent history has been slowed by increased hostilities among nations as well as a decline in funding.

The MRC is made up of three sections that serve different purposes. The Council is made up of a minister or cabinet member from each party, all empowered to make decisions on behalf of their countries. The Joint Committee is made up of a head of the department of water for each country, and the Secretariat provides technical and administrative expertise to the Council and Joint Committee. Another of ECAFE's suggestions, an expert advisory board, was adopted in 1958 and organized by ECAFE.

In 1995 the Mekong River Committee changed its name to the Mekong River Commission, after Cambodia was reinstated after a twenty-year absence. Since then, the new MRC has outlined ambitious programs—Basin Development Plan; Water Utilization Program; Environment Program; Flood Management Program; Capacity-Building Program; Agriculture, Irrigation and Forestry Program; Fisheries Program; Navigation Program; and Water Resources and Hydrology. However, it has actually implemented only several projects, none on the main branch of the river.[41]

Assessment and Possible Lessons

Moreover, neither of the two upstream countries (China and Burma) are party to the MRC, which means it cannot be a clear mechanism through which to resolve such conflicts. Unilateral developments have put additional pressures on the basin system. In particular, China has built two new dams and plans to build six to seven more, actions that could change the flow and navigability of the river.[42] Observers particularly worry that these actions have occurred in the absence of a cooperative legal framework.

Another criticism of the MRC has been that it has focused "too much on engineering, hydrological and economic aspects of projects, while de-emphasizing social and cultural issues."[43] Such large construction projects are more within the realm of the traditional water management approaches than looking at social solutions to basin development, but in a basin containing more than one hundred different ethnic groups, it might be wise for at least one of the branches of the MRC (most likely the Secretariat or the expert advisory panel) to build capacity along social or cultural lines.

Several lessons can be drawn from the MRC's experience that could possibly be relevant to the planning of other transboundary water agreements:

It was very helpful to have a disinterested third party doing the planning for the water agreement. That is particularly so in countries, like those newly seceded, that do not have the internal resources to plan and build a large-scale international cooperative water management structure. In this case, much of the international community provided expertise and resources to the process.

That said, dependence on third parties can prove a double-edged sword if the assistance ends. For instance, in 1975 the United States cut off its funding for the Lower Mekong River Commission, which had formerly been 12 percent of the total. While the funding was later reinstated, it was renewed at much lower levels. It is a fact of political life that outside interest in issues will be fleeting—especially issues as prosaic as water management. Thus, new cooperative water management institutions should strive to quickly set up their water management organizations to build a sustainable mode of operation.

As in the other cases, this one also suggests the wisdom of including all riparians in a watershed if cooperative management structures are to succeed. So, too, it reinforces the lesson that despite the inclinations of traditional water managers, water management agreements should not focus solely on the technical. They need also to take into account social and cultural aspects of water rights. If a management structure similar to that for the Mekong were the model elsewhere, it might be beneficial for people with expertise in social or cultural issues to be included in the secretariat or expert advisory council to bring these nontraditional dimensions to the table.

As in the chapter on oil and infrastructure, only one of the water cases involved a secession. Nevertheless they offer important lessons for new states that find themselves faced with the need to negotiate or renegotiate water agreements with neighboring states. Including all stakeholders is important. Outside groups can be very useful in advising, mediating, and providing material assistance. Current metrics, like population and irrigation needs, are more likely to lead to agreements on sharing ratios than is history, which too often turns into nationalist chest-thumping.

Trying to frame win-win arrangements is critical, perhaps with the prospect of new projects as part of the deal. Interim arrangements can be useful provided they aren't seen as permanent. Finally, states whose relations are not amicable can still frame limited agreements in the self-interest of both. Doing so requires recognizing that politics cannot be wished way while structuring arrangements for implementation that focus on the technical.

PART III

National Resources

CHAPTER 7

Assets and Liabilities

This chapter turns from natural resources to national and institutional ones. It begins with assets and liabilities that need to be divided in secessions. Negotiations over those include a number of specialized concepts. This chapter lays out the principal terms, which refer, first, to *the nature of the assets or liabilities* and, second, to *how the new states came into being*. It then provides examples of how those concepts have been employed in previous negotiations about secession, ending with several policy suggestions. The four cases then form the remainder of the chapter. They are the secession of Montenegro from Serbia, the dissolution of Czechoslovakia, the breakup of the Soviet Union, and the secession of Eritrea from Ethiopia.

Basic Concepts

Nature of Asset or Liability

Here, it is important to distinguish between *territorial* and *national* assets or liabilities. Territorial assets and liabilities have a location even if they may be movable, while national ones do not. Territorial assets include government infrastructure—from post offices and hospitals to military bases and state-owned companies. "Territorial liabilities" (or debt, sometimes called "localized debt") is a slightly odd term, but it refers, for instance, to debt incurred to construct a territorial asset, like a power plant.

By contrast, *national* assets and liabilities have no location and generally existed before the original state was divided. National debt is the most common national liability. National assets cover the range from currency accounts and federal (central government) movable property, to gold reserves and diplomatic and state property located abroad. New states may agree to divide national assets on the basis of population, territory, or some other formula.

How New States Came into Being

This also affects the negotiations. New states emerge from old ones in two ways: either part of the state secedes from the original state, or the original state dissolves into various new states. In either case, the states that emerge are called the *successor* states. The difference is that in the case of secession the original state is called the *continuing* state, while in the case of dissolution there is no continuing state, and both (or all) of the emerging states are simply successor states. The difference matters because it is usually presumed

Table 7.1. Policy Concepts for Assets and Liabilities

CONCEPT	Nature of assets and liabilities		How states came into being	
	TERRITORIAL	NATIONAL	SECESSION	DISSOLUTION
Description	Cannot be easily moved	Do not have physical locations	New state secedes from original state	Original state dissolves into several states
Examples	Military bases, state-owned companies	Gold, currency reserves, national debt	Soviet Union	Czechoslovakia
Special terms or provisions	Territorial principle: assets pass to the state on whose territory they are located	Efficiency principle: movable assets stay if integral to value of immovable ones	Continuing state: original state Zero-option agreement: continuing state takes on all original state assets and liabilities	Principles for dividing assets and liabilities: population, territory, or some other principle, like IMF "key principles"

that if there is a continuing state, it will inherit the legal status, international memberships, and, often, diplomatic properties of the original state—as, say, Russia did for the Soviet Union. Often, too, the simplest way to handle national assets and national liabilities after secession is for the continuing state to inherit all assets and liabilities. This is referred to as the *zero-option agreement*. Table 7.1 summarizes the policy concepts.

Examples of the Concepts in Negotiations

When the Soviet Union broke apart, Russia was regarded as the continuing state. In a zero-option agreement, it took all of the Soviet Union's national assets while assuming all the Soviet Union's national debts. In contrast, when the Czech and Slovak Republics were born out of former Czechoslovakia, the process was regarded as a dissolution, not a continuation. The two successor states agreed to allocate national assets and national liabilities, the national debt, in accord with the relative populations of the two states. By contrast, when Yugoslavia dissolved, the successor states agreed to divide most national assets—gold, reserves, and some diplomatic properties—according to the IMF's "key principles," which took into account the new republics' relative contributions to the federal budget of the former federation, their share in social product and export earnings of that federation, and their percentage of its population and territory.[1] The catch-22 was that Serbia, the dominant state, though not legally a continuing state, moved quickly to seize most of Yugoslavia's national assets before Bosnia and Croatia could reach an allocation agreement, while third-party states in which those assets existed were unwilling to freeze them until there was an agreement.

In negotiating territorial assets, the two successors to Czechoslovakia generally followed what is called the *territorial principle*, according to which assets pass to the state on whose territory they are located. In the case of movable assets, the two tried to distinguish between national assets that truly were moveable—which were then divided as other national assets (and debts)—and those that, if moved, would degrade the value of an asset that was not movable. Thus, for instance, movable property associated with factories remained with the factories because moving that property would have degraded the operations, hence value, of the factories themselves. This was the *efficiency principle* in operation.

In the case of the breakup of Yugoslavia, also regarded as a dissolution, the successor states also followed the territorial principle with regard to territorial assets, with two exceptions. One was military assets, which was the subject of a separate negotiation, and the other was property important to a particular successor state's "cultural heritage," which was to be the property of that state no matter where it was located. When Montenegro seceded from Serbia, the continuing state, the two agreed that all military assets, moveable and not, would remain with the state on whose territory they were located. That agreement left Serbia with the vast majority of the former Yugoslavia's military assets; moreover, Serbia used its control of the military to move more military assets into Serbia prior to the final division of the former country.

Liabilities, or debts, are different from assets mostly in that third parties—creditors—are often involved, sometimes intensely. For instance, when Yugoslavia broke up, the IMF first determined that the process was a dissolution, not a secession, then established the "key principles" as the formula for apportioning Yugoslavia's national debt. When, however, the IMF suggested to Serbia and Montenegro a zero-option solution for both IMF assets and debts, that solution did not come to pass, and Montenegro eventually agreed to take on 10 percent of the former state's IMF debt.

In still other cases, successor states have refused to accept responsibility for debt. Bangladesh did so when it split from Pakistan, even with regard to that portion of the World Bank debt that had been of some benefit to territory that became Bangladesh. Eritrea also refused when it split from Ethiopia. In both cases, the fact that the international community eventually accepted the refusals provides some support for the proposition that a seceding territory, especially one that was occupied, need not take on national debt obligations.

These experiences underscore several policy suggestions:

Start Discussions or Negotiations Early

Ethiopia and Eritrea offer a stark example of the risk of deferring these issues, and it is suggestive for other cases including Sudan because those two also were very focused on a referendum on secession. Other issues, including assets and liabilities, were deferred and later helped spur conflict. Starting early is especially critical on the asset side, for the continuing or dominant state has incentive and, often, opportunity to appropriate national assets and move territorial assets before the agreement is final.

Creditors Are Very Engaged Third Parties

This is the difference on the debt side. Multilateral international creditors, like the World Bank or IMF, may frame the negotiations, even set terms, and bilateral creditors will be deeply engaged in details of repayment and the like.

Serbia and Montenegro

Issue and Outcome

Serbia and Montenegro claimed to be the continuing state to Yugoslavia upon dissolution of the former state.[2] For more than a decade the two nations coexisted in a weak two-state union. In a last-ditch effort to hold the union together, Serbia and Montenegro reluctantly signed a Constitutional Charter that delayed a virtually inevitable dissolution by three years. Significantly, the Constitutional Charter outlined the division of assets and liabilities in the event of secession.

Thus, when Montenegro declared its independence from Serbia in 2006, what followed was a very rapid dissolution of the union and division of assets and liabilities. In some cases—for instance, military assets and membership in international organizations—the division was executed as had been agreed in the Constitutional Charter. In other cases (for instance, financial assets and outstanding loans with the IMF and European Commission), the division was renegotiated after the political split. While the zero-option agreement was exercised for some aspects of the division (international legal personality), provisions for a sharing arrangement were made in other instances (World Bank loans and grants).

Course of the Dispute

In the early 1990s, most of the republics that had formed the Socialist Federal Republic of Yugoslavia voted to secede. Serbia and Montenegro were the exceptions. The two republics banded together to form the Federal Republic of Yugoslavia in 1992, waged ethnic war against their neighbors, and claimed to be the continuing state of Yugoslavia. Moving quickly to appropriate assets, the new republic was successful in securing most of what had been Yugoslavia's financial and diplomatic assets and international memberships.

Over the next decade, aggressive Serbian policies in the region, among other issues, created tensions between the two states, and Montenegro's independence movement grew over time. Nevertheless, under pressure from the European Union, Serbia and Montenegro reluctantly signed the "Belgrade Agreement" in 2002, which created a two-state federation called the State Union of Serbia and Montenegro, formalized under the Constitutional Charter of the State Union. The weak union that resulted allowed each state its own economic and state structures. The free movement of people and capital was permitted within the state union, but each side maintained different currencies, tax policies, and budgetary and banking systems.[3] The common state had only five ministers and an indirectly elected president to oversee defense and foreign affairs on behalf of the union.[4]

In recognition of Montenegro's desire for independence, the Constitutional Charter of the State Union included specific provisions for the dissolution of the federation. In particular, after a three-year moratorium either party was permitted to hold a referendum on independence—although in practice this was designed specifically for Montenegro. It exercised that option as soon as the waiting period expired. The EU established the terms for the referendum on independence (that is, 55 percent approval and at least 55 percent voter participation) and monitored the voting process. The referendum was held on May 21, 2006, and it passed with 55.5 percent approval and 86 percent voter turnout. Montenegro formally declared independence from the State Union of Serbia and Montenegro on June 3, 2006. Serbia became an independent state shortly thereafter.

Serbia and Montenegro's previous experience with the dissolution of Yugoslavia proved informative for the state union. Thinking ahead, the two, in effect, negotiated their divorce in the document that constituted their union. In the event of succession, the continuing state would become the sole inheritor of the legal entity of the state union. Assets and liabilities were divided according to the Constitutional Charter, though some were renegotiated after the referendum. As per the Constitutional Charter, all military assets were split along territorial lines. Having appropriated many moveable military assets from Montenegro before the official split, however, Serbia assumed possession of nearly all military assets from the defunct state union.

Serbia was the continuing state, and the charter had codified a zero-option agreement, assigning Serbia all assets and liabilities of the former union. Despite that zero-option agreement, however, Serbia and Montenegro negotiated a split of the national assets and liabilities. While this was not made explicit by either party, Serbia's status as an international pariah state may have given Montenegro scope to demand some of the joint assets. It seems plausible that Montenegro was willing to assume the liabilities associated with Montenegrin affairs (e.g., IMF loans) in order to become truly separate from and independent of Serbia.

For its part, Serbia needed the international community to approve Serbia as the successor to the legal personality of the state union in order to move ahead with national affairs. By negotiating a division of assets and liabilities with Montenegro, Serbia garnered a modicum of political goodwill, which paved the way for ultimate recognition of the nation.

Just two months after the referendum dissolving the state union, the finance ministers and central bankers of Serbia and Montenegro agreed to a split of financial assets, in which Montenegro received 5.9 percent of the gold and convertible currency reserves. Similarly, in a bilateral agreement, Serbia and Montenegro split the financial liabilities to the EU ninety-ten, based on their relative shares of the use of funds. Ultimate liability for the outstanding loans remained with Serbia, however, since it had inherited the legal personality of the state union.[5]

Another important national asset is membership in international organizations. On that score, the division was very clear. Article 60 of the Constitutional Charter stated, "Should Montenegro break away from the state union of Serbia and Montenegro, the international instruments pertaining to the Federal Republic of Yugoslavia would concern and apply in their entirety to Serbia as the successor." Furthermore, "a member state that implements [the right to break away] shall not inherit the right to international personality and all disputable issues shall be separately regulated between the successor state and the newly independent state."[6] As a result, Serbia automatically inherited the state union's rights and obligations with regard to international treaties and membership organizations, including the UN, World Trade Organization, and Council of Europe.[7]

Montenegro did not dispute Serbia's claim to be the successor to the state union's international memberships. Instead, Montenegro was fast-tracked in becoming a member in its own right. Given the tensions between Serbia and Montenegro over Serbia's handling of war criminals and Kosovo, the international community was disposed to deal favorably with Montenegro even before the union had been formally dissolved. Thus its admittance as a new member state to regional and international organizations proceeded quickly, within a month or two.[8] The EU Council agreed to develop relations between the EU and Montenegro just nine days after the latter declared independence.[9] The expedited process was due in large part to the fact that in 2004 the EU had agreed to a "dual-track" approach to EU accession for Serbia and Montenegro, in anticipation of their eventual split.[10]

The division of the state union's debts was renegotiated after the split despite prior arrangements in the Constitutional Charter. In accordance with that document, Montenegro relinquished its claim to the state union's obligations and assets with respect to international donors upon declaring independence from Serbia. Thus, Serbia, by default, inherited the union's IMF debt and its attendant memberships (including the World Bank). However, Serbia and Montenegro were able to negotiate an alternative to the zero-option agreement specified the Constitutional Charter. Montenegro assumed responsibility for a portion of the former state union's portfolio of loans and grants from the World Bank. Serbia was subsequently released of those obligations.

An independent Montenegro was later admitted to the International Bank of Reconstruction and Development (IBRD) in January 2007. Indeed, the IBRD fast-tracked Montenegro's and Serbia's separate memberships in recognition of the fact that the two sides had been able to come to an agreement over the division of debts and assets on their own, which they communicated to the bank.[11]

In July 2006 Serbia and Montenegro agreed that the latter would submit its own application for new membership to the IMF.[12] In January 2007 Montenegro's application was officially approved. By accepting its IMF quota in the amount of US$41.2 million, Montenegro became a member of the IMF and World Bank.[13] Serbia continued membership and the rights and obligations of the state union. Its quota was approximately US$700 million as of the split in 2006.[14]

Negotiations over items that were not discussed in the Constitutional Charter proceeded slowly. These included pensions, health care, and social security. At issue was how Serbians in Montenegro and Montenegrins in Serbia would be provided for by each state.[15] In December 2006 these issues were resolved when Serbia and Montenegro each agreed to pay out the benefits accrued by citizens who had worked within their territory. That is, Serbia agreed to pay the pensions of Montenegrin citizens who had worked in Serbia, while Montenegro agreed to pay the pensions of Serbians who had worked in Montenegro, no matter in which of the two countries pensioners later settled.[16]

Assessment and Possible Lessons

Having recently emerged from a prior dissolution, Serbia and Montenegro knew what secession would involve. As a result, they had essentially agreed to a division of assets and liabilities prior to their split. Even so, they renegotiated the division once the split actually occurred, applying a variety of widely used principles. Their process conveys several lessons for other secessions:

International pressure played some role in the bilateral negotiations between Serbia and Montenegro. Serbia's status as an international pariah state in the early 2000s afforded Montenegro some advantage in its relations with international organizations, which in turn expedited the newly independent nation's membership process. In addition, negotiations between international member organizations and Serbia and Montenegro, respectively, were influenced by the outcome of the dissolution agreements. Several organizations, including the IMF and World Bank, cited the satisfactory split of national assets as a deciding factor in their separate negotiations with each party.

Negotiations prior to an official split can be helpful in preventing a winner-take-all confrontation between successor states. The agreement between Serbia and Montenegro governing the division of assets, one negotiated before the referendum took place, gave the parties a starting point and a fallback position should fresh negotiations fail. This undoubtedly contributed to the speed with which a new arrangement was struck.

It is not necessary to negotiate all the details of the split in advance. Serbia and Montenegro left several sticky issues (for instance, pensions) for discussion after independence. They were ultimately able to agree on these items, too.

There need not be a single approach to the division of all assets and liabilities across the board. For some assets and liabilities, the zero-option arrangement may make sense, while sharing may be appropriate for others. Similarly, while a prenegotiated arrangement may be helpful, flexibility can also be beneficial. The only critical factor is that both parties are able to agree on a division that balances assets against liabilities assumed by both countries.

The Dissolution of Czechoslovakia

The Issue and Outcome

After an uneasy seventy-four-year union, the Czech Republic and Slovakia became two independent nations on January 1, 1993, following the dissolution of Czechoslovakia.[17] The dissolution, which was ratified by the Federal Parliament on November 25, 1992, had been prepared well in advance and resulted in an uneventful and peaceful transition, so much so that the process was dubbed the "Velvet Divorce." Indeed, the split happened only after months of extensive negotiations between Czech and the Slovak leaders on a number of issues, including the division of assets and liabilities, which in effect reduced the tensions and potential sources of dispute after dissolution.

In summary, the two parties agreed to divide territorial assets according to the territorial principle—that is, unmovable assets were allocated to the state where the asset was located. National assets and liabilities were divided according to the population principle—that is, based on the population size—a two-to-one ratio, reflecting the fact that the Czech population was twice that of Slovakia.

In addition, the future of Czechoslovakia's position in international organizations such as the United Nations was discussed in the predissolution period; the two republics agreed to alternate Czechoslovakia's continuity in such bodies between the two countries. However, at independence they both separately applied for membership to these international bodies and both were admitted.[18] All in all, the two countries had agreed on most aspects of the division before the split, leaving only minor residual disagreements over financial assets and archived military documents. Both of these issues were resolved later, respectively in 2004 and 2007.[19]

Course of the Dispute

Czechoslovakia, a federation of the Czech lands and Slovakia, came into existence in 1918 after the fall of the Austro-Hungarian Empire at the end of

World War I. Differences in language, culture, and traditions, as well as in economic status, produced tension in the federation, which translated in the late 1980s and early 1990s into growing nationalism and political rivalry.[20] The rift between the two was aggravated by the end of communism, for, at that juncture, the Czechs were leaning toward the West and rapid economic reforms, while the Slovaks favored a slower pace of reform.

The parliamentary elections of June 1992 made this split vivid, as majorities of Slovaks and Czechs voted for diametric opposites—the Slovaks for Vladimir Meciar, a populist leader leaning left, and the Czechs for Vaclav Klaus, an economist on the center-right who championed free markets. At that point, the leaders of the two met to discuss the future of the country and agreed to loosen the federation, which would entail reducing the power of the federal government, or to look into splitting the country.[21] However, no referendum was held on the question,[22] as the two leading parties were opposed to it and blocked it in the federal parliament.[23]

On July 17, 1992, the Slovak parliament declared independence. This was shortly followed by a meeting between Meciar and Klaus in which both agreed in principle to the dissolution of Czechoslovakia. The Federal Assembly, the main legislative body at the federation level, approved the dissolution only five months later,[24] on November 25, 1992, when it finally passed legislation permitting the dissolution.[25] The two used the months between the declarations of sovereignty and the federal approval of dissolution for extensive negotiations over the modalities of separation and the future relationship of the two republics. As a result of these discussions, by October 1992, sixteen comprehensive agreements had been signed by Meciar and Klaus.[26]

The process of dividing assets and liabilities in Czechoslovakia followed a very formal approach in which first Czech and Slovak parties would negotiate and agree on provisions, then submit them to a vote at the federal level in the Federal Assembly of Czechoslovakia. If passed, the provisions would become law. In the negotiations, Czech leaders proposed that federal assets be divided, first, by the territorial principle, then all the other assets according to population—the two-to-one ratio in favor of the Czech Republic.

The Slovaks were initially apprehensive about the territorial division of federal assets because they stood to lose on, for instance, military assets, 80 percent of which were located on Czech territory. For their part, some Czechs also opposed the proposal—and particularly the division of all the other assets according to population—on the grounds that during the existence of Czechoslovakia, the Czech regions had produced more than twice as much as Slovak regions and were therefore entitled to more than twice as much of Czechoslovakia's assets.[27]

Ultimately, after months of negotiations, on November 4, 1992, the Federal Assembly of Czechoslovakia passed Constitution Act 541 on the Division of Property, a law at the federal level approving the division of the federation's assets. According to this law, 40 percent of assets, valued at approximately KCS 200 billion (US$6.6 billion),[28] would be divided according to the territorial principle and the remainder, worth approximately KCS 300 billion (US$10 billion), would be divided according to the population principle.[29] Military assets were divided according to the population principle while at the same time maintaining the operational capability of the two republics' forces. To that effect, one hundred thousand tons of military equipment would be transferred between the two armies going in both directions.[30] A commission with equal Czech and Slovak representation was set up to implement the division after the dissolution.[31]

Liabilities were estimated in 1992 at US$9.3 billion. One month prior to the scheduled breakup of Czechoslovakia, the would-be finance ministers of the Czech Republic and Slovakia notified international creditors, mainly the IMF and the World Bank, that they had agreed to divide liabilities the same way they had allocated assets—that is, according to the territorial principle for territorial debt and according to the population size for national debt.[32] The IMF, which made the final decision on the allocation of foreign debt, basically accepted this agreement, assigning 69.6 percent of assets, liabilities, and quotas of Czechoslovakia to the Czech Republic and 30.4 percent to Slovakia.[33]

Finally, the two countries reached a devolution agreement to alternate the continuity of Czechoslovakia in international organizations—that is, if one year Czechoslovakia was going to assume the presidency of a certain organization, then either the Czech Republic or Slovakia would take the position, and the next time would be the other country's turn. However, upon independence, both the Czech Republic and Slovakia were immediately recognized by the European Union and the United States, and both decided not to continue Czechoslovakia's membership but instead to apply separately to the UN. They were both admitted in January 1993, but membership to some of the UN auxiliary organizations was nonetheless done according to the devolution agreement.[34] The two countries were also admitted to the

Conference on Security and Co-operation in Europe and the European Bank for Reconstruction and Development shortly after their independence.[35] Later on, both countries joined NATO—the Czech Republic in 1999 and Slovakia in 2004. They also both joined the European Union in 2004.[36]

While for the most part the two nations were able to sort out the most significant issues prior to the breakup, some disputes remained. In particular, they came to an impasse over two, requiring the two countries to stay committed to some form of negotiation over a number of years after independence. The first issue was financial assets: the Czech Central Bank retained 4.1 million metric tons of Slovakian gold as collateral for a supposed debt of US$740 million owed to it by Slovakia, a debt that Slovakia refused to acknowledge. The second issue was Czechoslovakia's military archives containing files from communist-era military intelligence, which had remained under Czech possession. Both issues were resolved after years of negotiation. In 2004, the Czech Republic cancelled the US$740 million debt and relinquished the gold reserves to Slovakia, and in 2007 the two countries agreed to divide the military archives.[37]

Assessment and Possible Lessons

The peaceful nature of Czechoslovakia's dissolution, along with the careful agreements and implementation, make it an exemplary one. The example may not be easy to follow, especially in secessions that are more abrupt and less amicable. Still, it offers some best practices:

First, it is important to negotiate the details of how to split assets and liabilities prior to the actual dissolution of the state. On that score, Czechoslovakia was an admirable outlier: once it was agreed that Czechoslovakia would split, the two states did not rush toward independence. Instead, they achieved independence only once basic agreement on major issues had been reached.

Second, compromise is key to making headway in the negotiations: in the Czechoslovak case, both parties compromised in order to make progress in the negotiations.

Third, it is not necessary to resolve all the issues before the breakup as long as the two nations are committed to continuing to talk and work toward their resolution. That said, basic issues should not be left unresolved. After independence, the unresolved issues did produce some acrimony between

Czechs and Slovaks, but the two countries sustained a dialogue and managed to come up with a satisfactory solution.

The Breakup of the Soviet Union

Issue and Outcome

When the Former Soviet Union (FSU) disbanded in December 1991,[38] the ensuing fifteen republics had to negotiate, among other things, the division of the Soviet Union's assets and liabilities, as well as the allocation of the responsibilities and privileges associated with the Soviet Union's membership in international organizations and treaties.[39] The first issue was whether Russia would be considered a *continuing* state from which the others would be deemed to have seceded, or whether the Soviet Union would be regarded as having dissolved, leaving only successor states. Based on geography, demography, and history, the Russian Federation assumed the status of the continuing state of the Soviet Union in December 1991, without any opposition from the other republics or from the international community. Legally, it would assume all international privileges and obligations of the Soviet Union, including membership in international organizations and treaties. The other republics would have to apply for membership.

The Baltic states (Estonia, Latvia, and Lithuania) considered themselves occupied by the Soviet Union after 1940; nor was their inclusion in the Soviet Union recognized by most Western countries. For them, the disbanding of the Soviet Union restored their independence, rather than classifying them as seceding from the union. As a result, legally, Soviet rights and obligations did not extend to them.[40]

For the remaining twelve republics, the negotiations with regard to the division of assets and liabilities began shortly before the actual disbanding of the union, when it became clear that the Soviet Union would break up. International creditors, concerned about the repayment of the large debt that the Soviet Union had incurred over the 1980s and early 1990s, pressed to convene a meeting in October 1991. The outcome of the meeting was a temporary agreement among the parties that the successor states were jointly and severally liable for the debt, which would be serviced through the Soviet Foreign Exchange Bank (VEB).[41] The successor states also agreed to conduct internal negotiations to come up with a longer-term solution to the debt issue.[42]

Those deliberations proved difficult. The states disagreed over which criteria to use in assigning debt responsibilities, how able certain republics were to service debt, and how to disentangle the distribution of liabilities from those of assets. Two years of negotiations produced a number of agreements and mechanisms to allocate assets and liabilities, but none became fully operational because not all the successor states agreed to their terms.[43]

Ultimately, in 1993, the Russian Federation declared itself responsible for all the external debt of the Soviet Union, and started a process of bilateral negotiations with each of the other republics, pushing for "zero option agreements." By 1994, such agreements had been signed between Russia and all the republics save Ukraine.[44] With Ukraine, Russia agreed to cede 16.4 percent of assets as well as that percentage of liabilities.[45]

Course of the Dispute

In this case, determining that the Russian Federation was the continuing state was fairly straightforward. The announcement by the Russian Federation, on December 24, 1991, came as little surprise. It was geographically the largest entity within the Soviet Union, Russians represented the majority of the union's population, and historically the Soviet Union had been treated as the continuation of the Russian Empire. In fact, other nations, along with some of the new republics, were quick to recognize it, and no successor state presented any form of opposition to the declaration.[46]

The status of continuing state entitled Russia to the rights and obligations in the international organizations of which the Soviet Union had been a member, including permanent membership on the Security Council of the United Nations, as well as in the treaties to which the Soviet Union was signatory. Furthermore, as the continuing state of the Soviet Union, Russia was put in charge of the Soviet armed forces. All the other republics had to apply for new memberships in international organizations because, with the exception of the Baltic states, they were considered successor states of the Soviet Union.[47]

Before World War II, Estonia, Latvia, and Lithuania had been recognized as sovereign states by the international community, and they thought of their 1940 integration into the Soviet Union as an occupation. A number of Western governments had never recognized, de jure, the inclusion of the

Baltic states in the union. With the dissolution of the Soviet Union, these three states neither regarded themselves nor were considered by the international community as successor states; rather they were *reverted states* regaining their sovereignty. As a consequence, the rights and obligations of the Soviet Union did not apply to them, nor did any Soviet assets or liabilities.[48] They did, however, have to apply for membership in international organizations, most of which, including the most prominent, the UN, had come into being after they were incorporated in the Soviet Union.

When it became clear in the fall of 1991 that the Soviet Union would break up, international creditors, mostly member countries of the G7, became concerned about the repayment of Soviet debt, which by the end of 1992 amounted to US$78 billion.[49] They therefore convened a meeting with representatives of the would-be successor states on October 28, 1991, at the London G7 Summit to discuss repaying the Soviet debt on the disbanding of the Soviet Union.[50]

At the meeting, the parties settled on a memorandum of understanding (MOU) that delineated temporary arrangements for the repaying debt. In the MOU, the successors states agreed (1) to be jointly and severally responsible for the debt, (2) to designate the VEB, or its legal successor, as the debt manager, and (3) to continue discussions over how to divide the debt over the long term. The signing of the MOU enabled the ex-Soviet states to defer some of their scheduled debt repayments until the end of 1992.[51]

Internal deliberations continued as per the MOU, and in December 1991 a second agreement was reached: The parties agreed to a proportional division of assets and liabilities based on the joint-and-several formula, in which all successor states were to share responsibility for ensuring repayment of preexisting debts. The actual division rule was a formula based on GDP, imports, exports, and population. However, this agreement fell through almost immediately because only eight out of the twelve new states agreed to it. By mid-1992, only Russia had made payments to the VEB.

In March 1992, the heads of the new republics appointed the Interstate Commission, composed of representatives of the relevant parties, to prepare proposals and negotiate the terms of the division of assets and liabilities. The commission, however, also proved ineffective and was therefore suspended in November 1992, in favor of pursuing the issues basis between Russia and each of the twelve.[52]

In April 1993, Russia effectively declared itself responsible for the entirety of the FSU external debt, and started the bilateral negotiation process. By mid-1993, it had managed to sign zero-option agreements with eleven of the republics, assuming all the liabilities and the nonterritorial assets of the FSU. In so doing, Russia acquired an external debt of approximately US$100 billion, while it gained US$7.5 billion in usable reserves, along with a number of other assets of uncertain value, such as real estate abroad, stocks of precious metals (gold, diamonds, and copper), and FSU loans to other countries (primarily developing countries).[53]

Ukraine was the only country with which Russia was not able to reach a zero-option agreement. Instead, Ukraine wanted to assert its independence in world financial markets by taking its "fair share" of FSU debt. Russia ceded 16.4 percent of the FSU debt to Ukraine, along with the same share of assets. However, Ukraine contended that the assets were not adequately valued or transferred to Ukrainian parties at the time of the agreement, in January 1993, and announced that it would not continue under the agreed-upon arrangements. For its part, Russia refused to renegotiate the terms.[54]

Assessment and Possible Lessons

The negotiations were difficult and protracted, but the case of the FSU does suggest lessons for other states involved in dissolution or secession:

In the event of the dissolution of a country, deciding early on whether there will be a continuing state is helpful, for it simplifies the discussions with regard to membership in international organizations and treaties. In the FSU case, the fact that the Russian Federation was readily recognized as the continuing state of the Soviet Union facilitated discussions with regard to international rights and responsibilities.

The number of negotiating parties makes a difference. In this case, it proved difficult to reach agreement among Russia and all twelve new republics. What ultimately succeeded were bilateral negotiations, with the continuing state taking the lead.

A transparent valuation of the original state's assets and liabilities, one acceptable to all the negotiating parties, is necessary to forestall any future discord over the sharing agreement. Certainly, that was the main issue behind the Russia-Ukraine contretemps; had there been a transparent valuation process at the time of the negotiations, the issue of whether the transfer of the Soviet Union's assets to Ukrainian parties was adequate need never have arisen.

Secession of Eritrea from Ethiopia

Issue and Outcome

Eritrea's secession from Ethiopia, in May 1991, was unusually smooth because the Eritrean Popular Liberation Forces (EPLF), the group behind much of the independence movement, had been an ally of an Ethiopian resistance group, the Tigray People's Liberation Front (TPLF), which sought to overthrow the Derg, the Marxist regime in Ethiopia.[55] In 1991, both groups succeeded: the EPLF gained de facto independence of Eritrea, and the TPLF overthrew the Derg. Under mediation by the United States, the parties agreed that Eritrea would hold a UN-supervised referendum on independence. The vote, held in April 1993, produced an overwhelming "yes" vote, and Eritrea became formally independent in May.

Yet, because relations between the two countries were good and continued that way for several years, a number of important issues were left hanging, including the precise demarcation of the border, the division of assets and liabilities, and the monetary arrangements beyond a temporary agreement that both countries would use the Ethiopian currency, the birr. As relations between the two worsened, these issues provided more fuel for conflict. While the border issue probably triggered the disastrous war between the two from 1998 to 2000, the other unresolved issues played a role.

Course of the Dispute

After over two decades of fighting, Eritrea gained its independence from Ethiopia on May 24, 1991. During the struggle, the EPLF, the group behind much of the independence movement, had collaborated extensively with an Ethiopian resistance group, the TPLF, whose main goal was to topple the Derg, the Marxist regime in Ethiopia.[56] In 1991, the two groups jointly achieved their goals: the EPLF gained de facto independence of Eritrea, and the TPLF overthrew the Derg and formed a new government under the Ethiopian People's Revolutionary Democratic Front (EPRDF), which was in majority composed of TPLF members.

From May 26 to May 28, 1991, representatives from the EPLF and EPRDF, as well as other Ethiopian fractions, met in London, under the mediation of the United States, to discuss the transition.[57] The parties quickly agreed to a UN-supervised referendum on Eritrean independence. Subsequently, the EPLF formed a government in Eritrea, and the referendum was held in April 1993. Over 1.1 million Eritreans voted, and almost all (99.8 percent) voted for independence.[58]

Eritrea gained de jure independence in May 1993, and because of the close history of collaboration between the EPLF and the TPLF, the initial relations between the two countries were good. Over the next two years, they agreed on a number of issues, mainly economic, such as tax-free trade between them, using the Ethiopian birr as the common currency, and designating the port of Assab, located in Eritrea, as a free port for Ethiopia, which had become landlocked upon Eritrea's independence.[59]

However, the two parties neglected to adequately address critical outstanding issues that became bones of contention in their deteriorating relations after 1995, leading to the 1998–2000 war.[60] The border was not fully demarcated. While the two agreed to use the Italian colonial borders, there was confusion as to what exactly these borders were. Eritrea had been an Italian colony from 1890 to 1940. An original boundary had been drawn in 1890 and confirmed on two other occasions, in 1900 and 1902, between Italy and Menelik II, the emperor of Ethiopia at the time. Yet Italian Eritrea had slowly encroached into Ethiopian territory, and in 1935 Italy invaded the whole of Ethiopia. Thus, Ethiopia and Eritrea ultimately could not agree whether to use the 1890 established lines, as posited by Ethiopia, or the 1934 lines, as argued by Eritrea.[61]

The division of assets and liabilities was also left unsettled. No negotiations or deliberations of any kind were convened on that issue either before or immediately after the independence of Eritrea. The 1993 London Conference concentrated on negotiating the referendum, leaving most other issues to be worked out after the secession.[62] In addition, during the transition period (1992–1997), the Commercial Bank of Ethiopia had provided loans to the Eritrean government, some of which, worth 1.2 billion birr,[63] came to be considered bad debt.[64]

Assessment and Possible Lessons

While the border issue is generally regarded as the trigger for the 1998 war, other factors contributed to increasing tensions, and in the end the border became as much the pretext as the actual reason for war. In any case, the war devastated both countries. An estimated 70,000 people died in the conflict, which also caused massive displacements on both sides. Both countries expelled large numbers of people from the other country—an estimated 77,000 Eritreans were expelled from Ethiopia while 75,000 Ethiopians were expelled from Eritrea.[65]

The main lesson from the case is both obvious and paradoxical. While in many secession cases, ill will between the parties makes it difficult to settle outstanding issues, here the parties made the opposite mistake— believing their close relations would continue, thus making full settlement of issues appear unnecessary. Instead, the parties should have taken advantage of fair weather between them to nail down as many details as possible. While that surely would have been no guarantee that the agreement's terms would not become contested as relations worsened, it would have been a help.

The cases in this chapter all involved secessions, or dissolutions. The main lessons for dividing assets and liabilities are easy to state if hard to implement: start early and, if at all possible, leave time for negotiation between the decision to secede and the fact of secession, as occurred with Czechoslovakia and, in another way, the FSU. Designating a continuation state simplifies the negotiations and suggests the zero option as a starting point. To be sure, it helps if the divorce is amicable, yet Ethiopia and Eritrea illustrate the perils of assuming that comity will continue and so major issues can be deferred.

CHAPTER 8

Currency and Financial Arrangements

The question of currency after secession looks deceptively straightforward: the new state will either attempt to maintain a monetary union in some form with the existing state or opt for a separate currency of its own. Yet in fact the apparently simple choice entails much wider decisions not just about the nature of the new national banking system but also about monetary policy and fiscal policy. Because they directly affect the pocketbooks of citizens, currency issues can be politically emotive well beyond the apparently technical nature of, for instance, currency cross rates.

Policy Suggestions

Like the others, this chapter draws on various earlier secession experiences— the division of Czechoslovakia, Estonia, and Latvia after the dissolution of the Soviet Union, and Ethiopia and Eritrea—to look for lessons relevant to possible future secessions.

The case that perhaps most resembles the recent experience of Sudan and South Sudan is Ethiopia and Eritrea, in which a new country, smaller and poorer than the other, faced hard decisions about continued economic cooperation, of which currency was both the symbol and centerpiece. Eritrea gained de jure independence from Ethiopia in May 1993, but relations between the two remained good. As part of economic cooperation, it was decided that Eritrea would keep using the Ethiopian birr as its currency until it established its own institutions and eventually its own currency. As it turned out, both nations benefited for a time from free trade and Ethiopian access to Eritrean ports.

However, when Eritrea introduced a new currency, the nakfa, at the end of 1997, in an effort to achieve economic independence, Ethiopia retaliated, to the dismay of Eritrean authorities, rejecting parity between the nakfa and the birr, and immediately requiring the use of "hard" currencies for all transactions above 2,000 birr.[1] From there, economic cooperation went downhill rapidly, and increasing economic tensions played no small role in detonating the 1998 war between the two countries, which exacted a devastating human and economic toll on both.

In contrast, the dissolution of Czechoslovakia into the Czech Republic and Slovakia was approved in November 1992, and in preparation for a smooth transition, negotiations between the future leaders of the two states included currency arrangements. Each state would have its own central bank, but the two would maintain a monetary union temporarily—at least for the first six months after dissolution—with joint monetary policy decided by a joint Monetary Committee.[2]

However, it quickly became clear that the monetary union was not very credible given the stark differences in economic performance between the two countries. Inflation was much higher in Slovakia, and unemployment rates were four times those in the Czech lands.[3] Expectations of a future devaluation of the Slovak currency produced a major outflow of funds from Slovakia into Czech banks, and the two countries introduced their own currencies, the Czech koruna and the Slovak koruna, in February 1993, just one month after the dissolution of Czechoslovakia.[4] The Slovak koruna soon devalued against its neighbor.

The monetary transition in Latvia really began in the late 1980s when perestroika in the Soviet Union accorded more economic autonomy to Soviet states. That transition was both gradual and careful. The Bank of Latvia (BOLAT) became an independent central bank in March 1990 but did not start issuing currency until May 1992, first using the Russian ruble, then a temporary Latvian ruble.[5] When the permanent currency, the lat, was introduced, it was pegged to the IMF's basket of major currencies, known as the Special Drawing Rights (SDRs).

These careful policies were complemented with market-driven reforms, such as privatizing state-owned enterprises, reforming the tax code, and decontrolling prices.[6] Yet, despite the caution, a rapid and weakly supervised expansion of the banking sector plunged the country into a major banking crisis in 1994–1995, when commercial bank failures included the country's largest bank. Latvia was able to overcome the crisis, however, and tightened bank supervision while at the same time continuing to pursue overall prudent macroeconomic policies. As a result, the country grew 4.7 percent annually from 1995 to 2000, and continued to grow at fairly constant high rates until the recent global financial crisis.[7]

For Estonia, too, the monetary reform began with perestroika. In effect, by the time Estonia gained independence from the Soviet Union on August 20, 1991, the country had already set up a central bank and had clear plans to institute its own currency. It became the first country to leave the ruble zone, in June 1992, introducing the kroon as its new currency. To make the kroon credible and promote stability in the economy, the authorities chose to follow a currency board system in which the kroon would be backed by gold and foreign currency reserves. The new currency was also pegged to a more stable and widely traded foreign currency, the German deutsche mark, which had the added benefit of belonging to a country that was already a major trading partner of Estonia.

To further ensure that the currency board system would not be swayed by political influence, it was to be operated autonomously by the Issue Department of the Central Bank. The reforms in Estonia were so successful that many have dubbed it a "financial miracle" and model for other states.[8]

The cases suggest possible lessons for other secessions:

Currency Is Not Just Currency

Both the Ethiopia-Eritrea and Czechoslovakia cases drive home the point that a currency union requires agreement on macroeconomic policy. If there is no such agreement, or if the economic performance of the two states is very different, the union will impose perceived hardships and will not endure.

Plan for Future Contingencies

While Ethiopia and Eritrea agreed that eventually Eritrea would want its own policy and hence currency, they did not explicitly address how and when the transition would happen. When Eritrea came to feel that the Ethiopia's macroeconomic policies were not serving its interests, it adopted a new currency. Because Eritrea had done scant planning for that contingency, it was caught off guard by Ethiopia's harsh reception to the nakfa, precipitating a downward spiral in what had been mutually beneficial economic relations.

Try to Foresee the Market's Reaction

When the Czech Republic and Slovakia framed their joint policy, they did not take into account the possible reactions of the market, given the stark differences in the two countries' economic performance. They thus set out on distorting monetary policy provisions for the transition period.

Managing the Currency Is Not Enough

Central banks need also to monitor the banking system. In Latvia's case, the lack of experience with modern banking practices, coupled with an underdeveloped regulatory framework, was especially detrimental. Building a regulatory structure and monitoring capacity is a critical prerequisite to banking reform.

Learn from the Ideal

Estonia's experience as a relatively rich country suggests goals more than lessons that might apply other seceding but poor countries like Sudan.

Ensure That Monetary Reform Is Outside the Influence of Political Power

Estonia established the currency board system and avoided any political influences on the monetary reform.

Build Confidence and Credibility Around the New Currency

Estonia backed up the kroon with gold and foreign exchange reserves, thus enabling the full convertibility of the new currency with a more established and stronger currency.

Table 8.1. Policy Suggestions for Currency and Financial Arrangements

Country	Nature of experience	Lessons
Ethiopia-Eritrea	Initial cooperation good, in currency union But Eritrea came to feel union not in its interest Its introduction of new currency set a cycle of economic retaliation	Currency union requires agreement on broad macroeconomic policy Perhaps especially unlikely to endure if economies are very different Need to plan now for contingencies of new currency
Czechoslovakia	Careful planning, including monetary union for at least six moths But economic performance too different to sustain Separate currencies, Slovak koruna devalued	Careful planning important But must include foresight about reaction of markets
Latvia	Currency reform was careful and successful Interim currency Lat pegged to SDRs But wider banking reform failed	Again, careful planning important Need to build regulatory framework and monitoring capacity before embarking on monetary reform
Estonia	Long period of study and planning before independence Currency board with autonomy from politics New currency pegged to gold, German DM	Great success but not clear how relevant to Sudan Kept currency out of politics Built credibility of currency Coordinated economic reforms with monetary reform

Coordinate Economic Reforms with the Monetary Reforms

Concurrently with its monetary reforms, Estonia implemented economic policies such as the liberalization of external trade that reinforced its commitment to a liberalized economy, and with it the credibility of the new economic system in Estonia. Table 8.1 summarizes the policy suggestions for currency and financial arrangements.

Eritrea Secedes from Ethiopia

Issue and Outcome

Eritrea gained de jure independence from Ethiopia on May 24, 1993, after a three-decade war.[9] In the first years after independence, relations between the two countries were good and the two governments cooperated on a number of issues, including economic policies. As part of this cooperation, it was decided that Eritrea would keep using the Ethiopian birr as its currency until it established its own institutions and eventually its own currency. As it turned out, the economic arrangements were equally beneficial to both countries: The monetary union enabled Eritrea to gain access to the larger Ethiopian market and import food from Ethiopia without using foreign exchange reserves, while Ethiopia maintained free access to Eritrea's ports.[10]

The Eritrean government established the Bank of Eritrea in 1993 through a temporary proclamation and at the end of 1997 introduced a new currency, the nakfa. The decision to leave the monetary union was driven by several factors. First, Eritrea had a strong desire to achieve economic independence from Ethiopia. Second, and perhaps more important, the birr was being issued by the Bank of Ethiopia, and as a result Eritrea neither earned seigniorage revenue nor had much control over its own monetary policy,[11] which made it difficult for Eritrea to embark on its own economic path.[12]

To the dismay of Eritrean authorities, Ethiopia responded to the introduction of the nakfa by requiring the use of "hard" currencies, like U.S. dollars, for all transactions above two thousand birr.[13] To boot, Ethiopia rejected parity between the nakfa and the birr.[14] This set off a downward spiral of the two countries' economic cooperation: Eritrea increased import and export taxes on Ethiopia-bound goods, while Ethiopia announced that it would use the port of Djibouti, not Eritrea, as its main hub. The increasing economic tensions, along with lingering disputes on border demarcation, ultimately led to the 1998 war between the two countries, which had a devastating human and economic toll on both.[15]

Course of the Dispute

At independence, much of Eritrea's economy was in shambles as a result of decades of war and mismanagement under the overly centralized Soviet-style Ethiopian rule. Eritrea also had to build its economic institutions from scratch in the context of weak institutional capacity, as the country lacked qualified professionals and had little experience with managing macroeconomic policy. It was therefore decided that Eritrea would maintain the use of the Ethiopian birr in the interim period until it built enough experience to operate its own currency.[16]

In addition, the fact that both Ethiopia and Eritrea were coming out of a war and going through major political transitions provided incentive for a number of economic and political cooperation agreements between the two countries.[17] Indeed, in economic policy, recognizing their mutual interdependence, the two countries agreed to allow for the free movement of goods, capital, and people, as well as continued free access to Eritrean ports for Ethiopia under the Treaty of Friendship and Coordination signed in July 1993. Under the Protocol Agreement signed in September 1993, the two countries agreed to harmonize their macroeconomic policies, a move reinforced in July 1994, when the two governments issued a joint declaration on economic cooperation, announcing their desires to "advance gradually to a combined economic unit."[18]

These arrangements initially worked well for both countries. The Ethiopian birr, which had been artificially overvalued under the Marxist regime, was devalued in 1992, and the Ethiopian government introduced a foreign exchange auction system in May 1993 in order to let the currency's value be more determined by market forces. Devaluation spurred the exports of both. Moreover, the continued use of the birr in Eritrea opened up the larger Ethiopian market for Eritrean producers—until the 1998 war, over 60 percent of Eritrean external trade was with Ethiopia.[19] For Ethiopia, which had become landlocked as a result of Eritrean independence, the continued use of the Eritrean ports was of crucial benefit.[20]

Nevertheless, the macroeconomic policies being adopted in Ethiopia became increasingly mismatched to Eritrea's chosen strategy of economic development. Eritrean authorities were intent on setting up a fully liberalized economic system with an export-led growth strategy, encouraging free trade and foreign investment.[21] From this perspective, the common currency hurt because it remained overvalued in Eritrea's view.[22] In addition, Eritrea was denied the lever of monetary policy, such as setting interest rates, because monetary decisions were primarily made by the Bank of Ethiopia. Another corollary was the fact that because all the printing of the currency happened in Ethiopia, Eritrea was not earning any seigniorage revenue—revenue that was much needed for reconstruction after three decades of war.[23]

In 1997, Eritrea introduced the nakfa as its currency. Its authorities expected that the nakfa would be exchangeable one-to-one with the birr and would also circulate in Ethiopia. However, after some negotiations, the Ethiopian authorities rejected both propositions: the exchange rate between the nakfa and the birr was set to be five-to-one, and all trade between the two countries above two thousand birr would to be done in U.S. dollars.[24]

Eritrean authorities had not expected the negative reaction of the Ethiopian government with regard to the nakfa, and perceived the new rules as an Ethiopian-government-sponsored "sabotage" of the new currency. They responded by imposing higher import and export taxes on goods coming from and going to Ethiopia. In turn, Ethiopia announced that it would start using the port of Djibouti as its main hub and also started discussions with the Kenyan government to investigate potential use of the port of Mombasa. The direct effect of these new regulations was particularly harmful to the Eritrean economy, as the new regulations translated into higher-priced imports, the gradual depletion of foreign exchange reserves, and large price increases for consumer goods. Moreover, Ethiopia's shift to Djibouti from Eritrean represented a major loss of revenue for Eritrea.[25]

At the same time, border discussions between the two had stalled over how to demarcate a border area known as the Yirga Triangle.[26] Under the new trade rules, exact border lines became consequential, and attempts to control the border areas escalated.[27] On May 6, 1998, accumulating tensions between the two countries spilled into full-blown conflict when Eritrean troops crossed over the contested border into the city of Badme, and Ethiopian authorities retaliated with force.[28] The war lasted from 1998 to 2000, devastating both countries: in addition to the economic disruptions, an estimated seventy thousand people died in the conflict, and thousands more were displaced.[29]

The inflationary pressures in Eritrea further worsened as the government financed the war partly through monetary expansion. In addition, to keep foreign debt repayment low, Eritrean authorities kept the nominal exchange rate high despite the depreciation in the real value of the currency, which encouraged the growth of a parallel foreign exchange market.[30]

Assessment and Possible Lessons

This case illustrates how critical it is in order to avoid renewed conflict to get monetary (and more generally economic) arrangements right when two countries decide to split. Eritrea and Ethiopia failed to preserve the spirit of cooperation beyond the transition period, and at the core of the problem was the failure to think about and negotiate arrangements past that period. Several lessons relevant to other secessions emerge:

Negotiations on posttransition arrangements as early as possible during the secession process can help set clear guidelines, expectations, and timetables. While it was clear that Eritrea would eventually instate its own currency, Ethiopia and Eritrea did not explicitly address how and when the transition would happen as they put in place temporary measures.

If the nations opt for a monetary union during an interim period, macroeconomic policies need to be coordinated so that one party does not feel harmed by the policies implemented by the other. In the case of Ethiopia and Eritrea, Eritrean authorities felt that the macroeconomic policies implemented by the Bank of Ethiopia were not serving their interests, which in turn impelled them to introduce a new currency.

When a seceding state plans to introduce a new currency, it is important to discuss issues of convertibility and circulation before it is established. That is all the more the case if significant trade ties have been reinforced for years through the use of the same currency. Because of lack of such discussions in the Eritrea-Ethiopia case, Eritrea was caught off guard by Ethiopia's harsh reception to the nakfa. Surprise bred resentment and led to counterproductive tit-for-tat economic policies on both sides, effectively ending the era of economic cooperation between the two.

The Dissolution of Czechoslovakia

Issue and Outcome

The dissolution of Czechoslovakia into the Czech Republic and Slovakia was approved in November 1992, and in preparation for a smooth transition, future leaders of the two states held a number of negotiations, including some related to currency arrangements.[31] These resulted in a treaty on monetary arrangements under which the State Bank of Czechoslovakia (SBCS) would be disbanded and each new country would have its own central bank. To mute potential economic disruptions, the Czech Republic and Slovakia would maintain a monetary union temporarily—at least for the first six months after dissolution—with policy set by a Monetary Committee including representatives from both countries' central banks.[32]

However, the stark differences in economic performance between the two countries soon made it clear that the monetary union would have very little international credibility. In the event, expectations of future devaluations of the Slovak currency drove fund flows from Slovakia into Czech banks. For a time, Slovak banks were given credits to balance the outflow, but that could not be sustained. In the end, the two countries introduced their own currencies—the Czech koruna and the Slovak koruna—on February 8, 1993, just one month after the dissolution of Czechoslovakia.[33]

Course of the Dispute

With the fall of communism and the end of the centrally planned economy in Czechoslovakia, economic disparities between Czechs and Slovaks widened, with Slovakia lagging behind the Czech lands: by 1991, inflation was growing much faster in Slovakia and unemployment rates were four times as high as those in the Czech lands.[34] As a result, the two regions came to very different outlooks on the pace of economic reforms: Czechs leaned toward the West and rapid reforms, while Slovaks supported a slower pace. The differing outlooks were vividly displayed in the June 1992 parliamentary elections when a majority of Slovaks voted for Vladimir Meciar, a populist leader on left, and a majority of Czechs for Vaclav Klaus, an economist on the center-right who championed free markets.[35]

In the event, these disagreements over the pace of economic reforms played a central role in the dissolution of the Czechoslovak union.[36] Given the results of the June 1992 elections, the two leaders met and agreed to either loosen the federation, which would entail reducing the power of the federal government, or look into splitting the country. On July 17, 1992, the Slovak parliament declared independence, which was followed by a meeting between Meciar and Klaus in which both agreed in principle to the dissolution of Czechoslovakia. Shortly thereafter, on November 25, 1992, the Federal Assembly approved the split, and set the official dissolution date for January 1, 1993.[37]

In the months between the declarations of sovereignty and actual dissolution, the two republics negotiated intensely over the modalities of separation, and their future relations, including economic relations.[38] The two economics were highly interdependent, and so a badly managed separation risked severe economic consequences for both republics. The worst-case scenario entailed sharp reduction in trade between the two, loss of confidence from abroad and shortages in foreign currency.[39] Thus, harmonizing economic policies, including monetary policy, was necessary in order to minimize disruption in each of the economies.[40]

With regard to monetary policy, the two agreed to divide the SBCS into two entities—the Czech National Bank (CNB) and the National Bank of Slovakia (NBS)—and to put in place a temporary monetary union for the first six months after dissolution, managed by a Monetary Committee. This committee would be composed of the governors of the respective national banks and two senior officers from each bank. It would set a common monetary policy, with decisions being made by a simple majority vote.

The agreement stipulated that either country could pull out of the union if (1) it ran a fiscal deficit greater than 10 percent of the budget revenues, (2) it had foreign reserves that were less than the value of one month's imports, (3) capital transfers between the two republics were greater than 5 percent of total bank deposits, and (4) the Monetary Committee could not come up with an agreement on a fundamental monetary issue.[41]

From the very beginning, the arrangement lacked international credibility. The economic disparity between the two states gave rise to expectations in global markets that once each of the countries had their own currency, Slovakia would be forced to devalue. As a result, the announcement of the monetary provisions touched off an outflow of funds from Slovakian residents and firms into Czech commercial banks. The expectation of a Slovakian devaluation also introduced perverse incentives for trade and credit: Slovakian imports from the Czech Republic increased dramatically, and while Slovaks wanted to repay their debts immediately, Czechs had the opposite incentive and tried to delay repayment.[42]

Moreover, the continuing deterioration of the economic situation in Slovakia invited speculation against its koruna (CSK), which became instable. This only increased the need for exchange rate adjustments, which in turn triggered the decline of foreign exchange reserves. The development of a parallel market for the koruna was yet another sign of the lack of confidence in the monetary union: foreign commercial banks quoted the dollar-CSK exchange rate at 78 percent more than the official rate.[43]

To stem the outflow of currency from Slovakia and to stabilize the situation, the CNB started awarding credits to Slovakian banks in December 1992. However, by January 1993, it became clear that this arrangement could not be sustained. At that point, the Czech government decided that abandoning the monetary union was inevitable, and began secret negotiations with Slovakian counterparts to set the date for termination. The split occurred on February 8, 1993, and two new currencies, the Czech koruna and the Slovak koruna, came into existence.[44]

Initially, the Czech and Slovak korunas were at parity, but market forces soon compelled the anticipated devaluation, in July 1993. The depreciation of the Slovak koruna continued over the next several years as the economic gap between the two countries widened. By 1996, the Czech koruna was 20 to 30 percent more valuable than the Slovak one.[45]

Assessment and Possible Lessons

The main lesson that emerges from this case is that currency is not just currency. Rather, monetary arrangements after a secession or dissolution need to reflect the economic realities of the emerging nations. In this case, the future leaders of the Czech Republic and Slovakia did not take into account the reactions of the market to temporary monetary union, given the stark differences between the two economics, and so embarked on distortionary monetary policy provisions for the transition period. Their commitment to use the period before formal independence for serious negotiations, including about monetary policy, surely was a positive lesson. Nonetheless, the lack of foresight about market forces ended up increasing the instability of the monetary system, rendering it ineffective and ultimately leading to its failure—much sooner than the parties had anticipated.

Latvia

Issue and Outcome

The monetary transition in Latvia began in the late 1980s when Mikhail Gorbachev announced the restructuring of the Soviet Union under perestroika, which accorded more political and economic autonomy to Soviet states.[46] Under the new system, the Latvian Supreme Soviet established the BOLAT in 1987 and formed a Monetary Reform Committee in 1990.[47]

The BOLAT became an independent central bank with exclusive rights to issue the national currency on March 2, 1990, but did not do so until two years later. In the interim, Latvia first continued to use the Russian ruble. Yet high Russian inflation rates and the resulting instability of the ruble soon induced the BOLAT to create a temporary currency, the Latvian ruble (LVR). A year later, it created a permanent currency, the lat, which pegged in value to the IMF's basket of major currencies, known as the SDRs. Both the peg and the managed float against other currencies in which the bank engaged were designed to build the credibility of the new currency.[48]

Yet despite its careful approach to both monetary and fiscal policy, the country suffered a major banking crisis in 1994–1995, a crisis due to the rapid and weakly supervised expansion of the banking sector. However, Latvia weathered the crisis, and later tightened bank supervision, while at the same time continuing to pursue prudent macroeconomic policies. As a result, the country grew 4.7 percent annually from 1995 to 2000, and continued to grow at fairly constant high rates until the recent global financial crisis.[49]

Course of the Dispute

The first step toward monetary autonomy in Latvia came in 1987 when the Latvia Republican Office of the State Bank of the Soviet Union was renamed the Republican Bank of the State Bank of the Soviet Union, as part of the overarching reforms implemented in the Soviet Union under perestroika. In March 1990, two months before the independence of Latvia, the Supreme Council of the Latvian Supreme Soviet adopted the On the Bank of Latvia law establishing the BOLAT as a local central bank. Essentially, this move reinstated the BOLAT, which had functioned before Soviet occupation, as an independent national bank with the power to issue currency, the responsibility for monitoring commercial bank activities, and authority over monetary policy in the country. A Monetary Reform Committee was also formed at the time, under the On the Program of Creating Republic of Latvia Monetary System resolution, to manage the monetary transition. But only in September 1991, once Latvia had achieved independence and the Soviet Union had collapsed, was the restored central bank given the full right to issue national currency under the On the Reorganization of Banks in the Territory of the Republic of Latvia resolution.[50]

Immediately after independence, Latvia continued to use the Russian ruble. However, the removal of price controls in Russia, along with price adjustments for all exports of raw materials from Russia, led to hyperinflation in Latvia in the early 1990s, reaching 951 percent in 1992. At that point, Latvian authorities decided to break ties with the Russian monetary system, issuing a temporary currency, the LVR, which was initially exchangeable one-to-one with the Russian ruble. The temporary currency was intended primarily to tame inflation, but it also was used to counteract the potential shortage in bank notes arising from the imbalances in cash transactions with other states within the ruble zone.[51]

The BOLAT moved quickly to stabilize the LVR. Once all the Russian rubles within the country were exchanged for LVRs, transactions with countries in the ruble zone were done through corresponding accounts at the BOLAT, which also set the exchange rates for the currencies of former Soviet Union (FSU) states based on the cross rates of each of those currencies against the U.S. dollar. This resulted in the rapid appreciation of the LVR against the ruble and other currencies: for example, the LVR-ruble exchange rate rose from 1 to 1 in July 1992 to 0.31 to 1 in December 1992.[52]

In addition, to keep the value of the LVR steady against other currencies, the BOLAT started selling U.S. dollars and other convertible currencies (British pounds, French francs, deutsche marks, Japanese yen, and Estonian kroons) to commercial banks at slightly submarket rates. It did so until the exchange rate for LVR against the dollar stabilized at 170 LVR per dollar.[53] These monetary interventions were supplemented by tight monetary policies, which limited deficit financing through the issuing of currency, as well as market-oriented economic reforms, such as the gradual liberalization of trade and the privatization of state-owned enterprises.[54]

BOLAT introduced the permanent currency, the lat, in March 1993 at a rate of 200 LVR per lat. By that point, Latvian authorities had achieved international credibility for the country's monetary system. Yet to sustain that credibility, along with the stability of the currency, BOLAT implemented a fixed exchange rate regime, pegging the lat to the IMF's SDRs. In addition, BOLAT set up a managed float for the lat, just as it had done for the LVR, selling and buying convertible currencies to maintain the value of the lat against the SDR.[55]

Banking reform sought to modernize the sector from the Soviet-style banking to a more market-driven system. To that end, the BOLAT decided to keep the Soviet-era Savings Bank in the public sector for the time being, placing the branches temporarily under the BOLAT in preparation for privatization. By the end of 1993, nine of the forty-six had been sold to private commercial banks, while fifteen were consolidated into eight banks and sold through share offerings. Twenty-one of the remaining banks were restructured into one large state bank, the Universal Bank of Latvia (Unibank). In addition, licensing policy for new commercial banks was liberal on the rationale that more private banks would generate more competition, thus lowering deposit and lending rates, and so generating the large amount of capital lending needed for the growth of the private sector.[56]

Yet, while the BOLAT successfully managed the monetary transition, reforming the banking sector turned out to be more challenging. The liberal licensing rules, coupled with controls that permitted below-global-market prices for Russian commodities and Latvia's favorable location between Eastern and Western Europe, produced a proliferation of Latvian banks. They financed the highly profitable East-West trade, charging high interest rates for the loans associated with that trade. The number of commercial banks in the country increased from just six in 1990 to fifty-nine in 1993.

At the same time, in an aggressive attempt to increase their domestic market share, some banks expanded their lat-denominated deposits by offering above-market deposit rates, which were subsidized by the high interest rates charged on the loans associated with the East-West trade. For example, the largest commercial bank at the time, Baltija, offered annual deposit rates of around 90 percent in 1993 while market rates stood at 60 percent. In addition, a number of banks, including Baltija, converted large volumes of lats into U.S. dollars in expectation of a depreciation of the lat.[57]

However, as controls on Russian commodities prices were relaxed, those prices increased to near market rates, and the demand for the loans associated with East-West trade flows decreased. That led banks to look for other lending opportunities, including some that were highly risky. At the same time, the lat appreciated substantially against the dollar, forcing Baltija and other commercial banks into liquidity constraints, which meant they could no longer fulfill their commitments to depositors. The double bind of risky loans and liquidity constraints meant that the banks accumulated bad debt while losing deposits.[58] That ultimately caused the collapse of several important banks. All in all, by 1995, fourteen banks were failing, including Baltija, which alone had 212,000 depositors.[59]

Following advice from the World Bank and the IMF, the BOLAT responded to the crisis by taking full control over Baltija and letting the smaller banks fail. Out of the fifty-nine commercial banks that had been in existence in 1993, thirty-nine were allowed to operate but only fourteen were permitted to take household deposits; the rest were given restricted licenses.[60] Faced with the decline in public confidence in the banking sector, the authorities decided to compensate each depositor who lost funds in the collapse up to 500 lats immediately, followed by 100 lats a year for three years.[61]

Latvia also created two new institutions, a bank rehabilitation agency and a deposit insurance system, as part of that effort to restore public confidence.[62] The crisis prompted the BOLAT to take actions to improve the functioning of the banking sector: it hired more bank supervisory staff and required the banks that survived to establish control departments. Furthermore, BOLAT contracted with external accounting firms to place on-site examiners, who supplemented the supervisory work of the BOLAT.[63]

Assessment and Possible Lessons

As in other FSU countries, the initial stage of the reform process was difficult. Reforms translated into severe declines in GDP and wages. In Latvia, for instance, GDP in 1992 was only 59 percent of its level in 1989, and real wages fell by 60 percent between 1990 and 1992. Even so, there was a broad internal consensus that extensive reforms were needed in order for the country to enter an era of market-driven growth, and the Latvian government retained a strong mandate to continue pursuing the reforms.[64]

The gradual monetary transition in Latvia was successful in establishing the lat as a credible currency and in stabilizing the economy. In fact, the lat appreciated against the U.S. dollar, and the banking sector attracted a substantial amount of capital, particularly from Russia: In one year alone, from 1993 to 1994, deposits held by Latvian banks went from 99 million to 492 million lats.[65] Furthermore, annual GDP growth started to recover, turning around for a decline of about 5 percent in 1993 to a 2 percent growth rate in 1994 (the corresponding growth rates for income per capita were 3 percent in 1993 and 4 percent in 1994).[66]

By 1995, Latvian policies had restored confidence in the banking sector and more generally stabilized the country's macroeconomic conditions. Latvian authorities and the BOLAT continued prudent macroeconomic management, exercised budgetary restraint, and kept inflation low, accompanied by policies to strengthen the market economy and encourage private-sector-led growth. The policies paid off: between 1995 and 2000, Latvian GDP grew by 25.6 percent, and continued to grow at an average annual rate of 10 percent from 2001 through 2007.[67]

In the end, though, the results of Latvia's monetary and financial sector transition were mixed. On one hand, it established a credible new currency through gradual and well-thought-out policies. On the other, it initially failed in trying to establish a market-driven financial sector because the regulatory framework was inadequate. The failure in banking supervision threatened the overall economic stability achieved through monetary reform.

Ultimately, the Latvian case study highlights the two equally important roles of a central bank—managing the currency and monitoring the banking sector. Both need to be done concurrently in order to create a macroeconomic environment that will stimulate sustainable economic growth. The lack of experience with modern banking practices, coupled with an underdeveloped regulatory framework was especially detrimental in the case of Latvia. The lesson is that building a regulatory framework and monitoring capacity within the central bank before implementing banking reform are critical to establishing a sound market-driven macroeconomy.

Estonia

Issue and Outcome

The monetary transition in Estonia also began in the late 1980s when Mikhail Gorbachev announced the restructuring of the Soviet Union under perestroika, which among other things accorded more economic autonomy to Soviet states.[68] At that point, Estonian authorities convened a team of economists to think about the shift to a more autonomous economy, including a more decentralized management of monetary policy.

In effect, by the time Estonia gained independence from the Soviet Union on August 20 1991, the country had already set up a central bank (the EestiPank) and had concrete plans to institute its own currency. Remaining in the ruble zone made the country vulnerable to the economic turmoil in the Soviet Union, fueling inflation and holding up other economic reforms, such as trade liberalization and privatization.[69] On June 20, 1992, Estonia became the first country to leave the ruble zone, introducing the kroon as its new currency. As part of a strategy to instill credibility in the kroon and promote stability in the economy, the authorities chose to follow a currency board system in which the kroon would be backed by gold and foreign currency reserves. The new currency was also pegged to a more stable and widely traded foreign currency, the German deutsche mark, which had the added benefit of belonging to Estonia's favored trading partner.

The Estonian government further ensured that the currency board system would not be swayed by political influence by creating two main departments within the Central Bank—the Issue Department, which would operate the currency board outside of politics, and the Banking Department, which would hold any surplus foreign exchange reserves from the Issue Department and handle any remaining banking functions decided on by the government, such as emergency lending to the banking system.[70]

The monetary reforms in Estonia were so successful that many have dubbed it a "financial miracle," making it a model for other states.[71] Indeed, by following prudent macroeconomic policies, authorities fairly quickly established international confidence in the new currency. This in turn led to reduced inflation and increased foreign currency reserves, which ultimately contributed to a thriving local economy.[72]

Course of the Discussions

Starting in the early 1980s, Estonia, like much of the Soviet Union, was suffering economic stagnation marked by low productivity and widespread shortages of goods, which many attributed to the overcentralization of the Soviet economy.[73] In an attempt to redress the situation, in 1987 Moscow announced perestroika, a call for the restructuring of the Soviet economy by introducing some forms of private enterprise, allowing some foreign investment and trade, and decentralizing economic decisions. In essence, perestroika opened the door for the Soviet republics to start formulating their own economic reforms.

In Estonia, the leadership adopted the Isemajanoav Eesti (IME) plan, an ambitious plan of reform pushing for the economic independence of Estonia from the Soviet Union. The IME plan was approved by the Estonian Supreme Soviet in May 1989 and soon after by the Supreme Soviet in Moscow, but only on the condition that all reforms be in accordance with central Soviet laws.[74]

However, as it became clear over the following months that Estonia was moving closer toward independence from the Soviet Union, authorities started to build the economic infrastructure and implement reforms that went beyond the IME. Estonia created the Bank of Estonia (EestiPank) in 1989 and drew up plans for the adoption of an Estonian currency.[75] After independence in 1991, the need for that currency was precipitated by the ripple effect of rampant inflation, resulting from the economic crisis and poor monetary and fiscal policies in the Soviet Union. That inflation, in turn, was impeding other reforms such as the further liberalization of trade and the privatization of state-owned enterprises. Estonia introduced the kroon as its new currency on June 20, 1992, and most of the rubles in the economy were exchanged at the rate of 1 kroon for 10 rubles within a three-day transition period.[76]

In introducing the new currency, the Estonian government was keenly aware that the credibility in the kroon could not be assumed but would have to be established. To that end, it put in place a number of institutions and regulations. It established the currency board system to manage the currency. The board essentially committed the central bank to backing up, without any limitations, not only all the local currency bank notes but also the reserve deposits of commercial banks with hard currency and gold reserves.

These reserves came mostly from the restitution of 11.3 tons of gold from the Bank of England, which the pre–World War II EestiPank had deposited there. In addition, the bank had reserves of US$120 million in foreign currency reserves and had borrowed US$40 million in stabilization loans from the IMF.[77]

The kroon was pegged to the deutsche mark and could be exchanged by anyone at the fixed exchange rate of 8 kroons for 1 deutsche mark. The rate was set out to be equivalent to the market rate at the time for the deutsche mark in rubles.[78] Institutionally, to ensure the proper functioning of the currency board and minimize political interference, EestiPank was divided into two departments, the Issue Department, which was independent from policy, and the Banking Department, whose decisions would have to be in line government directives. The Issue Department was put in charge of operating the currency board and had the responsibility of ensuring that all of its assets (foreign exchange reserves) matched the liabilities (deposits in kroon). The Issue Department would not provide credit to the economy or loans to banks. In the event of surplus (due to interest earned or seigniorage), the proceeds would be passed onto the Banking Department, which was put in charge of dealing with any residual banking issues, including emergency loans to commercial banks and payment arrangements with former Soviet states.[79]

Assessment and Possible Lessons

The Estonian approach to monetary transition after independence from the Soviet Union has been widely praised as both well grounded in economic principles and disciplined. Estonian authorities were able to hold to reform even amid the financial crisis in late 1992 and early 1993 when a number of commercial banks with weak balance sheets were allowed to fail.[80] The currency board system and the full convertibility of kroons into deutsche marks quickly established the kroon as a credible currency.

Furthermore, coordinated economic policies—liberalized external trade, the privatizing of large government-owned enterprises, and the implementing of a bankruptcy law—reinforced the viability of the currency even as they enhanced the state of the economy, which in turn raised the demand for the kroon.[81]

The success of the reforms were felt almost immediately in the local economy; inflation fell from 500 percent in 1992 to around 30 percent in 1993, and during the period, foreign exchange reserves more than doubled. Not only did the stability of the kroon facilitate increased trade with Western countries, particularly neighbors like Finland, but it and the reforms also prompted a virtuous cycle: private sector activity grew, which in turn improved productivity and promoted economic growth.[82]

Its success makes Estonia monetary reform a model, even if perhaps one not easy to emulate by poorer seceding countries without the luxury of a relatively gradual transition. The lessons from its model include the following:

Estonian reform ensured that monetary reform was outside the influence of political power: by establishing the currency board system and muting political influences on the monetary reform, authorities in Estonia allowed the reform to be based on strong macroeconomic principles.

It built credibility around the new currency. Backing the kroon with gold and foreign exchange reserves and enabling the full convertibility of the new currency with a more established and stronger currency reduced the chance of panic at the introduction of the new currency. As a result, the economy remained stable and trade with foreign partners was maintained and even expanded.

It coordinated monetary reform with broader economic reforms, like liberalized trade, and so reinforced the commitment to a liberalized economy, and with it the credibility of the new economic system in Estonia.

Not surprisingly, the cases in this chapter echo some of the lessons of the previous chapter, which included the same countries. Starting to negotiate early is critical, as is providing as much time as possible for a transition to new arrangements. Indeed, a gradual process is perhaps more important for monetary arrangements than for assets and liabilities because of the need to build international credibility in those arrangements. The principal lesson that differs for monetary policy is the imperative of remembering that currency is not just currency. Rather decisions about currency and finance, even for transition periods, critically affect and are critically affected by underlying economic conditions and broader economic policy choices.

CONCLUSION

The context of any particular secession plainly will matter enormously. Like divorces, secessions are less painful if done amicably, and when there is trust. Yet in many cases those will be exactly the commodities in short supply. And in at least one of the secessions described in this book, Eritrea's departure from Ethiopia, the fact that the victors in the two states were allies led them to assume their comity would continue. They felt little immediate need for hard negotiations on specific issues. Yet when relations soured, these unresolved issues came back to haunt the parties, leading them to war in a scant few years.

Timing and Sequencing Are Important

Because context matters so much, the lessons of the cases in this book can hardly amount to a template. Yet those lessons are suggestive even if implementing them will be no mean feat. In terms of timing, two lessons stand out; they are the two sides of the same coin. One is the need to work out security arrangements early; the other, related, is to avoid drop-dead dates that will risk becoming the opening bell for mass migration or violence.

Paradoxically, security arrangements may be easier to work out than it might appear; that is the lesson of India and Pakistan after partition. The forces of the two sides are likely to exist and may be relatively well organized. And any security arrangements will almost surely be interim—even if that interim turns out to be lengthy—so the arrangements will be less freighted with the weight of permanence.

Starting security discussion early can improve people's understanding, thus muting the risk of drop-dead dates. It also provides time to assess the intentions of refugees, and to prepare for the returnees. Both Indian and Pakistani leaders simply assumed initially that most of the refugees were there only temporarily. In Bosnia, where ethnic conflict was the direct cause of displacement, it was naïve to view returning displaced persons to their homes as undoing the ethnic divides created by war.

In principle, the earlier negotiations can start on virtually all issues, the better. For instance, the water cases suggest the value of interim arrangements to bridge immediate needs while creating arrangements and projects that will make for win-win outcomes. It takes time to build confidence in currency and accompanying economic arrangements, so an early start there would be helpful. Mikhail Gorbachev did not intend perestroika to be a graceful way to end the Soviet empire. Yet it gave the Baltic nations the opportunity to build "state" banks well before formal statehood—a luxury seceding regions, save perhaps those in Europe, will not have. In the case of Sudan, deadlines imposed by the international community came and went without the parties sharing much sense of urgency.

Citizenship ranks with security as the most critical issues in secession. Yet because it is the essence of sovereignty, national discretion is high and international enforcement weak. It may be hard to negotiate until the states are in place. Indeed, outside parties have difficulty influencing decisions until it is too late, even when national track records are poor, as they were in the case of the government of Sudan. There is also a binary quality to citizenship, one that risks drop-dead dates, though that can be muted through permanent residency and long periods for individual decision making.

One of the complicating factors of secession negotiations is that the parties may feel they are operating on different timetables, ones driven by the formalities of the secession itself. For instance, the southern Sudanese negotiators felt that on many issues they would be in a stronger negotiating position after secession, once they were on equal footing with Sudan as a sovereign state. For the government of Sudan, the timeline was nearly the reverse: its negotiating team was more inclined to reach agreement prior to the South's independence but largely stuck to maximalist positions in the knowledge that South Sudan would remain economically dependent on access to the oil pipeline running through northern Sudan with or without a deal.

Borders were not specifically discussed in this book, for in most secessions the formal borders will be relatively clear (that may not be the case with regard to resources lying offshore or onshore in areas there was no other reason to demarcate, as in the Neutral Zone between Saudi Arabia and Kuwait). Yet virtually all secessions will leave some regions with very divided loyalties. That was predictable, sadly, in the case of Sudan's oil-rich Abyei region and led to fighting there shortly after the secession vote. Again, the challenges of regions with divided loyalties should push policy makers to forge sustainable, immediate arrangements for security and examine longer-term considerations of citizenship.

Precedents Matter but So Do Third Parties

Achieving statehood gives seceding region stature in the community of nations but does not in itself change preexisting arrangements or power relations. Its relative power meant that all the former Soviet states accepted Russia as the continuing state of the Soviet Union, which turned out on balance to be a good thing. On the other hand, Serbia's relative strength allowed it appropriate most of the movable assets of the former federation before negotiations began.

Timor-Leste sought to overturn the preexisting oil-sharing arrangement with Australia, and had a good case for doing so. In the end, though, it achieved only a modest improvement—a result in part of its wisdom in being generous with a large neighbor on which it would continue to depend. In the Sudan case it was painful for outside observers to hear southern politicians claim that "the oil will be entirely ours" when it was pretty plain that South Sudan would do well to sustain the fifty-fifty split of oil revenues it had before independence.

The water cases suggest focusing on more recent and more mundane precedents. Arguments for water rights based on history tend to become occasions to reiterate nationalist chest-thumping. By contrast, arguments based on population ratios or irrigable land areas are more concrete and tend to produce more progress between disputing parties. This was the case for both the Nile River and the Indus River.

Third parties, both states and UN or international financial organizations, were helpful in many of the cases across different issues. They were both providers of assistance and guarantors of agreements. Especially in secessions like Sudan's, where the countries are both poor and inexperienced in dealing with large population inflows, the international community can help the migration and settlement process. In Russia, for instance, the UN-HCR and the International Organization for Migration (IOM), along with several NGOs, not only helped the Russian government set up the institutional and legislative framework for dealing with migration, but also provided direct assistance to the migrants themselves, in the forms of both financial support and capacity building, in order to facilitate their integration within Russia. In the water cases, outside states suggested arrangements, and induced parties to negotiate, sometimes through providing assistance.

Leadership and Trust Are Critical

For the lessons outlined in this book to make a difference, those outsiders who would help need direct access to the principal interlocutors in the states involved. For their part, those interlocutors need to see that the experiences of other states, and the lessons that might be drawn from them, are directly relevant to them. Of course, each case has its own particularities, but this book's premise is that it is all too easy for those involved in a secession struggle to think their situation is absolutely unique. Looking at how others have handled similar issues can provide some reassurance that it is not necessary to reinvent the wheel. With luck, that process might even build some trust, suggesting that there were precedents for the other side's negotiating position.

These cases and the lessons emerging from them are probably most useful in the initial framing of the process. That seemed the case in the instance of Sudan, where this early engagement helped to frame the concepts around the postreferendum negotiations between Sudan and South Sudan for key negotiators on both side. A further benefit was to demonstrate early on the interconnectedness between issues and suggest possible sequencing of negotiations before the talks formally started—for instance, agreement x on citizenship will allow for options y and z on other refugees, and so forth. The challenge is to frame the issues in a way that breaks out of the zero-sum mind-set likely to hang over secessions. That requires not just a process but a vision.

In Sudan, that vision became integrated into the mediation process facilitated by the African Union. It was a vision of two viable Sudanese states and of continued North-South cooperation after secession. Alas, that vision did not extend to oil, where southern politicians continued to voice unrealistic aspiration, and the issue never could be reframed as win-win. All the uncertainty surrounding Sudan's future had led to too little investment in technology and infrastructure. As a result, the country was recovering considerably less oil than it could if the oil companies had sufficient confidence to invest in the latest technology. And the size of possible joint gains was large—estimated at US$20 billion, or about 70 percent of total oil revenues over the five years before secession.

The vision was tested immediately after secession, on July 9, 2011. Many key issues remained unresolved, and the commitment to cooperate was not strong enough to prevent a new conflict from starting on the northern side of the North-South border, between the government of Sudan and the ex-southern-aligned SPLM in the northern states of Southern Kordofan and, later, Blue Nile.

For secession to be relatively smooth, leaders have to own the process and its outcome. In this book's cases, that is probably most visible in the breakup of Czechoslovakia, where the two leaders, Klaus and Meciar, could speak for their respective republics. In Sudan, the contrast was striking between the negotiation of the Comprehensive Peace Agreement (CPA) in 2005 and the later negotiations over secession. In the earlier period, southern rebel (SPLM) chairman John Garang and Sudan's vice-president Ali Osman Taha provided serious and effective leadership; they were able to develop a working partnership grounded in trust and personal cooperation, which in turn they were able to sell to their respective parties.

However, John Garang's death in July 2005, the subsequent political weakening of Taha, and six years of arguments over the CPA's implementation left the secession negotiations without that leadership. For the most part, the presidents of Sudan and the future South Sudan articulated only abstract principles that subordinates could not put into practical agreements. Moreover, there was a logic to cooperation in the earlier negotiations, stemming from the fact the parties would need to work together within the same government during the CPA's six-year implementation period. That logic did not persist in the secession negotiations when the temptation to simply cut ties with the other side argued against cooperation—which in turn reduced the chances of finding sustainable, win-win agreements.

Looking across all the cases in this book, perhaps the most striking and unexpected success story is the lack of violence in the repatriation of literally hundreds of thousands of Russians from other former Soviet republics after the collapse of the Soviet Union. While the newly sovereign republics were not all entirely welcoming to Russians who remained, in no new nation was there large-scale violence directed at the Russians. In part, the more nationalistic of the new republics, like the Baltic states, were richer and thus less likely to hold grievances against the Russians even as they made their integration more difficult; meanwhile, the poorer new republics needed the ethnic Russians' economic skills.

The importance of particular issues in secession will change over time, and specific solutions that were possible prior to secession may be trickier after the fact—or even once the prospect of eventual secession enters the political equation. The disputed region of Abyei, for example, was at one time seen a bridge between North and South Sudan. Yet the expectation of southern secession hardened views on both sides prior to the independence vote, and a zero-sum approach to this disputed area carried on even after secession.

Ultimately, perhaps, the lesson of the Sudan case is the plain one: parties that have been at war are not likely to come to peace, much less negotiate their divorce amicably. Good models and good lessons will not count for much absent good luck or exceptional circumstances—inspired and inspiring leaders or major international intervention, including peacekeepers. Hard cases, as they say, make bad law. Yet this book offers guidance for the less hard cases of secession. And for the hard cases it at least offers some examples of dividing states constructing win-win arrangements despite considerable hostility. Doing so isn't easy. But it is possible.

APPENDIX

Table A.1. Seceding States

Seceding country	Original country	Date
Panama	Colombia	November 3, 1903
Norway	Sweden	1905
Albania	Ottoman Empire	November 28, 1912
Finland	Russia	December 6, 1917
Estonia	Russia	May 1918
Latvia	Russia	November 1918
Hungary	Austria-Hungary	November 16, 1918
Austria	Austria-Hungary	November 16, 1918
Lithuania	Russia	1919
Czechoslovakia	Austria-Hungary	1919
Mongolia	China	July 1921
Burma	India	April 1937
Iceland	Denmark	June 17, 1944
Pakistan	India	August 15, 1947
South Korea	Korea	August 15, 1948
East Germany	Germany	1949
West Germany	Germany	1949
Ireland	United Kingdom	April 18, 1949
North Korea	Korea	May 1, 1949
Taiwan	China	December 1949
North Vietnam	Vietnam	September 15, 1954
South Vietnam	Vietnam	September 15, 1954
Senegal	Mali Federation	August 20, 1960
Cameroon	Nigeria	October 1961
Burundi	Rwanda-Burundi	1964
Rwanda	Rwanda-Burundi	1964
Singapore	Federation of Malaya	August 9, 1965
Bangladesh	Pakistan	March 26, 1971

(continued)

Table A.1. *(continued)*

Seceding country	Original country	Date
Turkish Republic of Northern Cyprus	Cyprus	November 15, 1983
Namibia	South Africa	March 21, 1990
Georgia	Soviet Union	April 6, 1991
Croatia	Yugoslavia	June 25, 1991
Slovenia	Yugoslavia	June 25, 1991
Moldova	Soviet Union	August 23, 1991
Belarus	Soviet Union	August 25, 1991
Azerbaijan	Soviet Union	August 30, 1991
Kyrgyz Republic	Soviet Union	August 31, 1991
Uzbekistan	Soviet Union	August 31, 1991
Tajikistan	Soviet Union	September 1991
Estonia	Soviet Union	September 6, 1991
Latvia	Soviet Union	September 6, 1991
Lithuania	Soviet Union	September 6, 1991
Macedonia	Yugoslavia	September 8, 1991
Armenia	Soviet Union	September 23, 1991
Turkmenistan	Soviet Union	October 27, 1991
Ukraine	Soviet Union	December 1, 1991
Kazakhstan	Soviet Union	December 16, 1991
Bosnia-Herzegovina	Yugoslavia	March 3, 1992
Czech Republic	Czechoslovakia	January 1, 1993
Slovakia	Czechoslovakia	January 1, 1993
Eritrea	Ethiopia	May 3, 1993
East Timor	Indonesia	May 20, 2002
Montenegro	Serbia and Montenegro	June 3, 2006
Serbia	Serbia and Montenegro	June 5, 2006
Kosovo (unilaterally declared)	Serbia	February 17, 2008
South Sudan	Sudan	July 9, 2011

Sources: B. Carter David and H. E. Goemans, "The Making of the Territorial Order: New Borders and the Emergence of Interstate Conflict" (unpublished paper, August 22, 2010); and Matt Rosenberg, "New Countries of the World: The 34 New Countries Created Since 1990," available at http://geography.about.com/cs/countries/a/newcountries.htm.
Note: This table lists countries that divided as double secessions from the original state.

NOTES

Introduction

1. John Wood discusses the range of factors and argues that rather than creating an entirely new sovereign claim, secessionist movements tend to build off of a "separable territory which contains the bulk of the potentially secessionist population." See his "Secession: A Comparative Analytical Framework," *Canadian Journal of Political Science* 14 (1981).

2. Michael Hechter, "The Dynamics of Secession," *Acta Sociologica* 35 (1992): 280.

3. Donald Horowitz, *Ethnic Groups in Conflict* (Berkeley: University of California Press, 1985), 259.

4. Henry Hale, "The Parade of Sovereignties: Testing Theories of Secession in the Soviet Setting," *British Journal of Political Science* 30, no. 1 (2000): 32.

5. Viva Ona Bartkus, *The Dynamics of Secession* (Cambridge: Cambridge University Press, 1999).

6. African Union, "Declaration on the African Union Border Programme and Its Implementation Modalities as Adopted by the Conference of African Ministers in Charge of Border Issues, Held in Addis Ababa (Ethiopia), 7 June 2007," available at http://www.africa-union.org/root/au/publications/PSC/Border%20Issues.pdf.

Chapter 1

1. The Hague Convention on Certain Questions Relating to the Conflict of Nationality Laws mandates that it is "for each State to determine under its own law who are nationals." Hague Convention on Certain Questions Relating to the Conflict of Nationality Laws, article 1 (April 12, 1930).

2. In 1996, the Venice Commission adopted the Declaration on the Consequences of State Succession for the Nationality of Natural Persons (Venice Commission Declaration), which urges states to respect the principle that everyone has the right to a nationality. The Venice Commission Declaration urges successor states to grant nationality to everyone who meets its criteria, without discrimination based on ethnicity, race, religion, language, or political opinions. See Venice Commission, "Declaration on the Consequences of State Succession for the Nationality of Natural Persons, European Commission for Democracy Through Law" (September 13–14, 1996), pt. III (8b). Similarly, the International Law Commission's "Nationality of Natural Persons in

Relation to the Succession of States" (ILC Draft Articles) provides that every individual holding the nationality of the predecessor state at the time of succession has the right to the nationality of at least one of the states concerned. The ILC Draft Articles further prohibit discrimination and arbitrary decisions concerning nationality and presume that persons who have their habitual residence in the territory that secedes acquire the nationality of the successor state. See International Law Commission, "Nationality of Natural Persons in Relation to the Succession of States," articles 1, 5, 15, 16 (1999), available at http://untreaty.un.org/ilc/texts/instruments/english/draft %20articles/3_4_1999.pdf.

3. Venice Commission, "Declaration on the Consequences of State Succession," pt. V (15) (16).

4. Ibid.

5. International Law Commission, "Nationality of Natural Persons," articles 1, 5, 15, 16.

6. Each state is responsible for the establishment of rules and procedures for nationality. According to international law, these rules shall "avoid creating cases of statelessness" and "respect, as far as possible, the will of the person concerned." Venice Commission, "Declaration on the Consequences of State Succession," pt. II (5) (6) (quoting article 2.1(b) of the Vienna Convention of 1978 on Succession of States in Respect of Treaties and Article 2.1(a) of the 1983 Vienna Convention on Succession of States in Respect of State Property, Archives and Debts). See also Venice Commission, "Declaration on the Consequences of State Succession," pt. V (15) (16).

7. See James C. Bennett, *Network Commonwealth: The Future of Nations in the Internet Era* (forthcoming).

8. For background, see Veysel Oezcan, *Germany: Immigration in Transition* (Berlin: Social Science Centre, July 2004).

9. See Agreement on Security and Related Matters Between the Ministries of Internal Affairs of the Governments of Ethiopia and Eritrea (Ethiopia, Eritrea, 1993), referenced in Human Rights Watch, *Eritrea & Ethiopia, The Horn of Africa War: Mass Expulsions and the Nationality Issue (June 1998–April 2002)*, vol. 15 (January 2003), available at http://www.hrw.org/reports/2003/ethioerit0103/ethioerit 0103.pdf.

10. All the references in this and the following paragraph are from Interim Const. Sudan article 28 (2005), available at http://www.sudan-embassy.de/c_Sudan.pdf.

11. Ibid., article 157 ("A special commission shall be appointed by the Presidency to ensure that the rights of non-Muslims are protected in accordance with the aforementioned guidelines and not adversely affected by the application of Sharia Law in the Capital").

Chapter 2

1. P. Oberoi, "Indian Partition," in *Immigration and Asylum: From 1900 to Present*, ed. M. Gibney and R. Hansen (Santa Barbara, Calif.: ABC-CLIO, 2005).

2. "Sixty Bitter Years After Partition," *BBC News*, August 8, 2007, retrieved June 7, 2009, http://news.bbc.co.uk/2/hi/south_asia/6926057.stm.

3. Oberoi, "Indian Partition."

4. Ibid.

5. C. E. Haque, "The Dilemma of Nationhood and Religion: A Survey and Critique of Studies on Population Displacement Resulting from the Partition of the Indian Subcontinent," *Journal of Refugee Studies* 8, no. 2 (1995): 186–209.

6. The Radcliffe line was named after Sir Cyril Radcliffe, the British lawyer who led the two Boundary Commissions (one for the Punjab province and the other for the Bengal province) that determined the exact boundaries between the two countries. The commissions were set up by the British government and included four local representatives, two from the All India Muslim League (AIML) and two from the Indian National Congress (INC), which was the dominant political party in India.

7. L. Chester, "Commentary and Analysis: 'The 1947 Partition: Drawing the Indo-Pakistani Border,'" *American Diplomacy*, retrieved June 10, 2009, from http://www.unc.edu/depts/diplomat/archives_roll/2002_01-03/chester_partition/chester_partition.html; S. Keen, "The Partition of India" (Postcolonial Studies at Emory, 1998), retrieved June 10, 2009, from http://www.english.emory.edu/Bahri/Part.html.

8. Oberoi, "Indian Partition."

9. Ibid.; Haque, "Dilemma of Nationhood and Religion."

10. R. Jeffery, "The Punjab Boundary Force and the Problem of Order, August 1947," *Journal of Modern Asian Studies* 8, no. 4 (1974): 491–520.

11. Oberoi, "Indian Partition."

12. Ibid.

13. Because of the sheer number of refugees, it was impossible for the government to provide all refugees with employment, so it prioritized dispersing them around the country and incentivizing them to find their own employment.

14. The pact was named after the two countries' prime ministers—Jawaharlal Nehru of India and Liaquat Ali Khan of Pakistan. "Liaquat-Nehru Pact 1950," in *The Story of Pakistan: A Multimedia Journey*, retrieved June 11, 2009, from http://www.storyofpakistan.com/articletext.asp?artid=A096.

15. "Delhi Pact," *Encyclopedia Britannica*, 2009, retrieved June 11, 2009, from http://www.search.eb.com/eb/article-9029821.

16. Oberoi, "Indian Partition"; and Haque, "Dilemma of Nationhood and Religion."

17. This case was originally written by Tewodaj Mengistu.

18. The new republics are as follows: the Baltic states Estonia, Latvia, and Lithuania; the Central Asian states of Tajikistan, Uzbekistan, Turkmenistan, Kazakhstan, and Kyrgyzstan; the Transcaucasus states of Armenia, Azerbaijan, and Georgia; and the Slavic states Belarus, Moldova, Ukraine, and the Russian Federation, the latter considered legally as the continuing state of the Soviet Union.

19. T. Heleniak, "Migration of the Russian Diaspora After the Breakup of the Soviet Union," *Journal of International Affairs* 57, no. 2 (2004): 99–116.

20. M. Flynn, *Migrant Resettlement in the Russian Federation: Reconstructing Homes and Homelands* (London: Anthem Press, 2004).

21. W. R. Brubaker, "Migration and Ethnic Unmixing in Europe," *International Migration Review* 32, no. 4 (1998): 1047–1065.

22. Flynn, *Migrant Resettlement*.

23. Heleniak, "Migration of the Russian Diaspora"; "Russian Diaspora," in *Immigration and Asylum: From 1900 to Present*, ed. M. Gibney and R. Hansen (Santa Barbara, Calif.: ABC-CLIO, 2005).

24. W. R. Brubaker, "Citizenship Struggles in Soviet Successor States," *International Migration Review* 26, no. 2 (1992): 269–291.

25. "Russian Diaspora."

26. In these two states, Russian peasants had settled in rural areas prior to the creation of the Soviet Union and had farmed the land for generations.

27. Ibid.

28. Heleniak, "Migration of the Russian Diaspora," 102.

29. Brubaker, "Migration and Ethnic Unmixing in Europe."

30. Ibid.

31. Ibid.

32. Ibid.

33. "Russian Diaspora."

34. Heleniak, "Migration of the Russian Diaspora."

35. Ibid.; Brubaker, "Migration and Ethnic Unmixing in Europe."

36. Russia signed a dual citizenship agreement only with Turkmenistan in 1993 and with Tajikistan in 1997.

37. Heleniak, "Migration of the Russian Diaspora."

38. Flynn, *Migrant Resettlement*.

39. Ibid.

40. Ibid.

41. Ibid.

42. This case was originally written by Sarah Outcault.

43. Internal Displacement Monitoring Centre/Norwegian Refugee Council, "Georgia: New IDP Strategy Awaits Implementation" (October 11, 2007), 6.

44. Evgeny M. Kozhokin, "Georgia-Abkhazia," in *U.S. and Russian Policymaking with Respect to the Use of Force*, ed. Jeremy R. Azrael and Emil A. Payin. Santa Monica, Calif.: RAND Corporation, 1996.

45. Internal Displacement Monitoring Centre, "Georgia," http://www.internal-displacement.org/.

46. U.S. Institute of Peace, "Quadripartite Agreement on Voluntary Return of Refugees and Displaced Persons" (April 4, 1994), available at http://www.usip.org/library/pa/georgia/georgia_quad_19940504.html.

47. Internal Displacement Monitoring Centre/Norwegian Refugee Council, "Georgia," 43.

48. Ibid., 12.

49. United Nations Economic and Social Council, "Specific Groups and Individuals: Mass Exoduses and Displaced Persons, Addendum: Georgia" (Document E/CN.4/2001/5/Add.4), 11.

50. Internal Displacement Monitoring Centre/Norwegian Refugee Council, "Georgia," 10.

51. The high proportion of IDPs on the registry who could be verified ten years after the conflict suggests that very few refugees have either returned to their homes or fully integrated into Georgian society.

52. Internal Displacement Monitoring Centre/Norwegian Refugee Council, "Georgia," 116.

53. Ibid., 11.

54. Boutros Boutros-Ghali, "Annual Report of the Secretary-General on the Work of the Organization" (United Nations, 1995).

55. "Abkhaz Official: Confidence-Building Is Needed for IDP Return," *Civil Georgia* (Tbilisi), February 17, 2007.

56. United Nations Economic and Social Council, "Specific Groups and Individuals," 23.

57. Internal Displacement Monitoring Centre/Norwegian Refugee Council, "Georgia," 18.

58. Internal Displacement Monitoring Centre/Norwegian Refugee Council, "Protracted Internal Displacement in Europe: Current Trends and Ways Forward" (May 2009), 9.

59. United Nations Economic and Social Council, "Specific Groups and Individuals," 11.

60. Greg Hansen, "Displacement and Return," *Accord* 7 (September 1999).

61. Internal Displacement Monitoring Centre/Norwegian Refugee Council, "Georgia," 28.

62. This case was originally written by Sarah Outcault.

63. Office of the High Representative, "General Framework Agreement for Peace in Bosnia and Herzegovina" (annex 7, article I, 1995), http://www.ohr.int/dpa/default.asp?content_id=380; see the full text at http://www.usip.org/library/pa/bosnia/dayton_gfa.html.

64. Erin Mooney, "Securing Durable Solutions for Displaced Persons in Georgia: The Experience of Bosnia and Herzegovina" (paper, Conflict and Migration: The Georgian-Abkhazian Case in a European Context, Istanbul, June 18–19, 2008).

65. Internal Displacement Monitoring Centre/Norwegian Refugee Council, "Bosnia and Herzegovina: Broader and Improved Support for Durable Solutions Required" (August 28, 2008), 15.

66. "Briefing Note on UNHCR and Annex 7 in Bosnia and Herzegovina" (UN-HCR, October 2007), 1.

67. Office of the High Representative, "General Framework Agreement for Peace in Bosnia and Herzegovina."

68. Mooney, "Securing Durable Solutions," 3.

69. Internal Displacement Monitoring Centre, "Bosnia and Herzegovina."

70. Internal Displacement Monitoring Centre/Norwegian Refugee Council, "Bosnia and Herzegovina: Broader and Improved Support," 12.

71. Commission of the European Communities, "Bosnia and Herzegovina 2008 Progress Report" (Staff Working Document 5/11/08), 20.

72. Mooney, "Securing Durable Solutions," 6.

73. United Nations High Commissioner for Refugees, "The State of the World's Refugees: Human Displacement in the New Millennium" (2006), 157, available at http://www.unhcr.org/cgi-bin/texis/vtx/template?page=publ&src=static/sowr2006/toceng.htm.

74. Ibid., 169.

Chapter 3

1. Sara Pantuliano, Omer Egemi, Babo Fadlalla, and Mohammed Farah, *Put Out to Pasture: War, Oil and the Decline of Misseriyya Pastoralism in Sudan* (London: Overseas Development Institute, March 2009), 25.

2. This point came through strongly in both "Responses to Pastoral Wars" (Sudan Issue Brief 8, September 2007), available at http://www.smallarmssurvey.org/files/portal/spotlight/sudan/Sudan_pdf/SIB%208%20Responses.pdf; and Halakhe Waqo, "Peacebuilding and Small Arms: Experiences from Northern Kenya" (OXFAM Kenya Program, 2003), available at www.iansa.org/un/notes/peacebuilding_and_small_arms.doc.

3. John Agyei and Ezekiel Clottey, "Operationalizing ECOWAS Protocol on Free Movement of People Among the Member States" (2007), available at http://www.imi.ox.ac.uk/pdfs/CLOTTEY%20and%20AGYEI.pdf.

4. Guleid Abdulkarim A. Ato and Ato Kibre Jimmerra Kasa, "Improving Pastoral Welfare in Ethiopia" (Research Brief 04-04-PARIMA, Global Livestock Collaborative Research Support Program, 2004), 2, available at http://glcrsp.ucdavis.edu/publications/PARIMA/04-04-PARIMA.pdf; Economic Community of West African States, "Executive Secretary's Annual Report, Chapter 2: Implementation of the Community Work Programme" (2000), http://www.comm.ecowas.int/sec/index.php?id=es-rep2000-3-2&lang=en.

5. See Agyei and Clottey, "Operationalizing."

6. See Solomon Desta and D. Layne Coppock, "Pastoralism Under Pressure: Tracking System Change in Southern Ethiopia," *Human Ecology* 32, no. 4 (August 2004): 465–486; and Elliot Fratkin and Robin Mearns, "Sustainability and Pastoral Livelihoods:

Lessons from East African Maasai and Mongolia," *Human Organization* 62, no. 2 (2003): 112–122.

7. See, for instance, Li Ying, Douglas L. Johnson, and Abdelkrim Marzouk, "Pauperizing the Periphery," *Journal of Geographical Science* 12, no. 1 (2002): 1–14; and Abdurahman Ahe, "Cross-Border Livestock Trade and Small Arms and Conflict in Pastoral Areas in the Horn of Africa" (presentation, International Association for the Study of Common Property Biennial Conference, April 19, 2006), available at http://dlc.dlib.indiana.edu/archive/00001823/00/Ame_Abdurahman.pdf.

8. This case was originally written by David Howell.

9. Scott Forrest, "Territoriality and State-Sami Relations," retrieved December 2008 from http://arcticcircle.uconn.edu/HistoryCulture/Sami/samisf.html.

10. Tore Modeen, "The Lapps in Finland," *International Journal of Cultural Property* 8, no. 1 (1999): 133–150.

11. Ibid.

12. Mattias Ahrén, "Indigenous Peoples' Culture, Customs, and Traditions and Customary Law—The Saami People's Perspective," *Arizona Journal of International and Comparative Law* 21, no. 1 (2004): 73.

13. Lars Ivar Hansen, "The Sami Hunting Society in Transition: Approaches, Concepts and Context," *HistoriaFenno-Ugrica I* 1–2 (1996): 315–334, retrieved December 2008 from http://www.uit.no/ssweb/dok/Hansen/LarsIvar/96.htm#top.

14. Robert Layton, *Conflict in the Archaeology of Living Traditions* (New York: Routledge, 1986).

15. Ahrén, "Indigenous Peoples' Culture, Customs, and Traditions and Customary Law," 85.

16. Ibid., 87–88.

17. Fae L. Korsmo, "Nordic Security and the Saami Minority: Territorial Rights in Northern Fennoscandia," *Human Rights Quarterly* 10, no. 4 (1988); Mai Beijer and Staffan Bolin, "Curriculum Development for Social Inclusion in Sweden," *Prospects* 33, no. 1 (March 2003).

18. See, for example, Juliet Eilperin, "Norway Debates the Promise, Costs of New Drilling; Oil Means More Revenue But More Climate Change," *Washington Post*, August 21, 2007, p. A08.

19. Láilá Susanne Vars, "Sapmi—Norway," in *The Indigenous World* (Copenhagen: International Work Group for Indigenous Affairs, 2007), 42.

20. Johnny-Leo L. Jernsletten and Konstantin Klokov, "Sustainable Reindeer Husbandry" (Centre for Saami Studies, 2002), 5.

21. Birgitte Ulvevadet and Konstantin Klokov, "Family-Based Reindeer Herding and Hunting Economies, and the Status and Management of Wild Reindeer/Caribou Populations" (Centre for Saami Studies, 2004), 96.

22. B. C. Forbes, "The Challenges of Modernity for Reindeer Management in Northernmost Europe," *Ecological Studies* 184 (2006): 21.

23. Vars, "Sapmi—Norway," 38–40.

24. Ibid., 40.

25. Johan Strömgren, "Sapmi—Sweden," in *The Indigenous World* (Copenhagen: International Work Group for Indigenous Affairs, 2008), 30.

26. Ibid., 32.

27. Ahrén, "Indigenous Peoples' Culture, Customs, and Traditions and Customary Law," 94.

28. Pauliina Feodoroff and Rebecca Lawrence, "Sapmi—Finland," in *The Indigenous World* (Copenhagen: International Work Group for Indigenous Affairs, 2008), 32–33.

29. This case was originally written by David Howell.

30. These tribes—"Indians" in popular parlance—are usually called Native Americans in the United States, First Nations in Canada. Herein we refer to them as "indigenous peoples."

31. Joseph Charles, "The Jay Treaty: The Origins of the American Party System," *William and Mary Quarterly* 12, no. 4 (1955); Joseph M. Fewster, "The Jay Treaty and British Ship Seizures: The Martinique Cases," *William and Mary Quarterly* 45, no. 3 (1988).

32. Todd Estes, "Shaping the Politics of Public Opinion: Federalists and the Jay Treaty Debate," *Journal of the Early Republic* 20, no. 3 (2000).

33. Richard Osburn, "Problems and Solutions Regarding Indigenous Peoples Split by International Border," *American Indian Law Review* 24, no. 2 (2000).

34. T. A. Mahan, "The Negotiations at Ghent in 1814," *American Historical Review* 11, no. 1 (1905); Frank A. Updyke, "The Treaty of Ghent—A Centenary Estimate," *Proceedings of the American Political Science Association* 10 (1913).

35. Bryan Nickels, "Native American Free Passage Rights Under the 1794 Jay Treaty: Survival Under United States Statutory Law and Canadian Common Law," *Boston College International and Comparative Law Review* 24, no. 2 (2001).

36. Eileen M. Luna-Firebaugh, "The Border Crossed Us: Border Crossing Issues of the Indigenous Peoples of the Americas," *WicazoSa Review* 17, no. 1 (2002).

37. Marcia Yablon-Zug, "Gone but Not Forgotten: The Strange Afterlife of the 'Jay Treaty's' Indian Free Passage Right," *Queen's Law Journal* 33, no. 2 (2008).

38. United States ex rel. Diabo v. McCandless, 18 F.2d 282 (D. Pa. 1927).

39. McCandless v. United States ex rel. Diabo, 25 F.2d 71 (3d Cr. 1928).

40. Yablon-Zug, "Gone but Not Forgotten."

41. United States, on Petition of Albro, ex rel. Cook et al. v. Karnuth, 24 F.2d 649 (2d Cr. 1928).

42. Karnuth v. United States ex rel. Albro, 279 U.S. 231 (S. Ct. 1929).

43. United States ex rel. Goodwin v. Karnuth, 74 F. Supp. 660 (W.D.N.Y. 1947).

44. Eileen M. Luna-Firebaugh, "Contemporary and Comparative Perspectives on the Rights of Indigenous Peoples," *Washington University Journal of Law & Policy* 19 (2005).

45. Audra Simpson, "Subjects of Sovereignty: Indigeneity, the Revenue Rule, and Jurdics of Failed Consent," *Law and Contemporary Problems* 71, no. 3 (2008).

46. Yablon-Zug, "Gone but Not Forgotten."

47. Luna-Firebaugh, "Border Crossed Us."

48. Sharon O'Brien, "The Medicine Line: A Border Dividing Tribal Sovereignty, Economies and Families," *Fordham Law Review* 53, no. 2 (1984); William R. Di Iorio, "Mending Fences: The Fractured Relationship Between Native American Tribes and the Federal Government and Its Negative Impact on Border Security," *Syracuse Law Review* 57, no. 2 (2007).

49. Joshua J. Tonra, "The Threat of Border Security on Indigenous Free Passage Rights in North America," *Syracuse Journal of International Law and Commerce* 34, no. 1 (2006).

50. Yablon-Zug, "Gone but Not Forgotten."

51. This case was originally written by David Howell.

52. Courtney E. Ozer, "Make It Right: The Case for Granting Tohono O'odham Nation Members U.S. Citizenship," *Georgetown Immigration Law Journal* 16 (2002).

53. Tonra, "Threat of Border Security."

54. Luna-Firebaugh, "Contemporary and Comparative Perspectives"; Megan S. Austin, "A Culture Divided by the United States–Mexico Border: The Tohono O'odham Claim for Border Crossing Rights," *Arizona Journal of International and Comparative Law* 8 (1991).

55. Ozer, "Make It Right."

56. Leah Castella, "The United States Border: A Barrier to Cultural Survival," *Texas Journal on Civil Liberties & Civil Rights* 5 (2000).

57. Osburn, "Problems and Solutions Regarding Indigenous Peoples Split."

58. Luna-Firebaugh, "Border Crossed Us."

59. U.S. Department of Homeland Security, Bureau of Customs and Border Protection, "Documents Required for Travelers Departing from or Arriving in the United States at Sea and Land Ports-of-Entry from Within the Western Hemisphere" (US-CBP 2007-0061, 2007), retrieved January 28, 2009, from http://www.dhs.gov/xlibrary/assets/whti_landseafinalrule.pdf.

Chapter 4

1. This case was originally written by Tewodaj Mengistu.

2. Donald R. Norland, "Innovations of the Chad/Cameroon Pipeline Project: Thinking Outside the Box," *Mediterranean Quarterly* 14, no. 2 (2003).

3. Ibid.; World Bank and International Finance Corporation, "Chad-Cameroon Petroleum Development and Pipeline Project: An Overview" (Washington, D.C.: World Bank, 2006).

4. The project developed the Miandoum, Kome, and Bolobo oil fields, built the pipeline, 890 kilometers of which is located in Cameroon, and built an offshore terminal off the coast of Cameroon, near Kribi in the Gulf of Guinea.

5. World Bank, "The Chad-Cameroon Petroleum Development and Pipeline Project" (January 2006), retrieved December 18, 2008, from http://go.worldbank.org/504AW22GX0.

6. According to the United Nations Development Programme, in 2007 Chad ranked last among 108 developing countries in the Human Poverty Index, which measures the extent of extreme social depravation (health, education, and standard of living). United Nations Development Programme, "Chad: The Human Development Index—Going Beyond Income," in *Human Development Report 2007/2008* (New York: United Nations, 2007).

7. "Breaking the Bank: Chad," *Economist*, September 27, 2008.

8. Shell and Elf withdrew from the consortium in 1999 and were replaced by Petronas and ChevronTexaco.

9. World Bank and International Finance Corporation, "Chad-Cameroon Petroleum Development and Pipeline Project."

10. World Bank, "Implementation Completion Report on Two IBRD Loans in the Amount of US$39.5 Million and in the Amount of US$53.4 Respectively to the Republic of Chad and the Republic of Cameroon for a Petroleum Development and Pipeline Project" (Washington, D.C.: World Bank, 2006).

11. Jeremy H. Keenan, "Chad-Cameroon Oil Pipeline: World Bank and Exxon-Mobil in '*Last Chance Saloon*,'" *Review of African Political Economy* 104, no. 5 (2005).

12. The priority sectors were identified as education, health, social services, rural development, infrastructure, the environment, and water resources management.

13. World Bank and International Finance Corporation, "Chad-Cameroon Petroleum Development and Pipeline Project."

14. Of the shares, 40 percent by ExxonMobil and 35 and 15 percent, respectively, by Petronas and ChevronTexaco.

15. David Johnston and Anthony Rogers, "Economic Analysis Clarifies How Chad Benefits from Oil," *Oil and Gas Journal*, July 28, 2008.

16. World Bank and International Finance Corporation, "Chad-Cameroon Petroleum Development and Pipeline Project."

17. World Bank, "Chad-Cameroon Petroleum Development and Pipeline Project."

18. Ibid.

19. World Bank and International Finance Corporation, "Chad-Cameroon Petroleum Development and Pipeline Project."

20. Energy Information Administration, "Chad and Cameroon" (Country Analysis Briefs, January 2007).

21. Esso Exploration and Production Chad Inc., "Chad-Cameroon Development Project—Project Update No. 24 Mid-Year Report 2008" (Houston: Esso Exploration and Production Chad Inc., 2008).

22. Energy Information Administration, "Chad and Cameroon."

23. World Bank and International Finance Corporation, "Chad-Cameroon Petroleum Development and Pipeline Project."

24. World Bank, "Chad-Cameroon Petroleum Development and Pipeline Project."

25. Korinna Horta, "The Wolfowitz Pattern at World Bank," *Boston Globe*, May 19, 2007.

26. Lisa Margonelli, "The Short, Sad History of Chad's 'Model' Oil Project," *New York Times*, February 12, 2007.

27. This case was originally written by Sarah Outcault.

28. Energy Information Agency, "Algeria" (Country Analysis Briefs, March, 2007).

29. M. H. Hayes, "Algerian Gas to Europe: The Transmed Pipeline and Early Spanish Gas Import Projects" (Stanford University, Program on Energy and Sustainable Development Working Paper 27, 2004), 3.

30. Ibid., 8.

31. Joint UNDP/World Bank Energy Sector Management Assistance Program (ESMAP), "Cross-Border Oil and Gas Pipelines: Problems and Prospects" (2003), 54.

32. Hayes, "Algerian Gas to Europe," 4, 15.

33. UNDP/ESMAP, "Cross-Border Oil and Gas Pipelines," 36.

34. Sonatrach, "Annual Report 2007," http://www.sonatrach-dz.com/annual%20report2007-uk.pdf.

35. Ente Nazionale Idrocarboni, "Annual Report" (2007), http://www.eni.it/en_IT/attachments/publications/reports/reports-2007/2007-annual-report.pdf.

36. Hayes, "Algerian Gas to Europe," 10.

37. International Energy Agency, "Security of Gas Supply in Open Markets: LNG and Power at a Turning Point" (2004), 321.

38. UNDP/ESMAP, "Cross-Border Oil and Gas Pipelines," 28.

39. Paul Stevens, "Pipelines or Pipe Dreams? Lessons from the History of Arab Transit Pipelines," *Middle East Journal* 54, no. 2 (2000); Hayes, "Algerian Gas to Europe."

40. Ilan Stein, "EU Energy Policy vis-à-vis Algeria: Challenges and Opportunities," *Bologna Center Journal of International Affairs* (Fall 2008).

41. Stevens, "Pipelines or Pipe Dreams?"

42. This case was originally written by Sarah Outcault.

43. "Recent History (Timor-Leste)," *Europa World*.

44. Joseph Nevins, "Contesting the Boundaries of International Justice: State Countermapping and Offshore Resources Struggles Between East Timor and Australia," *Economic Geography* 80, no. 1 (January 2004): 1–22.

45. "Recent History (Timor-Leste)."

46. International Monetary Fund, "Democratic Republic of Timor-Leste: Selected Issues and Statistical Appendix" (Country Report 05/250, June 2005).

47. "With Independence, What Changes for the Timor Gap?" *La'oHamutuk Bulletin* 3, no. 4 (May 2002).

48. Department of Foreign Affairs and Trade, Government of Australia, "Timor Sea Treaty" (April 2003), http://www.austlii.edu.au/au/other/dfat/treaties/2003/13.

49. International Monetary Fund, "Democratic Republic of Timor-Leste: Selected Issues and Statistical Appendix" (Country Report 05/250).

50. "Economy (Timor-Leste)," *Europa World*.

51. "Australia and East Timor: Fair Dinkum," *Economist*, May 21, 2005, p. 70.

52. "Economy (Timor-Leste)," *Europa World*.

53. "Treaty Between Australia and the Democratic Republic of Timor-Leste on Certain Maritime Arrangements in the Timor Sea," *Australian Treaty Series* (2007), http://www.austlii.edu.au/au/other/dfat/treaties/2007/12/12.rtf.

54. International Monetary Fund, "Democratic Republic of Timor-Leste: Selected Issues and Statistical Appendix" (Country Report 05/250).

55. International Monetary Fund, "Democratic Republic of Timor-Leste: Selected Issues and Statistical Appendix" (Country Report 07/86, February 2007).

56. Nevins, "Contesting the Boundaries of International Justice."

57. International Monetary Fund, "Democratic Republic of Timor-Leste: Selected Issues and Statistical Appendix" (Country Report 05/250).

58. International Monetary Fund, "Democratic Republic of Timor-Leste: Selected Issues and Statistical Appendix" (Country Report 08/203, June 2008).

59. "Economy (Timor-Leste)," *Europa World*.

60. International Monetary Fund, "Democratic Republic of Timor-Leste: Selected Issues and Statistical Appendix" (Country Report 07/86).

61. International Monetary Fund, "Democratic Republic of Timor-Leste: Selected Issues and Statistical Appendix" (Country Report 05/250).

62. This case was originally written by Tewodaj Mengistu.

63. UK-Norway North Sea Co-operation Workgroup, "Value Creation from UK-Norway Co-operation, Evaluation of the Potential Gain from Improved Co-operation" (2002).

64. Examples are the May 1976 and October 1979 agreements to facilitate the exploitation of the Frigg, Statfjord, and Murchison fields and to transport the resulting hydrocarbons by pipeline infrastructure. "Framework Agreement Between the Government of the United Kingdom of Great Britain and Northern Ireland and the Government of the Kingdom of Norway Concerning Cross-Boundary Petroleum Co-operation—Oslo, April 4, 2005" (presented to Parliament by the Secretary of State for Foreign and Commonwealth Affairs by Command of Her Majesty, May 2006) (London: Stationery Office, 2006).

65. On the U.K. side, the industry representatives were from BP and Shell, while the contractor and government reps were respectively from Woods Group and from the Department of Trade and Industry. On the Norwegian side, industry reps were from Norske Shell and Statoil, while the contractor and government reps were respectively from Aker and the Ministry of Petroleum and Energy.

66. UK-Norway North Sea Co-operation Workgroup, "Unlocking Value Through Closer Relationships" (2002); Department of Trade and Industry, "First Strike for UK Norway Deal" (July 1, 2005).

67. "Framework Agreement Between the Government of the United Kingdom of Great Britain and Northern Ireland and the Government of the Kingdom of Norway."

68. Ibid.

69. The Enoch field was discovered in 1985, while Blane was discovered in 1989.

70. Department of Trade and Industry, "UK and Norway Approve Two New North Sea Developments" (April 7, 2005).

71. UK-Norway North Sea Co-operation Workgroup, "Unlocking Value Through Closer Relationships," 1.

72. Ibid.

73. UK-Norway North Sea Co-operation Workgroup, "Unlocking Value Through Strengthened Relationships" (2004).

74. UK-Norway North Sea Co-operation Workgroup, "Value Creation from UK-Norway Co-operation."

75. UK-Norway North Sea Co-operation Workgroup, "Unlocking Value Through Strengthened Relationships."

76. Ibid., 4; Department of Trade and Industry, "First Strike for UK Norway Deal."

77. "Framework Agreement Between the Government of the United Kingdom of Great Britain and Northern Ireland and the Government of the Kingdom of Norway."

78. Ibid.

79. Ibid.

80. Ibid.

81. Department of Trade and Industry, "UK and Norway Approve Two New North Sea Developments."

82. Nick Terdre, "Talisman Forging Ahead on Rev, Yme," *Offshore* 67, no. 10 (October 2007): 102; ROC Oil, "First Oil from UK North Sea Blane Field" (September 13, 2007).

83. Shortly after Paladin Resources was appointed unit operator for both fields, the company was sold to Talisman Energy Resources Ltd, also a U.K.-based company.

84. Department of Trade and Industry, "UK and Norway Approve Two New North Sea Developments."

85. Terdre, "Talisman Forging Ahead"; ROC Oil, "First Oil from UK North Sea Blane Field"; Department of Trade and Industry, "UK and Norway Approve Two New North Sea Developments."

86. This case was originally written by Sarah Outcault.

87. M. T. Ghoneimy, "The Legal Status of the Saudi-Kuwaiti Neutral Zone," *International and Comparative Law Quarterly* 15, no. 3 (July 1966).

88. H. St. J. Philby, in ibid.

89. Office of the Geographer, U.S. Department of State, "International Boundary Study: Kuwait-Saudi Arabia Boundary" (No. 103, September 15, 1970).

90. S. Hosni, "The Partition of the Neutral Zone," *American Journal of International Law* 60, no. 4 (October 1966).

91. "Physical and Social Geography (Kuwait)," *Europa World*.

92. S. Ciszuk, "Chevron Secures Saudi Extension to Long-Term Neutral Zone Oil Concession," *Global Insight*, September 11, 2008.

93. See the Chevron corporate website (www.chevron.com/countries/kuwait/) and www.sachevron.com/profile.

94. Ciszuk, "Chevron Secures Saudi Extension."

95. C. Baltimore, "Chevron Extends Agreement with Saudi Arabia," *Reuters*, September 10, 2008.

96. See the Chevron corporate website: www.chevron.com/countries/kuwait/.

97. "Japan's Oil Industry," *SourceWatch*, August 11, 2008, http://www.sourcewatch .org/index.php?title=Japan<#213>s_oil_industry.

98. Energy Information Agency, "Kuwait" (Country Analysis Briefs, November 2006).

Chapter 5

1. R. Wigglesworth and S. Kennedy, "Norway Provides Model on How to Manage Oil Revenue," *International Herald Tribune*, 2007.

2. S. Tsalik, R. E. Ebel, C.R. Watch, "Caspian Oil Windfalls: Who Will Benefit?" (Open Society Institute, Central Eurasia Project, 2003).

3. Clive Archer, "Economy (Norway)," *Europa World*, retrieved January 21, 2009, from http://www.europaworld.com/entry/no.ec.

4. U. G. O. Fasano, "Review of the Experience with Oil Stabilization and Savings Funds in Selected Countries" (International Monetary Fund Working Paper 00/112, 2000).

5. Juliette Bennett, "Conflict Prevention and Revenue-Sharing Regimes," *UN Global Compact* (2002): 25.

6. International Monetary Fund, "Guide on Resource Revenue Transparency" (2007).

7. See the Norges Bank website: http://www.norges-bank.no/templates/article ____69365.aspx.

8. See the Norwegian Ministry of Finance website: http://www.regjeringen.no/en/ dep/fin/Selected-topics/The-Government-Pension-Fund/performance-of-the-gov ernment-pension-fu.html?id=434514.

9. Tsalik et al., "Caspian Oil Windfalls," 38. Also see the Norges Bank website: http://www.norges-bank.no/templates/article____69365.aspx.

10. Bennett, "Conflict Prevention," 25.

11. Fasano, "Review of the Experience with Oil Stabilization," 13.

12. Tsalik et al., "Caspian Oil Windfalls," 23.

13. See the Alaska Permanent Fund website: http://www.apfc.org/home/Content /home/index.cfm.

14. Tsalik et al., "Caspian Oil Windfalls," 24.

15. Ibid., 22.

16. International Monetary Fund, "Guide on Resource Revenue Transparency," 51.

17. Several have argued that De Beers' control of the diamond supply has resulted in more stable prices, but to the extent that Botswana has no such control itself, the vulnerability to price shocks remains, if only in theory.

18. Bank of Botswana, "Annual Report," http://www.bankofbotswana.bw/files/attachments/section22.pdf.

19. See the Sovereign Wealth Fund Institute website: http://www.swfinstitute.org/fund/pula.php.

20. International Monetary Fund, "Guide on Resource Revenue Transparency," 51.

21. M. Sarraf and M. Jiwanji, *Beating the Resource Curse: The Case of Botswana* (Washington, D.C.: World Bank Environment Department, 2001).

22. Paul Stevens and Evelyn Dietsche, "Resource Curse: An Analysis of Causes, Experiences and Possible Ways Forward," *Energy Policy* 36, no. 1 (2008): 56–65; A. Iimi, "Did Botswana Escape from the Resource Curse?" (International Monetary Fund Working Paper 06/138, 2006); E. Weinthal and P. J. Luong, "Combating the Resource Curse: An Alternative Solution to Managing Mineral Wealth," *Perspectives on Politics* 4, no. 1 (2006): 35–53.

23. The Kuwaiti dinar is pegged to a currency index, which eliminates the need to use the General Reserve Fund to stabilize the currency.

24. Fasano, "Review of the Experience with Oil Stabilization," 15.

25. "Economic Affairs (Kuwait)," *Europa World*, retrieved January 22, 2009, from http://www.europaworld.com/entry/kw.is.49.

26. Fasano, "Review of the Experience with Oil Stabilization," 15.

27. Tsalik et al., "Caspian Oil Windfalls," 44.

28. J. Devlin and S. Titman, "Managing Oil Price Risk in Developing Countries," *World Bank Research Observer* 19, no. 1 (2004): 119–139.

29. Ibid., 129.

30. Tsalik et al., "Caspian Oil Windfalls," 45.

31. Shirin Akiner, "Economy (Kazakhstan)," *Europa World*, retrieved January 21, 2009, from http://www.europaworld.com/entry/kz.econ.

32. Tsalik et al., "Caspian Oil Windfalls," 145–152.

33. Akiner, "Economy (Kazakhstan)."

Chapter 6

1. This case was originally written by David Howell and Sarah Olmstead.

2. R. O. Collins, *The Nile* (New Haven, Conn.: Yale University Press, 2002).

3. Overall, the Blue Nile, which barely crosses the territory of southern Sudan, contributes 80 to 90 percent of the flow. During the dry season, however, the White may compose 70 to 90 percent. That is because the Blue varies by as much as a factor of 50 from wet season to dry—from 113 m³/s (4,000 cu ft/s) to 5,663 m³/s (200,000 cu ft/s).

4. M. T. Klare, *Resource Wars* (New York: Macmillan, 2002).

5. Aaron T. Wolf and Joshua T. Newton, "Case Study of Transboundary Dispute Resolution: The Nile Waters Agreement" (Oregon State University, 2007).

6. P. P. Howell and J. A. Allan, *The Nile* (Cambridge: Cambridge University Press, 1994).

7. I. H. Abdalla, "The 1959 Nile Waters Agreement in Sudanese-Egyptian Relations," *Middle Eastern Studies* 7, no. 3 (1971): 329–341.

8. Wolf and Newton, "Case Study of Transboundary Dispute Resolution: The Nile Waters Agreement."

9. A. Swain, "Ethiopia, the Sudan, and Egypt: The Nile River Dispute," *Journal of Modern African Studies* 35, no. 4 (1997): 675–694.

10. Ibid.

11. M. Hefny and S. Amer, "Egypt and the Nile Basin," *Aquatic Sciences* 67, no. 1 (2005): 42–50.

12. Ibid.

13. S. E. Amer, Y. Arsano, A. El-Battahani, O. El-Tom Hamad, Magdy Abd El-MoenimHefny, I. Tamrat, and S. A. Mason, "Sustainable Development and International Cooperation in the Eastern Nile Basin," *Aquatic Sciences* 67, no. 1 (2005): 3–14.

14. O. Hamad and A. El-Battahani, "Sudan and the Nile Basin," *Aquatic Sciences* 67, no. 1 (2005): 28–41.

15. Y. Arsano and I. Tamrat, "Ethiopia and the Eastern Nile Basin," *Aquatic Sciences* 67, no. 1 (2005): 15–27.

16. A. Swain, "Mission Not Yet Accomplished: Managing Water Resources in the Nile River Basin," *Journal of International Affairs* 61, no. 2 (2008): 201–214.

17. Aaron T. Wolf, "Criteria for Equitable Allocations: The Heart of International Water Conflict," *Natural Resources Forum* 23, no. 1 (1999): 3–30.

18. M. El-Fadel, Y. El-Sayegh, K. El-Fadl, and D. Khorbotly, "The Nile River Basin: A Case Study in Surface Water Conflict Resolution," *Journal of Natural Resources and Life Sciences Education* 23 (2003): 107–117.

19. This case was originally written by David Howell and Sarah Olmstead.

20. Aaron T. Wolf and Joshua T. Newton, "Case Study of Transboundary Dispute Resolution: The Indus Water Treaty" (Oregon State University, 2008).

21. Ibid.

22. U. Z. Alam, "Questioning the Water Wars Rationale: A Case Study of the Indus Waters Treaty," *Geographical Journal* 168, no. 4 (2002): 341–353.

23. Subrahmanyam Sridhar, "The Indus Water Treaty," *Security Research Review* 1, no. 3 (2005).

24. S. Jain, P. Agarwal, and V. Singh, *Hydrology and Water Resources of India* (Dordrecht, Netherlands, Springer, 2007), 1035–1064.

25. M. Miner, G. Patankar, S. Gamkhar, and D. J. Eaton, "Water Sharing Between India and Pakistan: A Critical Evaluation of the Indus Water Treaty," *International Water* 34, no. 2 (2009): 204–216.

26. C. D. Thatte, "Indus Waters and the 1960 Treaty Between India and Pakistan," in *Management of Transboundary Rivers and Lakes*, ed. O.Varis, C. Tortajada, and A. Biswas (Berlin: Springer, 2008), 165–206.

27. S. Jain, P. Agarwal, and V. Singh, *Hydrology and Water Resources of India* ((Dordrecht, Netherlands: Springer, 2007)2007), 473–511.

28. Wolf, "Criteria for Equitable Allocations."

29. This case was originally written by Sarah Olmstead.

30. Aaron T. Wolf and Joshua T. Newton, "The Jordan River—Johnston Negotiations 1953–1955: Yarmuk Mediations 1980s" (Oregon State University, Transboundary Freshwater Dispute Database, 2007), available at http://www.transboundarywaters .orst.edu/.

31. Ibid.

32. Ibid.

33. A. Jägerskog, "Why States Cooperate over Shared Water: The Water Negotiations in the Jordan River Basin" (Linköping University Studies in Arts and Science 281, 2003).

34. Ibid.

35. H. I. Shuval, "Are the Conflicts Between Israel and Her Neighbors over the Waters of the Jordan River Basin an Obstacle to Peace? Israel-Syria and a Case Study," *Water, Air, and Soil Pollution* 123 (2000): 605–630.

36. This case was originally written by Sarah Outcault.

37. Jeffrey W. Jacobs, "Mekong Committee History and Lessons for River Basin Development," *Geographical Journal* 161, no. 2 (July 1995): 135–148.

38. Vietnam National Mekong Committee, "The Mekong River Commission: General Information," retrieved July 5, 2009, from http://www.vnmc.gov.vn/newsdetail .asp?NewsId=113&CatId=41&lang=EN.

39. Jacobs, "Mekong Committee History."

40. Vietnam National Mekong Committee, "Mekong River Commission."

41. Aaron T. Wolf and Joshua T. Newton, "Case Study of Transboundary Dispute Resolution: The Mekong Committee," retrieved July 5, 2009, from http://www.trans boundarywaters.orst.edu/research/case_studies/Mekong_New.htm.

42. Oregon State University, "Transboundary Freshwater Dispute Database" (2007), available at http://www.transboundarywaters.orst.edu/.

43. Jacobs, "Mekong Committee History."

Chapter 7

1. Ana Stanic, "Financial Aspects of State Succession: The Case of Yugoslavia," *European Journal of International Law* 12, no. 4 (2001): 751–779, available at http://ejil .oxfordjournals.org/cgi/reprint/12/4/751.pdf.

2. This case was originally written by Sarah Outcault.

3. David A. Dyker, "Economy (Montenegro)," *Europa World*.

4. Florian Bieber, "History (Montenegro)," *Europa World*.

5. Commission of the European Communities, "Establishing a Separate Liability of Montenegro and Reducing Proportionately the Liability of Serbia with Regard to

the Long-Term Loans Granted by the Community of the State Union of Serbia and Montenegro" (April 29, 2008), 2.

6. Constitutional Charter of the State Union of Serbia and Montenegro, Article 60 (Serbia and Montenegro, 2003), available at http://www.mfa.gov.yu/Facts/const_scg.pdf.

7. Iulia Serafimescu, "Montenegro, One Year and One Constitution Later," *Sphere of Politics (SferaPoliticii)* (2008): 87.

8. "Recent History (Montenegro)," *Europa World*.

9. Canas Vitalino, "Independent Montenegro: Early Assessment and Prospects for Euro-Atlantic Integration" (NATO Parliamentary Assembly, 2007), available at http://www.nato-pa.int/Default.asp?SHORTCUT=1162.

10. David A. Dyker, "Economy (Montenegro)," *Europa World*.

11. Gennady Pilch and Adam Shayne, "Montenegro Joins the World Bank as Newest Member" (World Bank, April 23, 2007).

12. TV Crna Gora, *Podgorica*, July 10, 2006.

13. Dyker, "Economy (Montenegro)."

14. National Bank of Serbia, "Relations with the International Monetary Fund," available at http://www.nbs.yu/export/internet/english/40/40_1/index.html.

15. Vitalino, "Independent Montenegro."

16. TV Crna Gora, *Podgorica*.

17. This case was originally written by Tewodaj Mengistu.

18. M. Z. Bookman, "War and Peace: The Divergent Breakups of Yugoslavia and Czechoslovakia," *Journal of Peace Research* 21, no. 2 (1994): 174–187; and P. R. Williams, "State Succession and the International Financial Institutions: Political Criteria v. Protection of Outside Financial Obligation," *International and Comparative Law Quarterly* 43, no. 4 (1994): 776–808.

19. A. Ryder, "History (Slovakia)," *Europa World*, retrieved June 24, 2009, from http://www.europaworld.com/entry/sk.hi.

20. "Czechs and Slovaks Plan Velvet Divorce," *St. Petersburg Times*, June 20, 1992; "Recent History (The Czech Republic)," *Europa World*, retrieved June 24, 2009, from http://www.europaworld.com/entry/cz.is.4.

21. S. Engelberg, "Split Is Prepared by Czechoslovaks," *New York Times*, June 21, 1992.

22. A 1990 poll found that most Czechoslovaks were opposed to the dissolution, with only 16 percent in favor of the dissolution.

23. Bookman, "War and Peace."

24. Two previous attempts, one in early October and the other in mid-November, to pass the law permitting the dissolution of the federation had failed due to opposition from certain Slovak quarters.

25. "Recent History (The Czech Republic)."

26. Bookman, "War and Peace."

27. Ibid.

28. This is computed on the basis of the official exchange rate in the early 1990s, which was at KCS 30 for US$1.

29. "Federal Government Approves Bill on the Division of Federation's Assets. Summary of World Broadcasts," BBC, November 7, 1992.

30. "Further Report on Army Asset Division: Army CGS Explains Agreement on Division of Air Force and Anti-Air Defence. Summary of World Broadcasts," BBC, October 2, 1992.

31. "Federal Government Approves Bill."

32. Williams, "State Succession and the International Financial Institutions."

33. D. Rowlands, "International Aspects of the Division of Debt Under Secession: The Case of Quebec and Canada," *Canadian Public Policy* 23, no. 1 (1994); Bookman, "War and Peace."

34. Williams, "State Succession and the International Financial Institutions."

35. Ibid.; "Czechoslovakia in Brief: Czech and Slovak Republics Admitted as Regular Members from 1st January. Summary of World Broadcasts," BBC, December 15, 1992.

36. "Czech Republic," *CIA World Factbook*, retrieved June 28, 2009, from https://www.cia.gov/library/publications/the-world-factbook/geos/EZ.html; "Slovakia," *CIA World Factbook, retrieved* June 28, 2009, from https://www.cia.gov/library/publica tions/the-world-factbook/geos/LO.html.

37. A. Ryan, "History (Slovakia)," *Europa World*; "Recent History (The Czech Republic)."

38. This case was originally written by Tewodaj Mengistu.

39. The new republics are as follows: the Baltic states Estonia, Latvia, and Lithuania; the Central Asian states of Tajikistan, Uzbekistan, Turkmenistan, Kazakhstan, and Kyrgyzstan; the Transcaucasus states of Armenia, Azerbaijan, and Georgia; and the Slavic states Belarus, Moldova, Ukraine, and the Russian Federation, the latter considered legally as the continuing state of the Soviet Union.

40. R. Mullerson, "The Continuity and Succession of States, by Reference to the Former USSR and Yugoslavia," *International and Comparative Law Quarterly* 42, no. 3 (1993): 473–493.

41. "Jointly and severally responsible" means that even in the event that one country fails to make a payment, the other countries are still responsible for the share of nonpaid debt.

42. Public International Law and Policy Group, "State Succession to the Immovable Assets of Former Yugoslavia" (International Crisis Group (ICG) Bosnia Report 20, 1997).

43. B. V. Christensen, *The Russian Federation in Transition: External Developments* (Washington, D.C.: International Monetary Fund, 1994); Mullerson, "Continuity and Succession of States."

44. E. Hasani, "The Evolution of the Succession Process in the Former Yugoslavia," *Thomas Jefferson Law Review* 29 (2006): 111.

45. Mullerson, "Continuity and Succession of States."

46. Ibid.

47. Ibid.

48. Ibid.

49. The members of the G7 include Canada, France, Germany, Italy, Japan, the United Kingdom, and the United States.

50. Baltic states were present but only as observer states.

51. Christensen, *Russian Federation in Transition*; Mullerson, "Continuity and Succession of States."

52. Rowlands, "International Aspects of the Division of Debt Under Secession"; A. Santos, "Debt Crisis in Russia: The Road from Default to Sustainability," in *Russia Rebounds*, ed. D. Owens and D. O. Robinson (Washington, D.C.: International Monetary Fund, 2003); "Russia Against Negotiating with Ukraine over USSR Debt," *RIA Novosti*, April 6, 2006, retrieved July 22, 2009, from http://en.rian.ru/russia/20060406 /45398182.html; Mullerson, "Continuity and Succession of States."

53. Christensen, *Russian Federation in Transition*; Santos, A. 2003.

54. Rowlands, "International Aspects of the Division of Debt Under Secession"; Mullerson, "Continuity and Succession of States."

55. This case was originally written by Tewodaj Mengistu.

56. The Marxist regime in Ethiopia, called the Derg, was led by Mengistu Haile Mariam, who came into power through a coup d'état in 1974.

57. These include representatives from the Derg regime as well as from the Oromo Liberation Front (OLF), a resistance movement that had transformed itself to a political party upon the fall of the Derg.

58. Greg Cameron, Manickam Venkataraman, Patrick Gilkes, and Sarah Vaughan, "Recent History (Ethiopia)," *Europa World*, retrieved July 15, 2009, from http://www .europaworld.com/entry/et.hi.

59. Greg Cameron, Alan Rake, and Sara Rich Dorman, "Economy (Eritrea)," *Europa World*, retrieved July 15, 2009, from http://www.europaworld.com/entry/er.ec.

60. Leenco Lata, ed., *The Search for Peace: The Conflict Between Ethiopia and Eritrea* (Oslo: Fafo, 2007).

61. J. Abbink, "Briefing: The Eritrean-Ethiopian Border Dispute," *African Affairs* 97 (1998): 551–565.

62. Lata, *Search for Peace*.

63. In 1997, Birr 1.2 billion was equivalent to approximately US$182.9 million.

64. Abbink, "Briefing."

65. X. Rice, "Annan Warns of Another War Between Ethiopia and Eritrea," *Guardian*, October 31, 2006, retrieved July 16, 2009, from http://www.guardian.co.uk /world/2006/oct/31/ethiopia.

Chapter 8

1. Cameron et al., "Recent History (Ethiopia)"; Abbink, "Briefing."

2. J. Pehe, "Czechs and Slovaks Define Postdivorce Relations," *RFE/RL Research Report* 1, no. 45 (1992); J. Fidrmuc, J. Horvath, and J. Fidrmuc, "Stability of Monetary

Unions: Lessons from the Break-Up of Czechoslovakia" (Tilburg University, Center for Economic Research Discussion Paper 9874, 1998).

3. Ryder, "History (Slovakia)."

4. Fidrmuc, Horvath, and Fidrmuc, "Stability of Monetary Unions."

5. Ibid.

6. Ibid.

7. D. Auers, "Economy (Latvia)," *Europa World*, retrieved October 26, 2009, from http://www.europaworld.com/entry/lv.ec.

8. "Estonia Leads the Way in Reform Success," *Herald Sun*, July 12, 1993.

9. This case was originally written by Tewodaj Mengistu.

10. J. Rock, "Relief and Rehabilitation in Eritrea," *Third World Quarterly* 20, no. 1 (1999): 129–142.

11. Seigniorage revenue is the direct revenue associated with issuing currency. Essentially it is the difference between the face value of the printed currency and the cost of producing and distributing it.

12. G. Hanson, "Building New States: Lessons from Eritrea" (UNU/IWIDER Discussion Paper 2001).

13. This was at the time equivalent to US$305.

14. Cameron et al., "Recent History (Ethiopia)"; Abbink, "Briefing."

15. L. Santoro, "At the Root of an Odd African War: Money," *Christian Monitor* (Asmara), June 22, 1998.

16. Hanson, "Building New States."

17. In 1991, an Ethiopian resistance group, the Tigray People's Liberation Front (TPLF), aided by the Eritrean Popular Liberation Forces (EPLF), toppled the Marxist regime in Ethiopia that had been in power since 1974. The TPLF then formed the transitional government of Ethiopia under the Ethiopian People's Revolutionary Democratic Front (EPRDF).

18. M. Venkataraman, "Ethiopia-Eritrea Ties: Past, Present and Future," *African Quarterly* 47, no. 1 (2007): 52–61.

19. Ibid.

20. Rock, "Relief and Rehabilitation."

21. To that effect, Eritrean authorities privatized state-owned enterprises and implemented policies targeted toward fiscal reforms and deregulation.

22. "Africa's Forgotten War: Addis Ababa and Asmara," *Economist*, May 8, 1999.

23. Hanson, "Building New States."

24. R. Cornwell, "Ethiopia and Eritrea: Fratricidal Conflict in the Horn," *Africa Security Review* 7, no. 5 (1998).

25. Abbink, "Briefing."

26. When Eritrea gained independence in 1993, a border commission was set up to determine the borders between the two countries.

27. Cornwell, "Ethiopia and Eritrea."

28. Abbink, "Briefing."

29. Rice, "Annan Warns of Another War."

30. A. Yamauchi, "Fiscal Sustainability—The Case of Eritrea" (International Monetary Fund Working Paper WP/04/7, 2004).

31. This case was originally prepared by Tewodaj Mengistu.

32. Pehe, "Czechs and Slovaks"; Fidrmuc, Horvath, and Fidrmuc, "Stability of Monetary Unions."

33. Fidrmuc, Horvath, and Fidrmuc, "Stability of Monetary Unions."

34. Ryder, "History (Slovakia)."

35. Engelberg, "Split Is Prepared by Czechoslovaks."

36. Other reasons for breakup included differences in language, culture, and traditions.

37. "Recent History (The Czech Republic)," *Europa World*, retrieved June 24, 2009, from http://www.europaworld.com/entry/cz.is.4.

38. Bookman, "War and Peace."

39. It was expected that the economic costs of the split would be higher for Slovakia, which had benefitted from years of transfers from Czech lands during the communist era in the form of redistribution of tax revenues. For 1992, estimates of the amount of transfers range from 4 to 8 percent of the Slovak GDP, while for 1991 they range from 1.5 to 2.6 percent of the Slovak GDP (Fidrmuc, Horvath, and Fidrmuc, "Stability of Monetary Unions").

40. A. Capek and G. Sazama, "Czech and Slovak Economic Relations," *Europe-Asia Studies* 45, no. 2 (1992): 211–235.

41. Fidrmuc, Horvath, and Fidrmuc, "Stability of Monetary Unions."

42. Ibid.

43. Ibid.

44. Ibid.

45. R. Vintrová, "Lessons from the Czech and Slovak Economies Split," *Prague Economics Papers* 1 (2009); P. Pavlínek, "Regional Development and the Disintegration of Czechoslovakia," *Geoforum* 26, no. 4 (1995): 351–372.

46. This case was originally written by Tewodaj Mengistu.

47. In the Soviet Union, the Supreme Soviets were the legislative bodies of each of the Soviet republics and were subordinate to the Supreme Soviet of the Soviet Union. Bank of Latvia, "History of the Bank of Latvia," retrieved October 30, 2009, from http://www.bank.lv/eng/main/all/lvbank/uuv/vesture/.

48. A managed float regime is one where the currency is allowed to vary against other currencies but the central bank intervenes on occasion by selling and buying currencies in order to maintain control over the exchange rate. L. Korhonen, "Currency Boards in the Baltics: What Have We Learnt?" (Bank of Finland, Institute for Economies in Transition, 1999).

49. Auers, "Economy (Latvia)."

50. Bank of Latvia, "History of the Bank of Latvia."

51. N. Mygind, "Different Paths of Transition in the Baltics" (Copenhagen School of Business, Center for East European Studies, 1997); A. Vanags, "Macroeconomic Stabilization and Central Bank Policy in Latvia," *Communist Economies and Economic Transformation* 10, no. 2 (1998); T. Greenes, "The Economic Transition in Baltic Countries," *Journal of Baltic Studies* 28, no. 1 (1997); Korhonen, "Currency Boards in the Baltics."

52. Vanags, "Macroeconomic Stabilization."

53. Ibid.

54. Korhonen, "Currency Boards in the Baltics."

55. J. Dreifelds, *Latvia in Transition* (Cambridge: Cambridge University Press, 1996).

56. A. Fleming, L. Chu, and M. Bakker, "The Baltics—Banking Crisis Observed" (World Bank, Europe and Central Asia Department, Policy Research Working Paper 1647, 1999).

57. Fleming, Chu, and Bakker, "The Baltics"; S. Timewell, "Latvia: The Brutal Truth—A Radical Shakeout Is Promised After the Scandal Surrounding the Collapsed Banka Baltija," *The Banker*, August 1, 1995; Auers, "Economy (Latvia)."

58. Initially, mostly companies withdrew their deposits, as households were less aware of the gravity of the problems within the banking sector.

59. Auers, "Economy (Latvia)."

60. Fleming, Chu, and Bakker, "The Baltics."

61. These amounts correspond respectively to US$1,000 and US$200.

62. Fleming, Chu, and Bakker, "The Baltics."

63. Ibid.

64. Greenes, "Economic Transition in Baltic Countries"; Auers, "Economy (Latvia)."

65. This is equivalent to going from US$174 million to US$865 million.

66. M. Bivens, "Russians Pour Cash into Banks of Latvia," *Moscow Times*, March 11, 1994; World Bank, "World Development Indicators" (World Bank, 2008).

67. Auers, "Economy (Latvia)"; World Bank, "World Development Indicators."

68. This case was originally written by Tewodaj Mengistu.

69. W. Iwaskiw, ed., "Economic Reform History," in *Estonia: A Country Study* (Washington, D.C.: Library of Congress, 2005).

70. A. Reynolds, "Monetary Reform in Russia: The Case for Gold," *Cato Journal* 12, no. 3 (1993); A. Bennett, "The Operation of the Estonian Currency Board," *IMF Staff Papers* 40 (1993): 451–470.

71. "Estonia Leads the Way in Reform Success."

72. A. Bridge, "Baltic Republics Fly High After Breaking with the Ruble: Kroon, Lat and Litras—New Names in the World of International Currency," *Independent*, July 26, 1993.

73. In the mid-1980s, for example, 90 percent of the Estonian economy was controlled by Moscow.

74. Iwaskiw, "Economic Reform History."

75. More accurately, the Bank of Estonia was reinstated after fifty years of inactivity. Indeed, while the Bank of Estonia existed and was fully operational before 1939, all of its activities were seized when Estonia was annexed into the Soviet Union.

76. Residents were allowed to exchange up to fifteen hundred rubles in cash at a rate of ten to one, while any excess cash was exchanged at the rate of fifty to one. All ruble-denominated accounts were exchanged at the ten-to-one exchange rate.

77. Reynolds, "Monetary Reform in Russia"; Bridge, "Baltic Republics Fly High."

78. Bennett, "Operation of the Estonian Currency Board."

79. Estonian Institute, "The National Currency of Estonia: The Estonian Kroon" (2002), retrieved October 9, 2009, from http://www.einst.ee/factsheets/factsheets_uus _kuju/the_national_currency_of_estonia_the_estonian_kroon.htm.

80. Estonian Institute, "National Currency of Estonia."

81. Ibid.; Bennett, "Operation of the Estonian Currency Board."

82. Bridge, "Baltic Republics Fly High."

BIBLIOGRAPHY

Abbink, J. "Briefing: The Eritrean-Ethiopian Border Dispute." *African Affairs* 97 (1998): 551–565.

Abdalla, I. H. "The 1959 Nile Waters Agreement in Sudanese-Egyptian Relations." *Middle Eastern Studies* 7, no. 3 (1971): 329–341.

Abdulkarim A. Ato, Guleid and Ato Kibre Jimmerra Kasa. "Improving Pastoral Welfare in Ethiopia." Research Brief 04-04-PARIMA. Global Livestock Collaborative Research Support Program, 2004.

"Abkhaz Official: Confidence-Building Is Needed for IDP Return." *Civil Georgia* (Tbilisi), February 17, 2007.

"Africa's Forgotten War: Addis Ababa and Asmara." *Economist,* May 8, 1999.

African Union. "Declaration on the African Union Border Programme and Its Implementation Modalities as Adopted by the Conference of African Ministers in Charge of Border Issues, Held in Addis Ababa (Ethiopia), 7 June 2007." Available at http://www.africa-union.org/root/au/publications/PSC/Border%20Issues.pdf.

Agreement on Security and Related Matters Between the Ministries of Internal Affairs of the Governments of Ethiopia and Eritrea (Ethiopia, Eritrea, 1993). Referenced in Human Rights Watch, *Eritrea & Ethiopia, The Horn of Africa War: Mass Expulsions and the Nationality Issue (June 1998–April 2002),* vol. 15 (January 2003). Available at http://www.hrw.org/reports/2003/ethioerit0103/ethioerit0103.pdf.

Agyei, John and Ezekiel Clottey. "Operationalizing ECOWAS Protocol on Free Movement of People Among the Member States." 2007. Available at http://www.imi.ox .ac.uk/pdfs/CLOTTEY%20and%20AGYEI.pdf.

Ahe, Abdurahman. "Cross-Border Livestock Trade and Small Arms and Conflict in Pastoral Areas in the Horn of Africa." Presentation to Survival of the Commons: Mounting Challenges and New Realities, the Eleventh Conference of the International Association for the Study of Common Property, June 19–23, 2006. Available at http://dlc.dlib.indiana.edu/dlc/handle/10535/2262 (as of August 15, 2013).

Ahrén, Mattias. "Indigenous Peoples' Culture, Customs, and Traditions and Customary Law—The Saami People's Perspective." *Arizona Journal of International and Comparative Law* 21, no. 1 (2004): 73, 85, 87–88, 94.

Akiner, Shirin. "Economy (Kazakhstan)." *Europa World.* Retrieved January 21, 2009, from http://www.europaworld.com/entry/kz.econ.

Alam, U. Z. "Questioning the Water Wars Rationale: A Case Study of the Indus Waters Treaty." *Geographical Journal* 168, no. 4 (2002): 341–353.

Amer, S. E., Y. Arsano, A. El-Battahani, O. El-Tom Hamad, Magdy Abd El-MoenimHefny, I. Tamrat, and S. A. Mason. "Sustainable Development and International Cooperation in the Eastern Nile Basin." *Aquatic Sciences* 67, no. 1 (2005): 3–14.

Archer, Clive. "Economy (Norway)." *Europa World*. Retrieved January 21, 2009, from http://www.europaworld.com/entry/no.ec.

Arsano, Y. and I. Tamrat. "Ethiopia and the Eastern Nile Basin." *Aquatic Sciences* 67, no. 1 (2005): 15–27.

Auers, D. "Economy (Latvia)." *Europa World*. Retrieved October 26, 2009, from http://www.europaworld.com/entry/lv.ec.

Austin, Megan S. "A Culture Divided by the United States–Mexico Border: The Tohono O'odham Claim for Border Crossing Rights." *Arizona Journal of International and Comparative Law* 8 (1991): 97–116.

"Australia." *Economic Geography* 80, no. 1 (January 2004): 1–22.

"Australia and East Timor: Fair Dinkum." *Economist*, May 21, 2005, 70.

Baltimore, C. "Chevron Extends Agreement with Saudi Arabia." *Reuters*, September 10, 2008.

Bank of Botswana. "Annual Report," available at http://www.bankofbotswana.bw/index.php/content/2009110614010-annual-report.

Bank of Latvia. "History of the Bank of Latvia." Retrieved October 30, 2009, from http://www.bank.lv/eng/main/all/lvbank/uuv/vesture/.

Bartkus, Viva Ona. *The Dynamics of Secession*. Cambridge: Cambridge University Press, 1999.

Beijer, Mai and Staffan Bolin. "Curriculum Development for Social Inclusion in Sweden." *Prospects* 33, no. 1 (March 2003): 51–62

Bennett, A. "The Operation of the Estonian Currency Board." *IMF Staff Papers* 40 (1993): 451–470.

Bennett, James C. *An Anglosphere Primer,* available at http://explorersfoundation.org/archive/anglosphere_primer.pdf.

Bennett, Juliette. "Conflict Prevention and Revenue-Sharing Regimes." *UN Global Compact* (2002): 25. Available at http://www.unglobalcompact.org/docs/issues_doc/Peace_and_Business/RevenueSharingRegimes.pdf (as of August 12, 2013).

Bieber, Florian. "History (Montenegro)." *Europa World*. Available at http://www.europaworld.com/entry/me.hi?ssid=888867155&hit=3 (as of August 19, 2013).

Bivens, M. "Russians Pour Cash into Banks of Latvia." *Moscow Times*, March 11, 1994.

Bookman, M. Z. "War and Peace: The Divergent Breakups of Yugoslavia and Czechoslovakia." *Journal of Peace Research* 21, no. 2 (1994): 174–187.

Boutros-Ghali, Boutros. "Annual Report of the Secretary-General on the Work of the Organization." United Nations, 1995.

"Breaking the Bank: Chad." *Economist*, September 27, 2008.

Bridge, A. "Baltic Republics Fly High After Breaking with the Ruble: Kroon, Lat and Litras—New Names in the World of International Currency." *Independent*, July 26, 1993.

"British Empire: British India in 1947." *Britannica Student Encyclopedia*, 2009. Retrieved June 7, 2009, from http://student.britannica.com/comptons/art-1965/British-India -in-1947-showing-major-administrative-divisions-the-distribution.

Brubaker, W. R. "Citizenship Struggles in Soviet Successor States." *International Migration Review* 26, no. 2 (1992): 269–291

———. "Migration and Ethnic Unmixing in Europe." *International Migration Review* 32, no. 4 (1998): 1047–1065.

Cameron, Greg, Alan Rake, and Sara Rich Dorman. "Economy (Eritrea)." *Europa World*. Retrieved July 15, 2009, from http://www.europaworld.com/entry/er.ec.

Cameron, Greg, Manickam Venkataraman, Patrick Gilkes, and Sarah Vaughan. "Recent History (Ethiopia)." *Europa World*. Retrieved July 15, 2009, from http://www .europaworld.com/entry/et.hi.

Capek, A. and G. Sazama. "Czech and Slovak Economic Relations." *Europe-Asia Studies* 45, no. 2 (1992): 211–235.

Castella, Leah. "The United States Border: A Barrier to Cultural Survival." *Texas Journal on Civil Liberties & Civil Rights* 5 (2000): 191.

Charles, Joseph. "The Jay Treaty: The Origins of the American Party System." *William and Mary Quarterly* 12, no. 4 (1955): 581.

Chester, L. "Commentary and Analysis: 'The 1947 Partition: Drawing the Indo-Pakistani Border.'" *American Diplomacy*. Retrieved June 10, 2009, from http://www.unc .edu/depts/diplomat/archives_roll/2002_01-03/chester_partition/chester_partition .html.

Christensen, B. V. *The Russian Federation in Transition: External Developments*. Washington, D.C.: International Monetary Fund, 1994.

Ciszuk, S. "Chevron Secures Saudi Extension to Long-Term Neutral Zone Oil Concession." *Global Insight*, September 11, 2008.

Collins, R. O. *The Nile*. New Haven, Conn.: Yale University Press, 2002.

Commission of the European Communities. "Bosnia and Herzegovina 2008 Progress Report." Staff Working Document 5/11/08.

———. "Establishing a Separate Liability of Montenegro and Reducing Proportionately the Liability of Serbia with Regard to the Long-Term Loans Granted by the Community of the State Union of Serbia and Montenegro." April 29, 2008.

Constitutional Charter of the State Union of Serbia and Montenegro. Article 60. Serbia and Montenegro, 2003. Available at http://www.mfa.gov.yu/Facts/const_scg .pdf.

Cornwell, R. "Ethiopia and Eritrea: Fratricidal Conflict in the Horn." *Africa Security Review* 7, no. 5 (1998): 62–69.

Crib, Robert. "History (Timor-Leste). *Europa World.* Available at http://www.europa world.com/entry/tp.hi?ssid=98184664&hit=2 (as of August 19, 2013).

"Czech Republic." *CIA World Factbook.* Retrieved from https://www.cia.gov/library /publications/the-world-factbook/geos/ez.html (as of August 13, 2013).

"Czechoslovakia in Brief: Czech and Slovak Republics Admitted as Regular Members from 1st January. Summary of World Broadcasts." BBC, December 15, 1992.

"Czechs and Slovaks Plan Velvet Divorce." *St. Petersburg Times,* June 20, 1992.

David, B. Carter and H. E. Goemans. "The Making of the Territorial Order: New Borders and the Emergence of Interstate Conflict." Unpublished paper, August 22, 2010.

"Delhi Pact." *Encyclopedia Britannica,* 2009. Retrieved June 11, 2009, from http:// www.search.eb.com/eb/article-9029821.

Department of Foreign Affairs and Trade, Government of Australia. "Timor Sea Treaty." April 2003. http://www.austlii.edu.au/au/other/dfat/treaties/2003/13.

Department of Trade and Industry. "First Strike for UK Norway Deal." July 1, 2005.

———. "UK and Norway Approve Two New North Sea Developments." April 7, 2005.

Desta, Solomon and D. Layne Coppock. "Pastoralism Under Pressure: Tracking System Change in Southern Ethiopia." *Human Ecology* 32, no. 4 (August 2004): 465–486.

Devlin, J. and S. Titman. "Managing Oil Price Risk in Developing Countries." *World Bank Research Observer* 19, no. 1 (2004): 119–139.

Di Iorio, William R. "Mending Fences: The Fractured Relationship Between Native American Tribes and the Federal Government and Its Negative Impact on Border Security." *Syracuse Law Review* 57, no. 2 (2007): 407.

Dreifelds, J. *Latvia in Transition.* Cambridge: Cambridge University Press, 1996.

Dyker, David A. "Economy (Montenegro)." *Europa World.* Available at http://www .europaworld.com/entry/me.ec?ssid=14352035&hit=2 (as of August 19, 2013).

"Economic Affairs (Kuwait)." *Europa World.* Retrieved January 22, 2009, from http:// www.europaworld.com/entry/kw.is.49.

Economic Community of West African States. "Executive Secretary's Annual Report, Chapter 2: Implementation of the Community Work Programme." 2000. http:// www.comm.ecowas.int/sec/index.php?id=es-rep2000-3-2&lang=en.

Eilperin, Juliet. "Norway Debates the Promise, Costs of New Drilling; Oil Means More Revenue But More Climate Change." *Washington Post,* August 21, 2007, A08.

El-Fadel, M., Y. El-Sayegh, K. El-Fadl, and D. Khorbotly. "The Nile River Basin: A Case Study in Surface Water Conflict Resolution." *Journal of Natural Resources and Life Sciences Education* 23 (2003): 107–117.

Emizent, Kisangani and Vicki Hesli. "The Disposition to Secede: An Analysis of the Soviet Case." *Comparative Political Studies* 27 (January 1995): 493–536.

Energy Information Administration. "Chad and Cameroon." Country Analysis Briefs, January 2007.

Energy Information Agency. "Algeria." Country Analysis Briefs, March, 2007.

———. "Kuwait." Country Analysis Briefs, November 2006.

Engelberg, S. "Split Is Prepared by Czechoslovaks." *New York Times*, June 21, 1992.

Ente Nazionale Idrocarboni. "Annual Report." 2007. http://www.eni.it/en_IT/attach ments/publications/reports/reports-2007/2007-annual-report.pdf.

Esso Exploration and Production Chad Inc. "Chad-Cameroon Development Project—Project Update No. 24 Mid-Year Report 2008." Houston: Esso Exploration and Production Chad Inc., 2008.

Estes, Todd. "Shaping the Politics of Public Opinion: Federalists and the Jay Treaty Debate." *Journal of the Early Republic* 20, no. 3 (2000): 393–422.

"Estonia Leads the Way in Reform Success." *Herald Sun*, July 12, 1993.

Fasano, U. G. O. "Review of the Experience with Oil Stabilization and Savings Funds in Selected Countries." International Monetary Fund Working Paper 00/112, 2000.

"Federal Government Approves Bill on the Division of Federation's Assets. Summary of World Broadcasts." BBC, November 7, 1992.

Feodoroff, Pauliina and Rebecca Lawrence. "Sapmi—Finland." In *The Indigenous World*, 32–33. International Work Group for Indigenous Affairs, 2008.

Fewster, Joseph M. "The Jay Treaty and British Ship Seizures: The Martinique Cases." *William and Mary Quarterly* 45, no. 3 (1988): 426–452.

Fidrmuc, J., J. Horvath, and J. Fidrmuc. "Stability of Monetary Unions: Lessons from the Break-Up of Czechoslovakia." Tilburg University, Center for Economic Research Discussion Paper 9874, 1998.

Fleming, A., L. Chu, and M. Bakker. "The Baltics—Banking Crisis Observed." World Bank, Europe and Central Asia Department, Policy Research Working Paper 1647, 1999.

Flynn, M. *Migrant Resettlement in the Russian Federation: Reconstructing Homes and Homelands*. London: Anthem Press, 2004.

Forbes, B. C. "The Challenges of Modernity for Reindeer Management in Northern-most Europe." *Ecological Studies* 184 (2006): 11–26.

Forrest, Scott. "Territoriality and State-Sami Relations." Retrieved December 2008 from http://arcticcircle.uconn.edu/HistoryCulture/Sami/samisf.html.

"Framework Agreement Between the Government of the United Kingdom of Great Britain and Northern Ireland and the Government of the Kingdom of Norway Concerning Cross-Boundary Petroleum Co-operation—Oslo, April 4, 2005." Presented to Parliament by the Secretary of State for Foreign and Commonwealth Affairs by Command of Her Majesty, May 2006. London: Stationary Office, 2006.

Fratkin, Elliot and Robin Mearns. "Sustainability and Pastoral Livelihoods: Lessons from East African Maasai and Mongolia." *Human Organization* 62, no. 2 (2003): 112–122.

"Further Report on Army Asset Division: Army CGS Explains Agreement on Division of Air Force and Anti-Air Defence. Summary of World Broadcasts." BBC, October 2, 1992.

Ghoneimy, M. T. "The Legal Status of the Saudi-Kuwaiti Neutral Zone." *International and Comparative Law Quarterly* 15, no. 3 (July 1966): 690–717.

Greenes, T. "The Economic Transition in Baltic Countries." *Journal of Baltic Studies* 28, no. 1 (1997): 9–24.

Hale, Henry. "The Parade of Sovereignties: Testing Theories of Secession in the Soviet Setting." *British Journal of Political Science* 30, no. 1 (2000): 31–56.

Hamad, O. and A. El-Battahani. "Sudan and the Nile Basin." *Aquatic Sciences* 67, no. 1 (2005): 28–41.

Hansen, Greg. "Displacement and Return." *Accord* 7 (September 1999): 58–63.

Hansen, Lars Ivar. "The Sami Hunting Society in Transition: Approaches, Concepts and Context." *HistoriaFenno-Ugrica* I-1 (1996): 315–333.

Hanson, G. "Building New States: Lessons from Eritrea." UNU/IWIDER Discussion Paper, 2001.

Haque, C. E. "The Dilemma of Nationhood and Religion: A Survey and Critique of Studies on Population Displacement Resulting from the Partition of the Indian Subcontinent." *Journal of Refugee Studies* 8, no. 2 (1995): 186–209.

Hasani, E. "The Evolution of the Succession Process in the Former Yugoslavia." *Thomas Jefferson Law Review* 29 (2006): 111–150.

Hayes, M. H. "Algerian Gas to Europe: The Transmed Pipeline and Early Spanish Gas Import Projects." Stanford University, Program on Energy and Sustainable Development Working Paper 27, 2004.

Hechter, Michael. "The Dynamics of Secession." *Acta Sociologica* 35 (1992): 267–283.

Hefny, M. and S. Amer. "Egypt and the Nile Basin." *Aquatic Sciences* 67, no. 1 (2005): 42–50.

Heleniak, T. "Migration of the Russian Diaspora After the Breakup of the Soviet Union." *Journal of International Affairs* 57, no. 2 (2004): 99–116.

Horowitz, Donald. *Ethnic Groups in Conflict*. Berkeley: University of California Press, 1985.

Horta, Korinna. "The Wolfowitz Pattern at World Bank." *Boston Globe*, May 19, 2007.

Hosni, S. "The Partition of the Neutral Zone." *American Journal of International Law* 60, no. 4 (October 1966): 735–749.

Howell, P. P. and J. A. Allan. *The Nile*. Cambridge: Cambridge University Press, 1994.

Iimi, A. "Did Botswana Escape from the Resource Curse?" International Monetary Fund Working Paper 06/138, 2006.

Internal Displacement Monitoring Centre. "Bosnia and Herzegovina." http://www.internal-displacement.org/.

———. "Georgia." http://www.internal-displacement.org/.

Internal Displacement Monitoring Centre/Norwegian Refugee Council. "Bosnia and Herzegovina: Broader and Improved Support for Durable Solutions Required." August 28, 2008.

———. "Georgia: New IDP Strategy Awaits Implementation." October 11, 2007.

———. "Protracted Internal Displacement in Europe: Current Trends and Ways Forward." May 2009.

International Energy Agency. "Security of Gas Supply in Open Markets: LNG and Power at a Turning Point." 2004.

International Law Commission. "Nationality of Natural Persons in Relation to the Succession of States." Available at http://untreaty.un.org/ilc/texts/instruments/english /draft%20articles/3_4_1999.pdf.

International Monetary Fund. "Democratic Republic of Timor-Leste: Selected Issues and Statistical Appendix." Country Report 05/250, June 2005.

———. "Democratic Republic of Timor-Leste: Selected Issues and Statistical Appendix." Country Report 07/86, February 2007.

———. "Democratic Republic of Timor-Leste: Selected Issues and Statistical Appendix." Country Report 08/203, June 2008.

———. "Guide on Resource Revenue Transparency." 2007.

Iwaskiw, W., ed. "Economic Reform History." In *Estonia: A Country Study*. Washington, D.C.: Library of Congress, 1995. http://lcweb2.loc.gov/frd/cs/eetoc.html (as of August 15, 2013).

Jacobs, Jeffrey W. "Mekong Committee History and Lessons for River Basin Development." *Geographical Journal* 161, no. 2 (July 1995): 135–148.

Jägerskog, A. "Why States Cooperate over Shared Water: The Water Negotiations in the Jordan River Basin." Linköping University Studies in Arts and Science 281, 2003.

Jain, S., P. Agarwal, and V. Singh. "Constitutional Provisions, Inter-state Water Disputes and Treaties." In *Hydrology and Water Resources of India*, 1035–1064. New York: Springer, 2007.

———. "Indus Basin." In *Hydrology and Water Resources of India*, 473–511. New York: Springer, 2007.

"Japan's Oil Industry." *SourceWatch*, August 11, 2008. http://www.sourcewatch.org /index.php?title=Japan<#213>s_oil_industry.

Jeffery, R. "The Punjab Boundary Force and the Problem of Order, August 1947." *Journal of Modern Asian Studies* 8, no. 4 (1974): 491–520.

Jernsletten, Johnny-Leo L. and Konstantin Klokov. "Sustainable Reindeer Husbandry." Centre for Saami Studies, 2002.

Johnston, David and Anthony Rogers. "Economic Analysis Clarifies How Chad Benefits from Oil." *Oil and Gas Journal*, July 28, 2008.

Joint UNDP/World Bank Energy Sector Management Assistance Program. "Cross-Border Oil and Gas Pipelines: Problems and Prospects." 2003.

Karnuth v. United States ex rel. Albro, 279 U.S. 231 (S. Ct. 1929).

Keen, S. "The Partition of India." Postcolonial Studies at Emory, 1998. Retrieved June 10, 2009, from http://www.english.emory.edu/Bahri/Part.html.

Keenan, Jeremy H. "Chad-Cameroon Oil Pipeline: World Bank and ExxonMobil in 'Last Chance Saloon.'" *Review of African Political Economy* vol. 32, 104, no. 5 (2005): 395–405.

Klare, M. T. *Resource Wars*. New York: Macmillan, 2002.

Korhonen, L. "Currency Boards in the Baltics: What Have We Learnt?" Bank of Finland, Institute for Economies in Transition, 1999.

Kolsto, P. "Russian Diaspora." In *Immigration and Asylum: From 1900 to Present*, ed. M. Gibney and R. Hansen, 532–37. Santa Barbara, Calif.: ABC-CLIO, 2005.

Korsmo, Fae L. "Nordic Security and the Saami Minority: Territorial Rights in Northern Fennoscandia." *Human Rights Quarterly* 10, no. 4 (1988): 509–524.

Kozhokin, Evgeny M. "Georgia-Abkhazia." In *U.S. and Russian Policymaking with Respect to the Use of Force*, ed. Jeremy R. Azrael and Emil A. Payin, 75–83. Santa Monica, Calif.: RAND Corporation, 1996.

Lata, Leenco, ed. *The Search for Peace: The Conflict Between Ethiopia and Eritrea*. Oslo: Fafo, 2007.

Layton, Robert. *Conflict in the Archaeology of Living Traditions*. New York: Routledge, 1986.

"Liaquat-Nehru Pact 1950." In *The Story of Pakistan: A Multimedia Journey*. Retrieved June 11, 2009, from http://www.storyofpakistan.com/articletext.asp?artid=A096.

Luna-Firebaugh, Eileen M. "The Border Crossed Us: Border Crossing Issues of the Indigenous Peoples of the Americas." *WicazoSa Review* 17, no. 1 (2002): 159–181.

———. "Contemporary and Comparative Perspectives on the Rights of Indigenous Peoples." *Washington University Journal of Law & Policy* 19 (2005): 155–166.

Mahan, A.T. "The Negotiations at Ghent in 1814." *American Historical Review* 11, no. 1 (1905): 695–700.

Margonelli, Lisa. "The Short, Sad History of Chad's 'Model' Oil Project." *New York Times*, February 12, 2007.

McCandless v. United States ex rel. Diabo, 25 F.2d 71 (3d Cir. 1928).

Miner, M., G. Patankar, S. Gamkhar, and D. J. Eaton. "Water Sharing Between India and Pakistan: A Critical Evaluation of the Indus Water Treaty." *International Water* 34, no. 2 (2009): 204–216.

Modeen, Tore. "The Lapps in Finland." *International Journal of Cultural Property* 8, no. 1 (1999): 133–150.

Mooney, Erin. "Securing Durable Solutions for Displaced Persons in Georgia: The Experience of Bosnia and Herzegovina." Paper presented at Conflict and Migration: The Georgian-Abkhazian Case in a European Context, Istanbul, June 18–19, 2008.

Mullerson, R. "The Continuity and Succession of States, by Reference to the Former USSR and Yugoslavia." *International and Comparative Law Quarterly* 42, no. 3 (1993): 473–493.

Mwauar, Ciru. "Kenya and Uganda Pastoral Conflict Case Study." UN Human Development Report Office Occasional Paper, 2005. Available at http://hdr.undp.org/en/reports/global/hdr2005/papers/HDR2005_Mwaura_Ciru_20.pdf (as of August 15, 2013).

Mygind, N. "Different Paths of Transition in the Baltics." Copenhagen School of Business, Center for East European Studies, Working Paper No. 5, 1997.

National Bank of Serbia. "Relations with the International Monetary Fund." Available at http://www.nbs.yu/export/internet/english/40/40_1/index.html.

Nevins, Joseph. "Contesting the Boundaries of International Justice: State Countermapping and Offshore Resources Struggles Between East Timor and Australia." *Economic Geography* 80, no. 1 (January 2004): 1–22.

Nickels, Bryan. "Native American Free Passage Rights Under the 1794 Jay Treaty: Survival Under United States Statutory Law and Canadian Common Law." *Boston College International and Comparative Law Review* 24, no. 2 (2001): 313–340.

Norges Bank. Retrieved January 23, 2009, from http://www.norges-bank.no/templates /article____69365.aspx.

Norland, Donald R. "Innovations of the Chad/Cameroon Pipeline Project: Thinking Outside the Box." *Mediterranean Quarterly* 14, no. 2 (2003): 46–59.

Oberoi, P. "Indian Partition." In *Immigration and Asylum: From 1900 to Present*, ed. M. Gibney and R. Hansen, 302–306. Santa Barbara, Calif.: ABC-CLIO, 2005.

O'Brien, Sharon. "The Medicine Line: A Border Dividing Tribal Sovereignty, Economies and Families." *Fordham Law Review* 53, no. 2 (1984): 315–350

Oezcan, Veysel. *Germany: Immigration in Transition*. Berlin: Social Science Centre, July 2004.

Office of the Geographer, U.S. Department of State. "International Boundary Study: Kuwait-Saudi Arabia Boundary." No. 103, September 15, 1970.

Office of the High Representative. "General Framework Agreement for Peace in Bosnia and Herzegovina." Annex 7, Article I. 1995. http://www.ohr.int/dpa/default.asp ?content_id=380.

Oregon State University. "Transboundary Freshwater Dispute Database." 2007. Available at http://www.transboundarywaters.orst.edu/.

Osburn, Richard. "Problems and Solutions Regarding Indigenous Peoples Split by International Border." *American Indian Law Review* 24, no. 2 (2000): 471–485.

Ozer, Courtney E. "Make It Right: The Case for Granting Tohono O'odham Nation Members U.S. Citizenship." *Georgetown Immigration Law Journal* 16 (2002): 705–723

Pantuliano, Sara, Omer Egemi, Babo Fadlalla, and Mohammed Farah. *Put Out to Pasture: War, Oil and the Decline of Misseriyya Pastoralism in Sudan*. London: Overseas Development Institute, March 2009.

Pavlínek, P. "Regional Development and the Disintegration of Czechoslovakia." *Geoforum* 26, no. 4 (1995): 351–372.

Pehe, J. "Czechs and Slovaks Define Postdivorce Relations." *RFE/RL Research Report* 1, no. 45 (1992): 7–11.

Pilch, Gennady and Adam Shayne. "Montenegro Joins the World Bank as Newest Member." World Bank, April 23, 2007.

"Physical and Social Geography (Kuwait)." *Europa World*. Available at http://www
.europaworld.com/entry/kw.ge?ssid=824497381&hit=1 (as of August 19, 2013).

Public International Law and Policy Group. "State Succession to the Immovable Assets of Former Yugoslavia." International Crisis Group Bosnia Report 20, 1997.

"Recent History (The Czech Republic)." *Europa World*. Retrieved June 24, 2009, from
http://www.europaworld.com/entry/cz.is.4.

"Responses to Pastoral Wars." Sudan Issue Brief 8, September 2007. Available at http://
www.smallarmssurveysudan.org/fileadmin/docs/issue-briefs/HSBA-IB-08
-Responses.pdf (as of August 13, 2013)

Reynolds, A. "Monetary Reform in Russia: The Case for Gold." *Cato Journal* 12, no. 3
(1993): 657–686

Rice, X. "Annan Warns of Another War Between Ethiopia and Eritrea." *Guardian*,
October 31, 2006. Retrieved July 16, 2009, from http://www.guardian.co.uk/world
/2006/oct/31/ethiopia.

ROC Oil. "First Oil from UK North Sea Blane Field." September 13, 2007.

Rock, J. "Relief and Rehabilitation in Eritrea." *Third World Quarterly* 20, no. 1 (1999):
129–142.

Rosenberg, Matt. "New Countries of the World: The 34 New Countries Created Since
1990." Available at http://geography.about.com/cs/countries/a/newcountries.htm.

Rowlands, D. 1997. "International Aspects of the Division of Debt Under Secession:
The Case of Quebec and Canada." *Canadian Public Policy* 23, no. 1 (1994): 40–54.

"Russia Against Negotiating with Ukraine over USSR Debt." *RIA Novosti*, April 6,
2006. Retrieved July 22, 2009, from http://en.rian.ru/russia/20060406/45398182
.html.

Ryder, A. "History (Slovakia)." *Europa World*. Available at http://www.europaworld
.com/entry/sk.hi?ssid=1020751589&hit=3 (as of August 19, 2013).

Santoro, L. "At the Root of an Odd African War: Money." *Christian Monitor* (Asmara),
June 22, 1998.

Santos, A. "Debt Crisis in Russia: The Road from Default to Sustainability." In *Russia
Rebounds*, ed. D. Owens and D. O. Robinson, 154, 156–157. Washington, D.C.:
International Monetary Fund, 2003.

Sarraf, M. and M. Jiwanji. *Beating the Resource Curse: The Case of Botswana*. Washington, D.C.: World Bank, Environment Department, 2001.

Serafimescu, Iulia. "Montenegro, One Year and One Constitution Later." *Sphere of
Politics (SferaPoliticii)*, issue 129/130 (2008): 87.

Shuval, H. I. "Are the Conflicts Between Israel and Her Neighbors over the Waters of
the Jordan River Basin an Obstacle to Peace? Israel-Syria and a Case Study." *Water, Air, and Soil Pollution* 123 (2000): 605–630.

Simpson, Audra. "Subjects of Sovereignty: Indigeneity, the Revenue Rule, and Jurdics
of Failed Consent." *Law and Contemporary Problems* 71, no. 3 (2008): 191–216.

"Sixty Bitter Years After Partition." *BBC News*, August 8, 2007. Retrieved June 7, 2009,
http://news.bbc.co.uk/2/hi/south_asia/6926057.stm.

"Slovakia." *CIA World Factbook*. Retrieved June 28, 2009, from https://www.cia.gov /library/publications/the-world-factbook/geos/LO.html.

Sonatrach. "Annual Report 2007." http://www.sonatrach-dz.com/annual%20report2007 -uk.pdf.

Sridhar, Subrahmanyam. "The Indus Water Treaty." *Security Research Review* 1, no. 3 (2005). Available at http://www.bharat-rakshak.com/SRR/Volume13/sridhar.html (as of August 13, 2013)

Stanic, Ana. "Financial Aspects of State Succession: The Case of Yugoslavia." *European Journal of International Law* 12, no. 4 (2001): 751–779. Available at http://ejil .oxfordjournals.org/cgi/reprint/12/4/751.pdf.

Stein, Ilan. "EU Energy Policy vis-à-vis Algeria: Challenges and Opportunities." *Bologna Center Journal of International Affairs* 11 (Spring 2008). Available at http:// bcjournal.org/volume-11/eu-energy-policy-vis-a-vis-algeria.html (as of August 16, 2013).

Stevens, Paul. "Pipelines or Pipe Dreams? Lessons from the History of Arab Transit Pipelines." *Middle East Journal* 54, no. 2 (2000): 224–241.

Stevens, Paul and Evelyn Dietsche. "Resource Curse: An Analysis of Causes, Experiences and Possible Ways Forward." *Energy Policy* 36, no. 1 (2008): 56–65.

Strömgren, Johan. "Sapmi—Sweden." In *The Indigenous World*, 29–33. International Work Group for Indigenous Affairs, 2008.

Swain, A. "Ethiopia, the Sudan, and Egypt: The Nile River Dispute." *Journal of Modern African Studies* 35, no. 4 (1997): 675–694.

———. "Mission Not Yet Accomplished: Managing Water Resources in the Nile River Basin." *Journal of International Affairs* 61, no. 2 (2008): 201–214.

Taylor, John G. "Economy (Timor-Leste)." *Europa World*. Available at http://www .europaworld.com/entry/tp.ec?ssid=824482095&hit=1 (as of August 19, 2013).

Terdre, Nick. "Talisman Forging Ahead on Rev, Yme." *Offshore* 67, no. 10 (October 2007): 102.

Thatte, C. D. "Indus Waters and the 1960 Treaty Between India and Pakistan." In *Management of Transboundary Rivers and Lakes*, ed. Olli Varis, Asit K. Biswas, and Cecilia Tortajada, 165–206. Berlin: Springer, 2008.

Timewell, S. "Latvia: The Brutal Truth—A Radical Shakeout Is Promised After the Scandal Surrounding the Collapsed Banka Baltija." *The Banker*, August 1, 1995.

Tonra, Joshua J. "The Threat of Border Security on Indigenous Free Passage Rights in North America." *Syracuse Journal of International Law and Commerce* 34, no. 1 (2006): 221–258.

"Treaty Between Australia and the Democratic Republic of Timor-Leste on Certain Maritime Arrangements in the Timor Sea." *Australian Treaty Series*. 2007. Available at http://www.austlii.edu.au/au/other/dfat/treaties/2007/12.html.

Tsalik, Svetlana. "Caspian Oil Windfalls: Who Will Benefit?" Ed. Robert Ebel. Open Society Institute, Central Eurasia Project, 2003.

TV Crna Gora. *Podgorica*. July 10, 2006.

UK-Norway North Sea Co-operation Workgroup. "Unlocking Value Through Closer Relationships." 2002.

———. "Unlocking Value Through Strengthened Relationships." 2004.

———. "Value Creation from UK-Norway Co-operation Evaluation of the Potential Gain from Improved Co-operation." Draft, August 2002. Available at http://www .regjeringen.no/upload/kilde/oed/rap/2002/0005/ddd/pdfv/160010-value_creation _from_uk-norway.pdf (as of August 19, 2013).

Ulvevadet, Birgitte and Konstantin Klokov. "Family-Based Reindeer Herding and Hunting Economies, and the Status and Management of Wild Reindeer/Caribou Populations." Centre for Saami Studies, 2004.

United Nations Development Programme. "Human Development Indicators.." In *Human Development Report 2007/2008*, 229–254. New York: United Nations, 2007.

United Nations Economic and Social Council. "Specific Groups and Individuals: Mass Exoduses and Displaced Persons, Addendum: Georgia." Document E/CN.4/2001/5 /Add.4.

United Nations High Commissioner for Refugees. "Briefing Note on UNHCR and Annex 7 in Bosnia and Herzegovina." October 2007.

———. "The State of the World's Refugees: Human Displacement in the New Millennium." 2006. Available at http://www.unhcr.org/4a4dc1a89.html (as of August 15, 2013).

United States ex rel. Diabo v. McCandless, 18 F.2d 282 (D. Pa. 1927).

United States ex rel. Goodwin v. Karnuth, 74 F. Supp. 660 (W.D.N.Y. 1947).

United States, on Petition of Albro, ex rel. Cook et al. v. Karnuth, 24 F.2d 649 (2d Cr. 1928).

Updyke, Frank A. "The Treaty of Ghent—A Centenary Estimate." *Proceedings of the American Political Science Association* 10 (1913): 94–104.

U.S. Department of Homeland Security, Bureau of Customs and Border Protection. "Documents Required for Travelers Departing from or Arriving in the United States at Sea and Land Ports-of-Entry from Within the Western Hemisphere." USCBP 2007-0061, 2007. Retrieved January 28, 2009, from http://www.uscis.gov /ilink/docView/FR/HTML/FR/0-0-0-1/0-0-0-123038/0-0-0-126045/0-0-0-127539 .html (as of August 13, 2013).

U.S. Institute of Peace. "General Framework Agreement for Peace in Bosnia and Herzegovina." 1995. http://www.usip.org/sites/default/files/file/resources/collections /peace_agreements/dayton.pdf (as of August 13, 2013).

———. "Quadripartite Agreement on Voluntary Return of Refugees and Displaced Persons." April 4, 1994. Available at http://www.usip.org/sites/default/files/file/re sources/collections/peace_agreements/georgia_quad_19940504.pdf (as of August 13, 2013).

Vanags, Alf. "Macroeconomic Stabilization and Central Bank Policy in Latvia." *Communist Economies and Economic Transformation* 10, no. 2 (1998): 203–215.

Vars, Láilá Susanne. "Sapmi—Norway." In *The Indigenous World*, 38–42. Copenhagen: International Work Group for Indigenous Affairs, 2007.

Venice Commission. "Declaration on the Consequences of State Succession for the Nationality of Natural Persons, European Commission for Democracy Through Law." September 13–14, 1996.

Venkataraman, M. "Ethiopia-Eritrea Ties: Past, Present and Future." *African Quarterly* 47, no. 1 (2007): 52–61.

Vintrová, R. "Lessons from the Czech and Slovak Economies Split." *Prague Economics Papers* 1 (2009): 3–25.

Vitalino, Canas. "Independent Montenegro: Early Assessment and Prospects for Euro-Atlantic Integration." NATO Parliamentary Assembly, 2007. Available at http://www.nato-pa.int/Default.asp?SHORTCUT=1162.

Waqo, Halakhe. "Peacebuilding and Small Arms: Experiences from Northern Kenya." OXFAM GB. Paper presented at a conference July 7–11, 2003, UN Centre, New York.

Weinthal, E. and P. J. Luong. "Combating the Resource Curse: An Alternative Solution to Managing Mineral Wealth." *Perspectives on Politics* 4, no. 1 (2006): 35–53.

Wigglesworth, R. and S. Kennedy. "Norway Provides Model on How to Manage Oil Revenue." *International Herald Tribune*, October 17, 2007.

Williams, P. R. "State Succession and the International Financial Institutions: Political Criteria v. Protection of Outside Financial Obligation." *International and Comparative Law Quarterly* 43, no. 4 (1994): 776–808.

"With Independence, What Changes for the Timor Gap?" *La'o Hamutuk Bulletin* 3, no. 4 (May 2002). Available at http://www.etan.org/lh/bulletins/bulletinv3n4.html #With Independenc (as of August 15, 2013).

Wolf, Aaron T. "Criteria for Equitable Allocations: The Heart of International Water Conflict." *Natural Resources Forum* 23, no. 1 (1999): 3–30.

Wolf, Aaron T. and Joshua T. Newton. "Case Study of Transboundary Dispute Resolution: The Indus Water Treaty." Oregon State University, 2008.

———. "Case Study of Transboundary Dispute Resolution: The Mekong Committee." Retrieved July 5, 2009, from http://www.transboundarywaters.orst.edu/research /case_studies/Mekong_New.htm.

———. "Case Study of Transboundary Dispute Resolution: The Nile Waters Agreement." Oregon State University, 2007.

———. "The Jordan River—Johnston Negotiations 1953–1955: Yarmuk Mediations 1980s." Oregon State University, Transboundary Freshwater Dispute Database, 2007. Available at http://www.transboundarywaters.orst.edu/.

Wood, John. "Secession: A Comparative Analytical Framework." *Canadian Journal of Political Science* 14 (1981): 107–134.

World Bank. "The Chad-Cameroon Petroleum Development and Pipeline Project." January 2006. Retrieved December 18, 2008, from http://go.worldbank.org /504AW22GX0.

——. "Implementation Completion Report on Two IBRD Loans in the Amount of US$39.5 Million and in the Amount of US$53.4 Respectively to the Republic of Chad and the Republic of Cameroon for a Petroleum Development and Pipeline Project." Washington, D.C.: World Bank, 2006.

——. "World Development Indicators." Washington, D.C.: World Bank, 2008.

World Bank and International Finance Corporation. "Chad-Cameroon Petroleum Development and Pipeline Project: An Overview." Washington, D.C.: World Bank, 2006.

Yablon-Zug, Marcia. "Gone but Not Forgotten: The Strange Afterlife of the Jay Treaty's Indian Free Passage Right." *Queen's Law Journal* 33, no. 2 (2008): 564–617.

Yamauchi, A. "Fiscal Sustainability—The Case of Eritrea." International Monetary Fund Working Paper WP/04/7, 2004.

Ying, Li, Douglas L. Johnson, and Abdelkrim Marzouk. "Pauperizing the Periphery." *Journal of Geographical Science* 12, no. 1 (2002): 1–14.

INDEX

ACKNOWLEDGMENTS

This book grew out of an intriguing RAND project sponsored by Humanity United, a foundation committed to building peace and advancing human freedom through working to end mass atrocities and modern-day slavery. One Humanity United staffer, David Mozersky, coupled considerable experience in the region with the insight to realize that Sudan was approaching the secession vote with a host of important issues unaddressed. The injunction not to change African borders constrained governments, so there was a role for Track II—unofficial—diplomacy. He and his colleague—and earlier ours at RAND—Horacio Trujillo also had the wisdom to believe that any Track II process for Sudan would be enriched by looking at earlier episodes of secession. Thus was born the series of cases and issue analyses presented in this book. The idea was less to make specific policy suggestions, still to less to outline a solution, than to energize the Track II process by demonstrating that other secessions have handled similar issues, if not always well, and to inform the process with suggestions or lessons that emerge from those earlier experiences.

This project was conducted jointly by RAND's Frederick S. Pardee Center for Longer Range Global Policy and the Future Human Condition and its Center for Global Risk and Security. The RAND Pardee Center aims to enhance the overall future quality and condition of human life by aggressively disseminating and applying new methods for long-term policy analysis in a wide variety of policy areas where they are needed most. The Center for Global Risk and Security reflects the need for a focal point for crosscutting, multidisciplinary research and analysis on the increasingly complex issue of global security. It draws on RAND's unparalleled breadth of related expertise—from strategy to health to technology and criminal justice—and expands upon RAND's long history of excellence in informing security policy by exploring innovative new areas of inquiry that cut across traditional perspectives.

Comments are welcome. Please contact the author, Gregory F. Treverton, gregt@rand.org or phone 310-393-0411 ext. 7122. The Pardee Center and Center for Global Risk are within RAND's International Programs, which also include the Center for Asia Pacific Policy (CAPP), the Center for Middle East Public Policy (CMEPP), and the Center for Russia and Eurasia (CRE).

As author, I owe large debts, which I happily acknowledge. One is to Humanity United, which funded the work, and especially to its talented staffers, who both made the work happen and made it a pleasure. David Mozersky was a wonderful colleague and guide to matters Sudanese throughout, and the conclusions reflect his work. His colleague, Michael Kleinman, joined us not only in traveling to Sudan but in brainstorming about the issues at play. Horacio Trujillo drew on his knowledge of RAND to set the project in motion as director of research for Humanity United.

The book benefited from two careful reviews, one by a scholar commissioned by the University of Pennsylvania Press and the other by my colleague, Warren Bass. I appreciate them both, and especially thank Warren, who—in the spirit of one of RAND's founding giants, Nathan Leites—not only pointed out language that was infelicitous or unclear but also suggested a number of fixes, line by line.

The other debt I owe is to RAND colleagues. Robert Lempert was a partner, especially in initiating the project. I especially thank the graduate fellows at the Pardee RAND Graduate School who wrote the cases—especially Tewodaj Mengistu, who did the most cases, but also David Howell, Sarah Outcault, Sarah Olmstead, and Yashodhara Rana. The specific cases each wrote are credited to them throughout the book, and they, too, were wonderful colleagues. They worked hard, were ready for new challenges (including travel to Sudan), and met the tight deadlines sometimes required as events moved forward on the ground in Sudan. The most rewarding part of this project was the chance to work with colleagues from both Humanity United and RAND.